Breaking Through the Stained Glass Ceiling

Women Religious Leaders in Their Own Words

Maureen Fiedler, editor

Breaking Through the Stained Glass Ceiling

Women Religious Leaders in Their Own Words

Maureen Fiedler, editor

Seabury Books

NEW YORK

Cover art courtesy of Thinkstock
Cover design by Laurie Klein Westhafer
Typeset by MediaLynx

Library of Congress Cataloging-in-Publication Data

Breaking through the stained glass ceiling: women religious leaders in their own words / Maureen E. Fiedler, editor.
     p. cm.
Includes bibliographical references.
ISBN 978-1-59627-120-3 (pbk.)
1. Women and religion. 2. Women in Christianity.
I. Fiedler, Maureen.
BL458.B74 2010
206'.10820973--dc22
2010006100

Seabury Books
445 Fifth Avenue
New York, New York 10016
www.churchpublishing.org

An imprint of Church Publishing Incorporated

5 4 3 2 1

This book is dedicated to:

Sr. Mary Luke Tobin, SL (1908–2006)

An inspiring leader to women of many faith traditions

Woman of prayer and contemplation

Lover of community and the pioneer spirit of Loretto

Religious leader for nuclear disarmament

Ambassador for justice, peace, and human rights around the globe

Defender of the rights of women

Promoter of interfaith dialogue and understanding

Trailblazer and risk-taker for justice, peace, and equality

Graceful and joyous dancer

May her spirit be yours

Leadership roles:

Official Auditor, Second Vatican Council, 1964–1966
(one of only 15 women)

President of the Loretto Community, 1958–1970

President, Leadership Conference of Women Religious, 1964–1967

Director of Citizen Action, Church Women United, 1972–1978

Author, *Hope is an Open Door*

Contents

Foreword by Kathleen Kennedy Townsend xi

Acknowledgments xiii

Introduction xv

A Word about *Interfaith Voices* xxv

Chapter 1 1
Women as Denominational or Organizational Leaders

- Bishop Katharine Jefferts Schori 2
  First Woman Presiding Bishop of the Episcopal Church
  and First Woman Primate of the Anglican Community

- The Reverend Sharon Watkins 8
  First Woman General Minister and President of the Christian Church
  (Disciples of Christ) and First Woman to Preach at a Presidential
  Inauguration Prayer Service

- Bishop Vashti McKenzie 12
  First Woman Bishop of the African-Methodist Episcopal Church
  and First Woman President of the AME Council of Bishops

- The Reverend Susan Andrews 15
  First Woman National Moderator of the Presbyterian Church

- Dr. Ingrid Mattson 18
  First Woman President of the Islamic Society of North America (ISNA)

- Swami Krishna Priya Bognavati 22
  First Woman Hindu Acharya in the U.S.

- Ishani Chowdhury 25
  Director of Public Policy for the Hindu American Foundation

- Fatima Zahra Salhi, Ilham Chafik, and Nezha Nassi 28
  The Mourchidates of Morocco

- Starhawk 30
  Leader of the Earth-Based Wiccan/Goddess Tradition

Chapter 2 . . . . **36**
Women Leaders in Theological and Scriptural Scholarship

- Dr. Amy-Jill Levine 38
  on *The Misunderstood Jew: The Church and the Scandal of the Jewish Jesus*
- Rita Nakashima Brock and Rebecca Ann Parker 41
  on *Saving Paradise: How Christianity Traded Love of this World for Crucifixion and Empire*
- Dr. Elaine Pagels 47
  on *Beyond Belief: The Secret Gospel of Thomas*
- Dr. Karen King 51
  on the Nag Hammadi Library and *The Gospel of Judas*
- Dr. Julie Galambush 56
  on *The Reluctant Parting: How the New Testament's Jewish Writers Created a Christian Book*

Chapter 3 . . . . **61**
Women in Feminist Theology

- Dr. Mary Hunt and Dr. Judith Plaskow 61
  on Christian and Jewish Feminist Theology
- Dr. Rosemary Radford Ruether 67
  on *Goddesses and the Divine Feminine*
- Dr. Rosemary Radford Ruether and Dr. Delores Williams 70
  on Feminist and Womanist Theologies
- Dr. Amina Wadud 73
  on *Inside the Gender Jihad*
- Dr. Elizabeth Johnson 77
  on *She Who Is: The Mystery of God in Feminist Theological Discourse*
- Dr. Rena Pederson 81
  on *The Lost Apostle: Searching for the Truth about Junia*
- Dr. Phyllis Trible 84
  on *Hagar, Sarah, and Their Children*

Chapter 4 . . . . **87**
Religious Feminist Activists

- Rabbi Eveline Goodman-Thau 88
  First Woman Orthodox Rabbi
- Aisha Taylor 91
  Former Executive Director, Women's Ordination Conference on the Archeological Evidence for Women's Leadership

- The Reverend Andrea Johnson 96
  Roman Catholic Woman Bishop
- Rabbi Susan Talve 99
  Central Reform Congregation, St. Louis, Missouri
- Asra Nomani 101
  on *Standing Alone in Mecca*
- Daisy Khan 105
  Executive Director of ASMA, the American Society
  for Muslim Advancement and Muslim Women
  Organizing for Empowerment

Chapter 5 108
Women Leaders in Spirituality

- Sr. Joan Chittister, OSB 109
  on *Called to Question: A Spiritual Memoir*
- Barbara Brown Taylor 115
  on *Leaving Church: A Memoir of Faith*
- Ann Lamott 119
  on *Plan B: Further Thoughts on Faith*
- Immaculée Ilibagiza 121
  on *Left to Tell: Discovering God Amidst the Rwandan Holocaust*
- Sharon Salzberg 125
  on Buddhism in America
- Sallie Tisdale 126
  on *Women of the Way: Discovering 2,500 Years of Buddhist Wisdom*
- LaDonna Harris 129
  on Native American Spirituality
- The Reverend Dr. Renita Weems 134
  on Womanist Spirituality
- Jean Houston 137
  on *Mystical Dogs: Animals as Guides to Our Inner Life*
- Jeanette Rodriguez 139
  on *Our Lady of Gaudalupe: Faith and Empowerment among Mexican-American Women*

Chapter 6 143
Women Leaders in Social Justice, Peace, and Ecology

- Layli Miller-Muro 144
  on Caring About Women's Rights in the Baha'i Tradition
- Sr. Helen Prejean, CSJ 147
  on *The Death of Innocents*

- **Kathleen Kennedy Townsend** 150
  on Reclaiming the Catholic Social Justice Tradition
- **Julia Butterfly Hill** 156
  on Saving the Redwoods
- **Kim Bobo** 159
  on Defending the Rights of Working People
- **Lutheran Bishop Margaret Payne** 162
  on Seeking Peace and Human Rights in the Middle East
- **Leymah Gbowee and Abigail Disney** 168
  on Christian and Muslim Women in Liberia,
  Pray the Devil Back to Hell

Chapter 7 . . . . **172**
Women Leaders in Interfaith Relations
- **Diana Eck** 173
  on *A New Religious America*
- **Mary Heléne Rosenbaum** 176
  on the Challenges of Interfaith Marriage
- **Dr. Susanna Heschel** 180
  on the Interfaith Friendship of Her Father and Dr. Martin Luther King
- **Ranya Idliby, Suzanne Oliver, and Priscilla Warner** 185
  on *The Faith Club*—An Interfaith Movement in Living Rooms
- **Kathy Giese, Olivia Berardi, and Nafees Ahmed** 192
  on Conducting Teenage Interfaith Dialogue

Chapter 8 . . . . **195**
Women Leaders in Religious Media
- **Barbara Bradley Hagerty** 195
  NPR Religion Correspondent, on *Fingerprints of God:*
  The Search for the Science of Spirituality
- **Krista Tippett** 201
  on *Speaking of Faith*

Epilogue **207**

Bibliography **209**

Foreword

Congratulations to Maureen Fiedler for her groundbreaking work on *Interfaith Voices*, the public radio show she has hosted for more than eight years. In that role, she has been educating the public on the vast array of faith traditions, breaking down religious stereotypes, and promoting not only tolerance but collaboration among those of different traditions.

Now, she has taken her work to a new stage with this important book. Her radio interviews over the years revealed a hopeful trend: the rise of women's leadership in the world of religion. We often hear that women are assuming new leadership roles in politics, journalism, sports, and the professions. But we don't hear as much about women leaders in religious institutions.

That's because most of these institutions have been mired in patriarchy for centuries, and some religious institutions (like my own Catholic Church) still are. Many have demeaned women, and used theology and scriptural misinterpretations to keep them in second-class status. Women who challenged the religious status quo had to cope, not only with culture and tradition, but with the "will of God." The struggle has been difficult, and it's far from over. So, religious institutions, which ought to be prophetic voices for justice and equality, have, until recently, been very slow to recognize the leadership gifts of women.

But patriarchy is falling under its own weight. Its demise will take more time in some institutions than in others, but its days are numbered. And this book documents that crumbling of religious patriarchy. In some places, the bricks are just beginning to fall, but women are circling "outside the walls," demanding change they are confident will come. In other places, patriarchy is already rubble, and women's voices are heard with authority and frequency in houses of worship and official conferences.

In this book, we hear the voices of women who are denominational leaders, theologians, and scholars, feminist activists, leaders for justice and peace, innovators in interfaith relations and religion journalists. Most exciting of all, we hear women's voices across faith traditions: Christians, Jews, Muslims, Baha'is, Buddhists, Hindus, and more. I think of it as a Women's Hallelujah Chorus!

This fits the God I have known since childhood. The God I knew then, and know now, is a "Big God," a God who cares about large, societal issues: war and peace, poverty, discrimination, how we treat one another in society at large. This "Big God" is an inclusive God, not a God who leaves aside half the human race. This God calls forth the gifts and talents of all human beings in an age when our global community cries out for voices of moral clarity.

So, women (as well as men) in religious leadership face special challenges today. In the twenty-first century, it is not enough that they be leaders. They must be *good* leaders, sources of moral power and inspiration. They need to embrace a "Big God," an inclusive God, a God who cares—not just about a personal spiritual life, but about the way we treat each other in community, acting as neighbors, with justice, in a global society.

Many of these women are doing just that. And that's why this book is important. People of faith in the twenty-first century need to hear such hopeful leaders crying out for justice, equality, and peace. Just turn the page, and you can hear them.

Kathleen Kennedy Townsend

Acknowledgments

I owe a profound debt of gratitude to the great women I have had the privilege of interviewing. Their voices are the heart of this book. They have not only informed and inspired me; they have strengthened my own faith.

Special thanks go to those who have collaborated with me in producing *Interfaith Voices*, and its predecessor, *Faith Matters*. They include Paul Woodhull, Peter B. Collins, Linda Rabben, Josephine Reed, Alexandra West, Regina Anderson, Rev. Lauren Phelps, Fritzi Bodenheimer, John Parman, Katie Jones, Michael Leard, Laura Kwerel, Jane Flotte, and many talented young interns. John Parman encouraged me to produce a book, and arranged the initial interview with Church Publishing.

My gratitude reaches out to those who helped edit the book: my good friend and feminist theologian, Mary Hunt of the Women's Alliance for Theology, Ethics and Ritual and my long-time friend and colleague at the Quixote Center, Dolly Pomerleau.

Finally, I am grateful to all those who helped me understand the importance of gender equality over the years. My father, Frank Fiedler, insisted that women were the equals of men so he taught me how to change a tire and change the oil in a car. My long-time colleagues at the Quixote Center—Dolly Pomerleau and Bill Callahan—nurtured my belief in gender equality, and helped me translate ideals into concrete programs, as did the women and men with whom I shared the struggles for the Equal Rights Amendment and for women's rights in the Roman Catholic Church. Many dear friends in the Loretto Community inspire me every day with the brilliance of women's leadership. The spirit of all these people lives in these pages.

Maureen Fiedler, SL

Introduction

When I became actively interested in gender equality in 1970, the horizon was bleak. There were few women in the U.S. Congress, and the only woman who dared run for president, Shirley Chisholm, was seen—at best—as a protest candidate. There were intact "glass ceilings" everywhere. Only one woman—Katharine Graham, publisher of the *Washington Post*—was the CEO of a Fortune 500 company, and she did not assume the formal title until 1979. And in the mid-1970s, none of the top elected positions in the AFL-CIO were filled by women.

The "*stained* glass ceiling" seemed especially impenetrable. Women were ministers in most mainstream Protestant traditions, but they usually found themselves in small churches with small incomes and little influence within the larger body. The Episcopal Church had not yet ordained women as priests, much less bishops. It was not until 1974 that the famous "Philadelphia Eleven" caused a firestorm with their irregular ordinations, and the drive for women Episcopal priests moved ahead in earnest.

There weren't even any women rabbis in the United States when I became active in 1970. The Reform Movement in American Judaism ordained its first woman rabbi in 1972, the Reconstructionist Movement in 1974, and the Conservative Movement in 1985. The Orthodox Movement has not done it yet, officially. The status of women in Islam was not on the radar screens of the West. Almost no one in the United States was asking about women's status in traditions like Buddhism and Hinduism.

But, as the host of *Interfaith Voices*, a public radio show heard across North America, I have begun to realize that the dream of gender equality in the world of religion is beginning to be realized. In fact, the acceptance of women leaders in religion appears to have reached a "tipping point" in many faith traditions. Gender equality has become an accepted norm, culturally and theologically. It's just a question of how soon the new order of equality is actually realized.

This story needs to be told. There are outstanding achievements like the election of Bishop Katharine Jefferts Schori as the presiding bishop and primate of the Episcopal Church, and the election of Dr. Ingrid Mattson as the first woman president of the Islamic Society of North America, but the gradual rise of women leaders in the world of religion over the last forty to fifty years has been largely "under the radar." That is what I seek to bring to light in this book.

Women *are* emerging as religious leaders in faith traditions across the board, in many different roles and capacities, even though some who defend patriarchy still disapprove. Women are not only denominational and organizational leaders, but leading theologians and scripture scholars, prolific writers in the field of spirituality, prominent activists for social justice, peace and ecological sanity, leaders in forging positive interfaith relations, and leaders in religious media.

In this book, you will meet many of these women, as I have had the pleasure of meeting them—in interviews for *Interfaith Voices*.

Why Should We Care?

Why is this trend important? First of all, human equality is a question of justice. Even faith traditions that deny women access to leadership roles in practice usually affirm gender equality in principle. The rise of women in religious leadership affirms publicly that such teachings are not just abstract theological principles, but norms for acting justly in the real world. Once in leadership, these women serve as models for what is possible across the spectrum of faith.

But more is at stake. Religious institutions are highly influential in society at large. They are arbiters of right and wrong. What they teach about gender roles is quoted everywhere. Their practices offer models for the rest of society. When religious institutions exhibit injustice of any kind, they give tacit permission for everyone else to do it.

The most glaring example of this is racial discrimination in the United States. Until the civil rights era of the 1960s, there were churches and religious schools that practiced racial segregation. Some even preached that it was permissible. So if the preacher said it was okay, in word or deed . . . then it became permissible for the rest of society.

That is why it was especially important that religious leaders, like Dr. Martin Luther King and Rabbi Abraham Joshua Heschel, led the Civil Rights Movement in the 1960s. It was important that ministers, priests, rabbis, and nuns marched at Selma. It said in blunt English, "It is not *morally* permissible to discriminate."

The same holds for gender equality. When religious institutions refuse to allow women to assume leadership positions, ordained or otherwise, they give tacit "permission" to businesses, secular organizations, and government to exclude women from leadership at all levels.

Finally, women's leadership in religion is important for the world at large. The vast majority of the world's poor, the world's illiterate, and the victims of crimes like human trafficking and sex slavery are women. Although some male religious leaders—to their credit—are actively involved in these issues, women have a personal identity with these victims, and offer the potential for acting more resolutely to find solutions.

But It's Not Nirvana Yet

A few caveats are in order. The increase in women's leadership does not mean that we are headed for a religious feminist "Nirvana" in the next few years. What we are seeing is the front edge of a trend that will continue, and must continue, for many decades until women's leadership in religion is taken for granted. Realism demands that we recognize the formidable obstacles that remain.

Discrimination in many faith traditions is still bolstered by theological arguments. In my own Roman Catholic Church, where ordained ministry is a necessary prerequisite for institutional leadership, women cannot even be ordained as deacons, much less priests or bishops. The Vatican justified this because the priest is supposed to image Christ, and women cannot resemble a male. The Southern Baptist tradition, relying on a literal reading of scripture, has backtracked on its earlier practice of allowing women pastors; they are no longer ordained. And the Southern Baptist Convention tells women that they must submit to the "headship" of their husbands. Many right-wing evangelicals in non-denominational churches also preach the "headship" of men, and refuse to allow women pastors. Even in mainline Protestant denominations, where women ministers have been around for decades, there remain pockets of resistance.

In Judaism, the struggle continues. The Conservative, Reform, and Reconstuctionist traditions ordain women rabbis, but Orthodox Judaism does not yet permit them, although a few Orthodox women have been ordained in some seminaries, and the quest for equality goes on.

In Islam, although women in some countries are Qur'anic scholars and even *muftis* (authoritative teachers), women are not generally permitted to become imams, or lead mixed-gender prayer services. Instead, they are usually relegated to the rear of mosques for Friday prayers, sometimes even to separate rooms.

The structures are much more informal in Buddhism and Hinduism, but women still struggle for recognition as gurus or spiritual mentors. In Thailand, Theravada Buddhist women struggle for "ordination" as monks.

Even in the Baha'i tradition, where gender equality is a central tenet, the Universal House of Justice, an international body charged with guiding the growth and development of the global Baha'i community, is all male. Women are not eligible for election.

Sikhism is especially strong in recognizing and practicing the equality of men and women. It advocates active and equal participation in the congregation, in academia, in healthcare, and the military, among other aspects of society. Female subordination, the practice of taking a father's or husband's last name, practicing rituals that imply dependence or subordination, are all alien to Sikh principles. That does not mean that Sikhs always practice what they preach, but the theological basis for equality is firm.

Two major religions in the world claim a woman founder. One is Christian Science, founded by Mary Baker Eddy. The other is the Seventh Day Adventists, founded by Ellen White.

The Sikhs, Seventh Day Adventists, and Christian Scientists notwithstanding, we have a long road to go.

Yet the tide has clearly shifted. The issue is out in the open everywhere. Questions about gender equality and women's leadership have been raised in just about all denominations. *A Woman's Nation*, the 2009 report from the Center for American Progress, authored by Maria Shriver, underlines the rise of women and women's influence in every aspect of American life. Consequently, it is increasingly difficult to defend the second-class status of women in religious institutions and roles. We are entering a new era. We can note—and celebrate—the progress to date.

How Did I Get to This Place?
A Personal Note

My personal feminism began at about age eight or nine. I loved school, enjoyed reading, and even began my global awareness as a "pen pal" correspondent with a girl my age in Africa. I remember a moment of serious self-questioning one day. I watched my mother spend hours ironing clothes and curtains and just about anything in the house that could be ironed. I distinctly remember asking myself, "Is this my future?" I was thinking of household roles, and I could not see myself doing those chores for a lifetime.

In the religious realm, I was one of those Catholic girls who "played Mass" in the living room. I was the priest, with my younger brother serving as an "altar boy." It was only later that I discovered that those roles would not play out that way in real life. However, I was quite inclined toward a life of prayer and dedication to others, and so in 1962, after two years of college, I entered the Sisters of Mercy of Erie, Pennsylvania. As I young nun, I lived through the turbulent yet exhilarating years of the Second Vatican Council, when just about every aspect of Catholic life changed. I reveled in it, especially its message of social justice. And I was active in moving my Mercy community to implement changes.

When my community seemed to be backsliding away from the practices we had adopted with the Second Vatican Council, I searched out a new community that lived in that spirit. I began exploring the Sisters of Loretto in 1980, and formally transferred in 1984. I have never regretted it.

In the 1970s, I attended graduate school at Georgetown University, studying government. My doctoral dissertation asked why women were not elected political leaders in the same numbers as men, and why—even as the "second wave" feminist movement was burgeoning—women were not running for office in increased numbers. The answers were complex, but they indicated that many women in the 1970s, even those active in politics, still accepted restrictive cultural norms that limited them largely to traditional roles, and the data also documented discriminatory attitudes among men who are the gate-keepers to power.

Between 1978 and 1982, I became an all-day, every-day activist for the Equal Rights Amendment. In the last months before ratification failed, I was one of eight women who fasted for thirty-seven days in Springfield, Illinois, as a public witness to the need for gender equality written into law. "Women Hunger for Justice" read the banner under which we sat every day in the rotunda in the state capitol building. It was a profound experience.

And then there was church! My church, the Roman Catholic Church, I decided, needed an "equal rights amendment" or at least "equal rites" when it came to ordination. In the 1970s, I began working at the Quixote Center where a fledgling group called "Priests for Equality" had published a charter of equality, calling for—among many other items—the ordination of women. I attended the first Women's Ordination Conference in Detroit in 1975, where hope for change ran high.

It had been only eleven years since the Second Vatican Council had "let in the fresh air" of new thinking, new practices, new openings to the rest of the world. And although the Council had not approved the ordination of women to any role, even the diaconate, the spirit of that Council made everything seem possible. So why not take it to the next step? We at the Quixote Center began to write, publish, and commission Gallup polls on the issue of women's ordination. We tracked results showing that increasing majorities of Catholics were ready for women priests. (Today, more than 60 percent of American Catholics favor women priests).

In the 1980s, as I worked for an end to U.S.-sponsored wars in Central America, I took time on my trips to the region to talk to Latina women who had been leaders (some even *commandantes*) in regional struggles for justice, and hear their aspirations for equality.

In the 1990s, I worked with the international movement for reform of the Catholic Church, called the "We Are Church" movement, and realized that European women, and indeed women across the globe, shared this quest for equality.

Finally, in the twenty-first century, as I moved strongly into interfaith work, I learned of the struggles and triumphs of women throughout the major faith traditions. I found that the barriers are similar, and the struggles have a lot in common.

My interviews on *Interfaith Voices* have revealed over time the trend that is the central thesis of this book: women are indeed emerging as leaders in the world of religion. It is a development that will continue. The reasons for this rise organically from recent history.

Why This Trend?

First, women's secular leadership roles are establishing new parameters for the possible. Religious institutions have *not* been "prophetic" beacons of hope for women's leadership; they are simply following trends established by secular feminist "prophets." Many of those prophets led the women's movement that emerged in the 1960s and 1970s. Over the decades, they successfully communicated to the public an ethic of gender equality that paved the way for women in new leadership roles.

Many women have become prime ministers, presidents, or equivalents: Margaret Thatcher in Great Britain, Angela Merkel in Germany, Golda Meir in Israel, Indira Gandhi in India, Benazir Bhutto in Pakistan, Corozon Aquino in the Philippines, Michelle Bachelet in Chile, Ellen Johnson Sirleaf in Liberia—to name but a few.

In the United States, when Nancy Pelosi is speaker of the house and Hillary Clinton can run for president as a credible, serious candidate, being a bishop no longer looks like an impossible dream. This entire trend toward women's secular leadership makes it more "thinkable" that women can become religious leaders as well.

Second, with women's rising successes in the secular world, the theological and scriptural arguments barring women from religious leadership roles sound archaic, out of touch with reality. They no longer seem to fit the "facts on the ground" that people see everywhere.

More than that, women theologians and scripture scholars have challenged patriarchal thinking and traditions for decades now. They have answered the traditional arguments that have defended misogyny, and they have convinced millions with their fresh understandings of scripture, new theological insights, or historical proofs that women were indeed leaders in earlier centuries in Judaism, Christianity, Buddhism, and Islam.

Feminist scholars are not usually quiet, retiring academics. They write, speak, blog, and are interviewed by the media. Their ideas make sense, especially to the younger generation who take women's leadership in government, business, and the professions for granted.

Third, women are not only finding their theological voice, they are developing new attitudes, believing that they can preach, they can lead, and they can do it as well as men. They look to the women who are already bishops and renowned preachers like Bishop Vashti McKenzie of the African-Methodist Episcopal Church, or women like the Rev. Sharon Watkins, president of the Christian Church/Disciples, who preached at the official Inaugural Prayer Service of President Barack Obama. And they ask themselves, why not me? I, too, can aspire to leadership. Role models are producing a multiplier effect.

Finally, we live in an age of mass, democratized communication. The news that women are leaders, and the new theologies that underlie this, are everywhere. Feminist theology is not only in books, but at conferences, in the media, and on the Internet. We're long past the time when an "Index" of forbidden books is even conceivable.

This egalitarian movement has become so pervasive that religions that still exclude women from official roles now face a new cultural reality that accepts, and believes in, gender equality, at least in the West. When a religious body refuses to practice it (like the Roman Catholic Church or much of Islam, for example), movements arise from within to challenge the status quo.

In Catholicism, for example, what began in 1975 as polite theological opposition to the all-male priesthood, with a few protests and street demonstrations, has now been transformed into at least two movements that challenge the establishment in different ways.

One is the "Women Church" movement. Those who are part of this movement believe that the entire structure of the Catholic Church is so unredeemable that they counsel women not to seek ordination in a male hierarchical system. Instead, they promote informal feminist communities and liturgies, some Christian and some not.

The truly threatening movement, institutionally speaking, is called "Roman Catholic Women Priests." The women who are a part of this movement refuse to drop the word "Catholic," and have moved ahead to ordain women as priests, and then bishops.* This burgeoning movement

---

* The ordinations are done using traditional Catholic rules: a bona fide Roman Catholic bishop ordained the first women priests and bishops on the condition that his name be kept secret until after his death. This allows the women bishops to claim what is central in the Catholic ordination tradition: "apostolic succession." They can claim a spiritual lineage back to the apostles, and ordain other women.

has now ordained more than forty women in the United States, with many more in training.

In the Baptist world, Shirley Taylor has formed Baptist Women for Equality. The New Baptist Covenant—which explicitly accepts gender equality and women pastors—was formed by Southern Baptists who find gender discrimination contrary to their beliefs. Those dissenters include former presidents Jimmy Carter and Bill Clinton. In fact, Jimmy Carter left the Southern Baptist Church specifically over the question of gender equality.

In Islam, Dr. Amina Wadud openly challenged patriarchy by delivering the sermon at Friday prayers at a mosque in Capetown, South Africa, in 1994, and by holding the first mixed-gender Friday prayer services in New York in 2005. Both were revolutionary in the Muslim world. She justified her actions theologically in a book called *Inside the Gender Jihad: Women's Reform in Islam*.

Asra Nomani, a Muslim feminist from Morgantown, West Virginia, entered her mosque, where women were expected to pray behind the men, and moved to the front to pray. She wrote about it in her book *Standing Alone in Mecca: An American Woman's Struggle for the Soul of Islam*. Women all over the Islamic world are challenging discriminatory practices, which they believe have sullied the traditions of the Prophet Mohammed.

In Orthodox Judaism, women are working to become rabbis. One woman, Eveline Goodman-Thau, whom I interviewed several years ago, found a rabbi in Israel to ordain her in 2000, and had begun her ministry. Her story reminds me of the Roman Catholic Women Priests movement.

Even the Church of Jesus Christ of the Latter Day Saints is not without challenge. When I fasted for the ERA, one of my colleagues was Sonja Johnson, who had been excommunicated from that church—not for wanting an official role, but simply because she favored the Equal Rights Amendment, and her church did not. She may be "out," but the unequal treatment of women continues to be an embarrassment for many Mormons.

When protest does not work, and there is no official indication that gender equality is in the offing, many members, men as well as women, drift away from their religious homelands. Mainstream Protestants and Unitarians will tell you that many former Roman Catholics now sit in their pews these days. Some women want to join a faith tradition where women have long been the dominant leaders, and they look to Wicca, or Neo-paganism.

Beyond Ordination or Denominational Leadership Roles

Ordinations, consecrations, or election to various denominational offices are not the only forms of "leadership" that women occupy in the world of religion today. Many have led religious institutions like universities and hospitals. In fact, many Catholic nuns filled such roles in decades when their secular counterparts were almost exclusively male.

Other women across faith traditions are theologians and scripture scholars. They are distinguished professors, acclaimed authors, and sought-after lecturers. Many break new ground theologically, not only when it comes to gender roles, but in many other dimensions of theology as well.

Hundreds of women are leaders in a field that has never really been "closed" to women: spirituality. Women today are not keeping their prayer lives or contemplative practices to themselves; they are publishing, speaking, and blogging everywhere.

Other women of faith are leaders in social justice, peace activism, or ecology from a faith-base. Again, these are fields that have not traditionally been closed to women, but women are emerging today in new and groundbreaking roles. I think, for example, of the Christian and Muslim women of Liberia who rose up and created a nonviolent, interfaith movement of public prayer and protest, and brought a bloody civil war in their country to an end. Their leadership was so successful that it provided an electoral base for the presidency of Ellen Johnson Sirleaf, the first democratically elected woman president in Africa.

In the United States, I think of women-led communities like Genesis Farm, Green Mountain Monastery, and Santuario Sister Farm in the world of ecology. These women are not just talking; they are offering concrete examples of eco-spiritual lifestyles that offer hope for saving the planet.

Finally, women have assumed leadership in the relatively new field of interfaith relations, promoting dialogue and collaboration on a global scale.

And many women, including myself, are reporting all of this to the world through religious media.

An Invitation to Meet Some of these Leaders

This book invites you to meet many of the women who are emerging as religious leaders today. They speak their own truth in their own words. They offer insights and relate experiences shared with me in interviews on *Interfaith Voices*. These are hopeful women in the midst of life and leadership, speaking about many different issues and challenges.

This selection of women leaders does not pretend to be all-inclusive. It reflects the religious makeup of North America where *Interfaith Voices* is broadcast, and thus, it emphasizes the Abrahamic traditions, especially Christianity.

One thing they have in common: they are all serious women of faith. When they challenge the traditions or norms of their spiritual homeland, it is usually out of love and concern. They generally fear that unjust treatment of women is clouding a larger message of love and compassion, and that it is keeping many of their sisters from being spiritually comfortable in their own traditions.

I invite you to hear these women, each speaking in her own voice, heralding a future that is still in the birthing process.

A Word about
Interfaith Voices

All the interviews in this book were produced for *Interfaith Voices*, the leading religion news magazine in public radio. It is an innovative and growing show heard nationwide across the United States and in parts of Canada.

Launched in 2002, only months after the attacks of September 11, 2001, the show seeks to promote interfaith understanding, dialogue, and collaboration at all levels. It offers both compelling interviews and produced pieces that deal with all major religious traditions, and with interfaith relations generally. Many segments focus on faith, ethics, or spirituality as these intersect with public policy or culture.

Interfaith Voices received the Media Excellence Award from the Rumi Forum in 2009 for promoting interfaith and intercultural dialogue. In 2010, *Interfaith Voices* won the Wilbur Award for Radio for its special series, "Soundscapes of Faith."

Interfaith Voices partners with WAMU-88.5 FM in Washington, DC, to produce the show. It is a one-hour show, broadcast weekly.

Interfaith Voices can be heard online, or by podcast.
Go to: www.interfaithradio.org.

Chapter 1
Women as Denominational or Organizational Leaders

Denominational leadership is hardest for women to achieve because it involves real power, and because those who elect or appoint such leaders must overcome any lingering gender bias in their decision-making. Still, the numbers of women in such positions are growing. In the Christian world, women now serve as bishops in major American denominations, including the Episcopal, Methodist, Evangelical Lutheran, Reformed, and African-Methodist Episcopal churches. And of course, the presiding bishop and primate of the Episcopal Church is a woman, Katharine Jefferts Schori.

In churches that do not have the office of bishop, women have also made strides. Rev. Susan Andrews became the first woman elected to head the Presbyterian Church (U.S.A.) in 2003. Rev. Sharon Watkins is the president and general minister of the Christian Church (Disciples of Christ). She was also the first woman ever to preach at an Inaugural Prayer Service, that for President Barack Obama in January 2009. The Unitarian Universalists have yet to elect a woman as denominational president, but they were among the earliest to ordain women as pastors. In 1999, they became the first religious denomination in the United States where ordained women outnumbered ordained men.

In the Jewish world, women have been elected presidents of the Central Conference of American Rabbis, the umbrella group for the Reform tradition in Judaism. The first was Rabbi Janet Marder; the second was Rabbi Ellen Weinberg Dreyfus. In the Reconstructionist tradition, Rabbi Toba Spitzer was chosen to lead the Reconstructionist Rabbinical Association in 2007, and Rabbi Julie Schoenfeld became the first woman to chair the Rabbinical Assembly of Conservative Judaism.

In the Muslim world, Dr. Ingrid Mattson is the first woman (and the first convert) to become president of the Islamic Society of North America. In some parts of the world, Muslim women are now recognized as *muftis*, or Islamic scholars with the right to issue *fatwas* (authoritative religious edicts). This has been the practice in India for some time, and there are movements in that direction in the United Arab Emirates and Turkey.

There are also signs of new leadership roles for women in Islam. For example, Muslim women have recently been installed as *mourchidates* in Morocco. This is a social service role, not unlike deacons in Christianity, but it is an attempt to institutionalize women's leadership, and it may be a step toward other leadership roles for women in Islam.

Leadership and structures in the Eastern religious traditions like Hinduism and Buddhism are informal, and leaders are less often elected than "proclaimed" and then ultimately recognized and accepted by a sizeable following. Ma Jaya Sati Bhagavati is a prominent woman guru in the Hindu tradition at Kashi Ashram in Florida. The Venerable Tenzin Palmo is a highly respected Buddhist nun and spiritual leader, as is Pema Chodron, who has a following in Europe, Australia, and North America. Ishani Chowdhury became the face of Hinduism in official Washington, especially during her tenure as director of public policy for the Hindu American Foundation. Karen Pechelis emphasized the growth of female gurus in the Hindu tradition in her book, *The Graceful Guru: Hindu Female Gurus in India and the United States.*

When I interviewed women in these roles, I sometimes addressed questions about women's leadership, but most of these women—while recognizing their historic roles—do not dwell on their "firsts." They are concerned about issues that challenge their respective denominations.

Bishop Katharine Jefferts Schori

First Woman Presiding Bishop of the Episcopal Church and First Woman Primate of the Anglican Communion

Bishop Katharine Jefferts Schori is the twenty-sixth presiding bishop of the Episcopal Church, and the first woman primate in the worldwide Anglican Communion. She was elected in 2006 at the 75th General Convention of the Episcopal Church. Before that, she served as the bishop of the Episcopal Diocese of Nevada. She is also an oceanographer and a licensed pilot. Appropriately, her first book is called *A Wing and a Prayer.*

I spoke with Bishop Katharine Jefferts Schori in June 2007 when she was dealing with severe splits in the Episcopal Church over the ordination of openly gay and lesbian priests and bishops.

MAUREEN FIEDLER: You are one of those rare firsts among women who make it to the top. How has that been for you? Do you celebrate it? Do you find it a challenge to be the first woman, or do you mostly not think about it?

KATHARINE JEFFERTS SCHORI: It's not a big issue for me. I'm certainly aware that for some people, I am a symbol of something far larger. But I've spent most of my adult life in professions that are dominated by men, and so it really does not feel like anything terribly unusual to me.

FIEDLER: How have others received you as a woman in the Episcopal Church of the United States and in the worldwide Anglican Communion?

JEFFERTS SCHORI: Mostly with graciousness. When we meet each other as human beings face-to-face, there's usually abundant graciousness. We find it generally difficult to be rude to other people when we meet them for the first time.

FIEDLER: I know from your new book, *A Wing and a Prayer*, that you are deeply concerned about what you call bodybuilding, which means in your case building the body of Christ, or the community of the faithful. But as we all know, the Episcopal Church body has some splinters these days; some churches have even said they are seceding from the Episcopal Church. How serious is this split in your view?

JEFFERTS SCHORI: Numerically, it's fairly minor. And that's not something that's always evident in the media. We have about 7,400 congregations in the Episcopal Church. And those, in which a majority of dissenters are a sizable number, have voted to disassociate from the Episcopal Church. They number about forty-five, so it's well under one percent of the total. That said, there are clearly more people than that who are unhappy with some of the decisions of the last couple of General Conventions, but they're not going anywhere.

FIEDLER: So you're not really expecting more parishes to say that they are splitting themselves from the parent body?

JEFFERTS SCHORI: No, I don't expect a significant increase. Most of the ones who are exceedingly unhappy have probably already acted.

FIEDLER: What is your understanding of the issues that caused this split?

JEFFERTS SCHORI: First of all, I would not call it a split. I would call it some individuals deciding to leave the church.

FIEDLER: Just to be technically clear—in the Episcopal tradition, churches can't secede, but individuals can leave the church?

JEFFERTS SCHORI: That's absolutely correct. We have always struggled about who is a member of the community, and who is not. If you look at the very earliest history of Christianity, there were significant struggles over whether Gentiles could be followers of Jesus. The first great church councils, if we can call them by so august a name, were about whether Gentile converts had to be circumcised and follow the Jewish dietary laws.

And certainly in our own country, we've had a long series of challenging conversations about the place of slaves in the church, about the place of immigrants in the church, about the place of women in the church. And today, the conversation is about the place of gay and lesbian people in the church. And I remain convinced that there will be another group yet to come. I don't know who it's going be, but it seems to be part of the fallen nature of humanity to want to define ourselves over against some other group.

FIEDLER: Does the split, in your view, have anything to do with the Episcopal Church's moving away from traditional understandings of authority? Or treating theological teaching, or truth, as somehow relative? That's what some critics claim.

JEFFERTS SCHORI: Anglicanism has always held up as a high value a broad understanding of theological belief. We have said that we are comprehensive, for the sake of truth. We're willing to live with some tension without having to define everything in black and white. The great genius of the Elizabethan Settlement was that people worshiped together and were permitted to hold a variety of theological understandings of what actually happened at Communion in the Eucharist.* That's been part of our gift and value, and some people find it uncomfortable, especially in a culture that is not supportive of that.

FIEDLER: In other words, the Episcopal Church is tolerant of different theological views, within certain boundaries?

JEFFERTS SCHORI: Not just tolerant, but affirming of differences as a sign of health.

FIEDLER: Some critics have raised the question of the centrality of Christ in the church. Is that an issue for Episcopalians: new understandings of Christ that are troubling some people?

JEFFERTS SCHORI: I think that it's another expression of discomfort with a variety of understandings.

FIEDLER: Was the consecration of Bishop Gene Robinson of New Hampshire, who is, as we know, the first openly gay bishop in the Episcopal Church, the precipitating moment for much of discomfort, in your view?

JEFFERTS SCHORI: In some people's view, certainly. But Gene is not the first openly gay bishop in the Episcopal Church. The Bishop of Utah, when he retired, wrote to the elder members of the House of Bishops and came out. So Gene is not the first, but he's certainly the first who was elected as an openly gay man. There have clearly been numerous gay priests and bishops throughout the history of the church. Gene Robinson is the first

---

* The Elizabethan Settlement refers to the Act of Supremacy and the Act of Uniformity passed by the British Parliament in 1559, under the reign of Elizabeth I. These, in essence, established the Church of England (Anglican Church), and the Act of Uniformity permitted flexibility in belief about the Real Presence in communion.

who's been willing to be open in public about that during the election process.

FIEDLER: How about comfort with the role of women in the Episcopal Church? It's in fairly recent history, beginning with the irregular ordinations in '74, followed by regular ordinations in '76, that you even began to have women as priests. And within several years there were women bishops, and now you are the first woman presiding bishop. Is there general comfort with that, or is it still an underlying issue in the Episcopal Church?

JEFFERTS SCHORI: It is an underlying issue for some people in the Episcopal Church. Out of 110 dioceses, there are still three diocesan bishops who do not recognize the validity of ordained women as priests or bishops. A couple of them do permit women deacons. And there are certainly some of the faithful in our church who are uncomfortable with the idea of women in ordained leadership. Some theologians, feminist theologians in particular, point to the connection between the place of women and the place of gay and lesbian people in the church as challenging the traditional patriarchal understanding of authority and leadership.

FIEDLER: With some churches claiming to secede, there is the question of who owns the church property. Where does that stand legally?

JEFFERTS SCHORI: We've been very clear over the recent decades, and clear in our canons, that all property is held in trust for the larger body, and that congregations do not own their property. They may hold title to it, but that title is held in trust for the larger community, because in most cases, that property is the result of the gifts, and the legacy of generations for the mission and ministry of generations yet to come.

FIEDLER: But there will be a contest in civil court over this, will there not? There are lawsuits pending.

JEFFERTS SCHORI: There are some in process now, and most of them have been decided in favor of the national body.

FIEDLER: Aren't some of the issues within the Episcopal Church writ a bit larger in the worldwide Anglican Communion?

JEFFERTS SCHORI: Yes, and the problems are complex. We're dealing with a history of colonialism, and colonialism that's beginning to be turned against the United States. And it's important to remember that the Episcopal Church is not just the church in the United States. We also have ten overseas dioceses in places like Taiwan, Honduras, Venezuela, and Haiti. Often, decisions that this church makes are equated with policies and actions of our government.

It's also important to remember that in places where there appear to be protests about actions of this church, that voice often comes from the archbishop of Canterbury. There is a diversity of opinion in every part of the Anglican Communion.

FIEDLER: And that diversity of the opinion within the Anglican Communion was expressed, for example, in your meeting in Tanzania earlier this year, in a discussion of gay and lesbian issues, was it not?

JEFFERTS SCHORI: Certainly, and that's probably an important thing to talk about. In that gathering of thirty-four or thirty-five bishops, leaders of their provinces, there were certainly a handful who are exceedingly unhappy with actions of the Episcopal Church. There is a much larger number who are tremendously annoyed that we are spending so much time and energy on this because people in their own provinces are dying of hunger, lack of medication, or medical care. And honestly, they are seeking for us as a Communion to move toward those life and death issues.*

FIEDLER: What can be done to heal the rift?

JEFFERTS SCHORI: Healing or reconciliation happens between individuals. It's not something that happens as easily between institutions or groups of people. For bodies that have separated to reconcile takes the kind of laborious work that we see in ecumenical dialogue. It takes meetings of individuals over months, years, sometimes decades, and centuries to find common ground.

The current conflict certainly has its roots in some earlier decisions of this church that were also problematic: our introduction of a new Prayer Book in 1979, the introduction of a new hymnal, the ordination of women. In some places, those were handled with more pastoral effectiveness than in others. But wounds remain in some places. The conversations about sexuality, in places where they cause significant pain, are often connected to places where those earlier decisions have been very painful. And pain often causes people to separate.

FIEDLER: Your book, *A Wing and a Prayer*, is a collection of your finest sermons, or homilies. There are many marvelous images and stories in it. I'm wondering, as you look at the book now, what part is most relevant to your role today as presiding bishop?

JEFFERTS SCHORI: Probably the focus on building *shalom*, building the reign of God, a community of justice and peace, where people's basic human dignity is attended to, where people can begin to value the diversity of creation, rather than seeing it as inordinate challenge, and where we can learn to live with others who are different from us.

FIEDLER: You talk about "shalom" not simply as a surface word that can be translated easily as "peace," but as something deeper.

---

* At the General Convention in Anaheim, California in July 2009, the Episcopal Church reaffirmed a long-standing policy that says the ordination process is open to all including gay and lesbian members and committed to begin a process for collecting rituals appropriate for the blessing of same-sex unions.

Jefferts Schori: Absolutely; it's about transformed life, which is the focus of Christianity.

Fiedler: You also talk a great deal in your book about issues like poverty, peace, and justice. Does it trouble you that issues like those that are involved in the split in the church deflect attention from these more pressing global issues?

Jefferts Schori: It's abundantly clear that the conversation about human sexuality is part of the vocation of this church in this season. And it has been for several decades. But it's not the whole of our vocation. Our mission as a church is about building a healed world, one that looks more like the reign of God.

Fiedler: If you had your druthers, into what issues would you pour yourself?

Jefferts Schori: I continue to pour myself into a secular understanding of what shalom might look like, framed by the Millennium Development Goals—a community vision for what the reign of God might look like. But the Millennium Development Goals go only part way toward that vision.

Fiedler: What exactly are the Millennium Development Goals?

Jefferts Schori: They're about solving abject human poverty. They're about making sure that all girls and boys have access to primary education, working on preventable and treatable diseases, like AIDS and tuberculosis and malaria. They're about ensuring environmental sustainability, addressing issues like third-world debt and trade policies, so that people really do have equal access to the good things of this life.

Fiedler: And the Episcopal Church, I assume, has programs to try to carry these ideals forward?

Jefferts Schori: That's absolutely right. The primary focus for our work happens through Episcopal Relief and Development. I was in Honduras a couple of weeks ago, and I got to see some on-the-ground examples of how clean water, adequate sanitation, and dignified housing transformed people's lives.

Fiedler: I know that you are a pilot, and you love to fly. And I'm wondering, using that image of a pilot, how has the flight seemed for you thus far as presiding bishop of the Episcopal Church? Has it been bumpy? Has it been mixed? Do you ever think an engine has conked out, or is it still exhilarating?

Jefferts Schori: It's always exhilarating. One has a very different perspective from above the earth.

Fiedler: And do you still fly?

Jefferts Schori: When I go back to Nevada, yes. But the airplane I fly there is rather unsuitable for the international travel I'm doing now.

The Reverend Sharon Watkins

First Woman General Minister and President of the
Christian Church (Disciples of Christ) and First Woman to Preach
at a Presidential Inaugural Prayer Service

The Reverend Sharon Watkins is the president and general minister of the Christian Church/Disciples in the United States and Canada, a denomination with about seven hundred thousand members. She is a member of the Central Committee of the World Council of Churches based in Geneva, and serves on the governing board of the National Council of Churches. Before her current leadership position, she was a missionary in the Congo for two years, a pastor in Bartlesville, Oklahoma, and held various positions in theological academia. I interviewed her in January 2009 at the time of the inauguration of President Barack Obama.

MAUREEN FIEDLER: I caught up with Sharon Watkins in Washington, DC two days before her historic sermon. I began by asking her how it was that then President-elect Obama tapped her to give the sermon.

SHARON WATKINS: I didn't have a strong connection with President-elect Obama. I was, however, included in a meeting of a broad range of religious leaders back in the summer, at which then candidate Obama had a pretty wide-ranging discussion about matters of concern to religious people. And because the group was very diverse, the conversation was strong and direct.

Barack Obama does not shy away from direct exchange. And he seemed quite honest about his opinions. In that kind of a group any one opinion is going to not sit well with somebody in the room. At the end of that discussion, I was asked to offer the closing prayer. And somehow or another, this invitation to preach at the Inaugural Prayer Service seems to have stemmed from that event.

FIEDLER: Did you expect to be asked? When did you get the invitation?

WATKINS: This came completely out of the blue—before Christmas. I had already decided I was coming to Washington for the inauguration. I planned to find a spot on the curb where I could sit and watch the parade and the swearing in on the Jumbo Tron. I wanted to be there because it's so huge to have, after all of these centuries, an African-American sworn in as president of the United States. And I wanted to be able to say to my grandchildren, "I was there."

FIEDLER: What did it feel like to get this invitation?

WATKINS: Honestly, preachers aren't very often without words, but I have to say it was a few long seconds before I could manage any words at all.

FIEDLER: You were the first woman, of course, ever to deliver the sermon. And you're also the first woman to lead your denomination, the Christian

Church (Disciples of Christ). How does it feel to be a pioneering woman in these roles?

WATKINS: In one sense, I don't feel like a pioneer. I went to seminary with women who are pioneers. I have been taught by professors, by women, who really had to do the heavy lifting. And it feels to me like I have the privilege of walking pretty easily down a path that those pioneering women opened for me.

FIEDLER: And these pioneering women are those that were first ordained in your denomination or other Protestant denominations?

WATKINS: The first ordinations of women happened in other Protestant denominations. Actually we've been ordaining women in Disciples since the late 1800s. So while we have had ebbs and flows of women's ordination that have somewhat corresponded to the rising and falling tides of women's opportunities generally, woman have been ordained in Disciples for many, many years.

FIEDLER: Your denomination has been ordaining women since the late 1800s, yet you are the first woman to head it. Did you meet any opposition?

WATKINS: There was not much opposition. It seemed to be the right thing at the right time.

FIEDLER: When were you elected?

WATKINS: It was in 2005.

FIEDLER: It seems to me that women are moving into increasingly significant roles in the world of religion—not just as denominational heads, but as theologians, as scripture scholars, as leaders in interfaith relations. Would you have any thoughts as to why?

WATKINS: I hope it means that we as a human family are realizing that the gifts of the whole family are necessary in order for us to move forward. God has made us diverse, and unique, and has gifted each one of us in particular ways. And if one whole segment of the human family is not participating in the general conversation, then we are missing out on some piece of what God has created. So I am grateful and joyful any time that more voices are a part of a conversation.

FIEDLER: Have you ever been in dialogue with women of other faith traditions, Muslim women, Jewish women, Hindu women, Buddhist women about the roles of women in those various traditions?

WATKINS: I haven't had the opportunity to do that so much. But I would welcome it. I really do believe that the frontier for us right now is global interfaith conversation. And I look forward to finding the opportunities to dialogue with other women.

FIEDLER: And what do you think are the key obstacles that women still have to overcome today when it comes to leadership roles in religion?

WATKINS: The biggest is probably just the habits of thinking that people around us have, and that we have ourselves. Sometimes we don't have the imagination to see anybody in a role. . . where we haven't seen them before. And I think that it's a matter of moving beyond our limited imagination on these things.

FIEDLER: Your denomination, the Christian Church Disciples, is not large, about seven hundred thousand members in the U.S. and Canada, so many people may not have heard of it. Can you say what is theologically distinctive about the Disciples?

WATKINS: The particular gift that we think we bring—and it was our founding insight—is that there is a deeper human unity than the differences that we experience in human life, that from the very beginning God made us one. And our desire is to live out of that unity more than to be divided by our differences.

We really had our beginning in the 1800s, on the American frontier. People were frustrated that the divisions of the church from Europe had been imported onto American soil. And here in the United States, they thought: this is crazy. We need to live out a deeper unity. And their desire was not to start a new denomination. Their desire was to sink into the body of Christ at large—that was the language that they used. They wanted to find a way to be simply Christian. We might say today that the denomination was to be generic Christian in the most fundamental way. And they had this belief that everybody would see that and come.

FIEDLER: What strikes me is how similar that message is to what President-elect Obama is saying about unity in the country. Does that similarity strike you?

WATKINS: It does, it does. Disciples have been around for two hundred years, but now more than ever, I think it could be our time. Because we're trying to peel back the layers of division to reveal the essential unity that God already made in creating one human family in the first place.

FIEDLER: With that in mind, do you think that the Obama family might consider worshiping at a church of your denomination, like the National City Christian Church that we're at right now, which is not far from the White House?

WATKINS: Of course we open our arms to embrace anybody who comes through the church doors. I do have to say in all fairness though, that the Obama family has a tradition, and has had a strong relationship in a congregation of another denomination.

FIEDLER: Which is the United Church of Christ, but that's not terribly different from you theologically, is it?

WATKINS: No, in fact, we have a strong partnership with the United Church of Christ. But with my sense of integrity I would always want to urge any family, even the presidential family, to stay within their own roots to the extent possible. Certainly I wouldn't want to be engaged in what we in the trade we call "sheep stealing."

FIEDLER: Sheep stealing?

WATKINS: You have pastoral flock imagery out there. And it's really more important, I think, to get the word about the love of God to people who've never heard, than to be trying to go from one brand of Christianity to another.

FIEDLER: In this case, it's a pretty important sheep.

WATKINS: It is, but I just want the Obama family to be in a faith community that nurtures them, and helps to feed their spirit. They will need it in the days ahead.

FIEDLER: What would you say is the central message of your sermon at the Inaugural Prayer Service?

WATKINS: The central message has to do with reminding us that at this particular moment, where we face so many crises, there is a tendency and temptation for us to get drawn away from our moral or ethical center. And my hope in the sermon is to say a word that urges all of us, the president in particular, to stay centered on those bedrock values, which people of many faiths share. They are core to what I think of as the best in the United States of America, what Abraham Lincoln called "the better angels of our nature."

FIEDLER: I know that you personally have been very concerned about issues like torture and ending the war in Iraq. In talking about coming to our moral center, do those issues come to the fore for you?

WATKINS: Yes, they do. And my moral core is also core for Disciples, is a sense that each person is a child of God. The image of God is stamped on each one of our faces. And it doesn't matter where we live; it doesn't matter what country we live in. It doesn't matter in what capacity I get to know you. I need to look into your face and see in you another child of God, a member of the human family.

And so in the speech that Barack Obama, not even yet Senator Obama, gave in 2004 at the Democratic National Convention, he said, "If there's a child on the south side of Chicago, who's not my child, who's not your child, a child who cannot read, that matters to me." And what I would add to that is, "If there's a child in the eastern part of the Democratic Republic of the Congo, who cannot rest easy because he doesn't know from which side the next militia is going to come, that's not my child or your child, but it is God's child, and that matters to me." We need to have that big of a view, of what it means to be part of a human family.

FIEDLER: And I understand that nobody vetted your sermon, that you can say whatever you want to say.

WATKINS: That's correct.

FIEDLER: We conclude with an excerpt from the sermon that the Reverend Sharon actually delivered at the Washington National Cathedral on January 21, 2009.

> *There is a story attributed to the Cherokee wisdom. One evening a grandfather was teaching his young grandson about the internal battle that each person faces. There are two wolves struggling inside of us, the old man said. One wolf is vengefulness, anger, resentment, self pity, fear. The other wolf is compassion, faithfulness, hope, truth and love. The grandson sat thinking, then asked: "Which wolf wins, Grandfather?" His grandfather replied, "The one you feed."*
>
> *There are crises banging on the door right now, pawing at us, trying to draw us off our ethical center, crises that tempt us to feed the wolf of vengefulness and fear. We need you, Mr. President, to hold your ground. We need you leaders of this nation to stay centered on the values that have guided us in the past, values that have empowered us to move through the perils of the present, of earlier times, and can guide us now into a future of renewed promise. We need you to feed the good wolf within you. To listen to the better angels of your nature, and by your example encourage us to do the same.*
>
> *In international hard times our instinct is to fight, to pick up the sword, to seek out enemies, to build walls against each other, and why not? They just might be out to get us. We've got plenty of evidence to that effect. Someone has to stand watch and be ready to defend, and Mr. President, tag! You're it! But on the way to those tough decisions, which American promises will frame those decisions? In the complex swirl of international interest, will you reason from your ethical center, from the bedrock of our best hopes? Which wolf will you feed?**

~~~~~~

Bishop Vashti McKenzie

First Woman Bishop in the
African-Methodist Episcopal Church and
First Woman President of the AME Council of Bishops

Bishop Vashti McKenzie was the first woman elected a bishop in the African-Methodist Episcopal Church, in 2000, and the first woman ever to serve as bishop in the African-Methodist Episcopal Church in America. In November of 2004 she became the first woman elected president of the AME Council of Bishops, and titular head of the church. She currently serves as the presiding prelate of the 13th Episcopal District which

---

* The whole sermon can be read or heard at: http://www.disciples.org/OfficeoftheGeneralMinisterand President/NewsandUpdates/HarmoniesofLiberty/tabid/483/Default.aspx

encompasses Tennessee and Kentucky. Prior to that, she was the chief pastor of the 18th Episcopal District in southeast Africa. Before her rise to the episcopate, she served as a pastor at Payne Memorial AME Church in Baltimore, Maryland. Two of my former colleagues at *Interfaith Voices*, Josephine Reed and Regina Anderson, interviewed her upon her election as head of the AME Council of Bishops.

JOSEPHINE REED: *Interfaith Voices* producer Regina Anderson and I recently attended a service at the famous Rankin Memorial Chapel at Howard University, where Bishop McKenzie was the guest preacher. After the service, Regina and I had the opportunity to speak with Bishop McKenzie.

REGINA ANDERSON: You are a very accomplished preacher, wife, and mother—among the other roles that you play. So I imagine you draw most of your inspiration and work from your faith. When your faith is tested, what do you do to overcome that difficult period?

VASHTI MCKENZIE: When my faith is tested, I go to three different sources. One is prayer, for prayer brings the presence of God into your life. Fasting, of course, is a part of the spiritual discipline. . . . But when I preach it's also preaching to me. And so, going back over the sermons that I have preached becomes nourishment to my soul.

REED: You are certainly one of the agents of change, the first woman bishop of the African-American Methodist Episcopal Church. And you stated upon your election, and this is a direct quote, "The stained glass ceiling has been pierced and broken." That was you piercing and breaking it. So talk about your elevation to bishop.

MCKENZIE: The election and consecration really was an exciting time—not only for me and the family, and for the AME Church, but also for women everywhere—for those who have to be salmon, to swim upstream, to go against the odds. You're out-gunned, out-numbered, out-manned, out-woman-ed, out-everything. Yet God can bless you and bring about a positive reality.

So my goal was not to become the first woman bishop. My goal was not to break the glass ceiling. I was put into that position, so it happened. And so my goal is to be the best Episcopal leader that I can be. But really, it was just a totally—you know—out-of-body experience, mind-blowing, life-rearranging, life-changing moment for me and my family. At this past General Conference in 2004, in Indianapolis, we elected two more women.

Bishop H.H. Brookins, who assigned me to Payne Memorial, which was really a launching pad for this Episcopal run . . . he said, "Can you handle this?" And I said, "What's different about this church?" He said,

"This church is a connectional church; it was one of the mother churches of the conference. And if you fail, it'll be a long time before another woman will have this opportunity. But if you succeed, it'll never be your success; it'll always be someone else's."

And so the night that I was elected, he was standing right on the podium next to me, and we looked at each other. And he's saying the same thing, "If you fail, it'll be a long time before another woman is elected in your position. But if you succeed, it'll never be your success." And so I think the church's response to four years of being in the episcopacy helped the other two women to be elected this past time.

REED: Bishop McKenzie, you come from a family of pioneers. Your great-grandfather started the *Afro-American*, which is one of *the* newspapers in the United States. And four generations of your family studied at Howard University. Talk about how both served to propel you forward and, at the same time, how you might have found this heritage a bit daunting.

MCKENZIE: Coming from a family of leaders, there are certain things that are not options. And in my family everyone went to college. College is what you did. There was no other option. Leadership and managerial issues, employee-employer relationships, human relationships—all those tools and skills—those were topics at our dinner table.

When the whole family came together and my grandmother had all five daughters, and all five of their husbands, and sixteen grandchildren every Sunday at the house around the dinner table, all of these things were a part of discussions. It was like breathing.

Many leaders came through my grandfather's house. I met Althea Gibson, Thurgood Marshall, and Martin King. As a young child, standing there looking at these great marvelous people, you begin to wonder—where is my place, what is my role, what is going to be my contribution? And so that's what my father said to me while we were in the midst of the civil rights era. He said, "Don't let anyone have to ask you what you did for your people, or for your community." In a lifetime there's always something that someone can do. And all of us have to find the pulpits from which we preach.

REED: You began as a journalist, and then you felt called by preaching ministry. Can you talk about that transition?

MCKENZIE: Everybody who believes in God has a role to play in the kingdom, or in ministry. Some people sing, some people usher, some people work in outreach ministry. Everybody has a role to play. And so when I gave my heart to God, I was a church child, but still there's a point where you make the transition. I began to look to see what role I would play.

And I felt that I would be in the media. I was in gospel broadcasting. And so I figured, hey, this is what God wants me to do. But it's the hand of God in your life just pushing and pushing and pushing, saying this is not enough; there's more I want you to do. Then he called me to preach and to pastor, and now to serve as an Episcopal leader.

The Reverend Susan Andrews
First Woman National Moderator
of the Presbyterian Church

In 2003, Rev. Susan Andrews became the first woman elected as National Moderator of the Presbyterian Church (U.S.A.), a position with a one-year term of office. Before that, she served as pastor of Bradley Hills Presbyterian Church in Bethesda, Maryland. In 2006, a second woman, the Reverend Joan Gray of Birmingham, Alabama, was elected national moderator. I interviewed Rev. Andrews at her church office in Bethesda in June of 2003, shortly after her historic election. This interview was aired in a narration format, rather than questions and answers.

MAUREEN FIEDLER: Susan Andrews defeated two male candidates at the annual Presbyterian Conference, wining 53 percent of the vote on the second ballot.

SUSAN ANDREWS: Given the fact that I was a female pastor, given the fact that I was the progressive candidate, it was unknown whether or not I could muster a majority of the delegates. But I did, and I was elected.

FIEDLER: Women were first ordained elders in the Presbyterian Church in 1949, and as clergy in 1956. And they now make up more than 25 percent of the Presbyterian clergy. Rev. Andrews says that the struggle over ordaining Presbyterian women is finished. But a report on the status of clergy women made public at the annual conference, revealed that Presbyterian women already ordained are still faced with a stained glass ceiling.

ANDREWS: The vast majority of women are in tiny churches, they're in associate positions, or in some instances they don't have jobs at all. So there still is a discrepancy for women, in terms of the kinds of positions they're called to, and there's still a discrepancy in terms of salary.

FIEDLER: Rev. Andrews' parish is unique in many ways. First of all, the location has made it imperative to deal with important and sensitive issues of religion, science, and medicine.

ANDREWS: Our location, one mile from the National Institutes of Health (NIH), puts us right smack in the middle of the scientific community. We have many NIH scientists, physicians, folks who are very involved in the cutting edge of scientific theory, research, and development. And so the conversation between theology and science, between faith and science is something that we really focus on here. And I think that we've become a leader on that issue within our denomination.

FIEDLER: Thirty-five years ago, her church began to share its worship space with the Bethesda Jewish congregation. This is now the longest interfaith space-sharing arrangement of any house of worship in the United States. The two congregations even built a new space together called Covenant Hall.

ANDREWS: We understand ourselves to be spiritual siblings, sharing sacred space. We actually have a signed covenant between our two communities, talking about what this relationship means, how we celebrate our differences. We're utterly unique in our theologies, and yet we constantly have dialogue, adult education seminars, worship, and conversations.

FIEDLER: Rev. Andrews says that ongoing Jewish-Christian dialogue has both stretched her and enriched her.

ANDREWS: If my goal were to convert my Jewish brothers and sisters into being Christians, this relationship would never work. My goal is to be the most joyful, impassioned Christian that I can be, and speak that freely, but at the same time to be totally open to listening to the Jewish tradition, and to be totally hospitable to having these friends in our space sharing this location. . . . I leave the "who's saved and who's not saved" up to God, because ultimately it's God's invitation, and it's God's mystery. I am a stronger Christian today than I was fifteen years ago, because of what I've learned about the Torah, because of what I've learned about Jesus as a Jew, because of what I've learned about the ethical roots of my Christian faith. And in learning about Judaism, I have also learned why I'm a Christian, which has to do with the personal relationship with Jesus Christ.

FIEDLER: Her congregation's support of Palestinian Christians created a bit of tension, but it has never broken the mutual respect nurtured by dialog.

ANDREWS: We had ten sessions looking at the Middle East, from both a Jewish and a Christian perspective, with both a Palestinian focus and an Israeli focus. Because we have been so strong in supporting Palestinian Christians, that has been fertile ground for some very electric conversation with the Jewish congregation.

FIEDLER: Bradley Hills Presbyterian Church also welcomes gays and lesbians, and advocates their rights.

ANDREWS: In teaching and preaching and advocacy, we have been openly for the full inclusion of gays and lesbians within our congregation and within the Presbyterian Church.

FIEDLER: Rev. Andrews says she supports the ordination of gay and lesbian clergy in the Presbyterian Church, even though she supported postponing the decision at this year's conference.

ANDREWS: Although I'm in favor of removing the prohibition on the ordination of gays and lesbians from our Constitution, our Book of Order, I did believe that it was not the year to do that, because we have a theological taskforce that is doing some very important work trying to come up with a process by which we can move through this issue. And they will not report till the year 2006. And I believe that we need to give them time to do their work.*

FIEDLER: Rev. Andrews says she would not have any problem personally officiating at a same-sex union, but she would consult her vestry or church board before doing it in the parish. She believes that the church as a whole should be open to blessing such unions. That, she says, ironically would put the church in a strong position to advocate a traditional sexual ethic.

ANDREWS: If the church could get to the point where it openly welcomes gays and lesbians, then we have the right to begin to help the gay and lesbian community, along with the heterosexual community, embrace a very traditional sexual ethic of long-term monogamist relationships. I think this is a growing edge in the gay community.

FIEDLER: As moderator of the church for a year, she sees herself in a three-fold role, first—listener and story teller.

ANDREWS: Listening to the stories of the various communities of faith, to the various racial and ethnic caucuses, to the various theological groups within the church, be they conservative or liberal, and then telling their stories in other places.

FIEDLER: Then—peacemaker and reconciler.

ANDREWS: To truly reach out, particularly to those theologically in a different place than I am, so that I can honor where they are, and begin to find some common ground.

FIEDLER: And finally, visionary and catalyst for church growth.

ANDREWS: Our denomination has been losing members, as many mainline churches have. And I don't think that that's a foregone conclusion. So I think we need to talk about each congregation's making a commitment to grow. And because I'm in a congregation that has been growing for the last fourteen years, I think that I can help congregations figure out a strategy to do that.

FIEDLER: She also has a fervent hope for mainline U.S. Protestantism generally.

---

* In 2006, the Presbyterian Church (U.S.A.) voted to allow regional governing bodies flexibility in enforcing the rule about ordaining non-celibate gays and lesbians. However, in October, 2009, the highest court of the Presbyterian Church (U.S.A.) ruled that there are no exceptions to the church's ban on ordaining non-celibate gays and lesbians.

ANDREWS: That kind of prophetic, social justice, progressive understanding of the world that mainline Protestants have always had, has been sidelined in our public life. And I would love my role as moderator to give some visibility and some voice to that particular Christian vision.

Dr. Ingrid Mattson

First Woman President of the
Islamic Society of North America (ISNA)

If there's any faith tradition in which the popular stereotypes put women in inferior roles, it's Islam. But Muslim women are making real progress.

Dr. Ingrid Mattson is a Canadian and a convert, who was raised a Catholic. She is now the first woman (and the first convert) elected president of the Islamic Society of North America (ISNA). After she embraced Islam in her younger years, she went on to get a Ph.D. in Islamic studies from the University of Chicago. She is now director of Islamic Chaplaincy and a professor at the Macdonald Center for Islamic Studies and Christian-Muslim Relations at Hartford Seminary in Hartford, Connecticut, the first Islamic chaplaincy program in the United States. I interviewed Dr. Ingrid Mattson in February 2008.

MAUREEN FIEDLER: How difficult was it to get elected as the first woman president of the Islamic Society of North America? Did your gender create opposition?

INGRID MATTSON: Not at all. I had served two terms as vice-president, and our membership considered it to be a natural transition for me to move into the presidency, and there was very little discussion of my gender. But I was the first female *vice*-president. At that time, I remember hearing from the election committee that they had a few calls from various members who were wondering what was going on. But it was a small minority, and that surprised all of us. You know, our community perhaps was further along than most people expected them to be.

FIEDLER: And how about reactions since you've been elected?

MATTSON: Even those organizations that are more socially conservative than ours, who I don't think would, anytime in the near future, consider a woman in an executive role, have been very collegial and have treated me as a peer.

FIEDLER: What about internationally? I'm sure you travel as part of this job.

MATTSON: I do. And the reaction has been extraordinary, very supportive, even from people in the conservative countries, in the Arab Gulf, for example. So I think that sometimes we (and I include myself here) stereotype societies, and think that these people are not open-minded.

FIEDLER: Do those Middle Eastern visits include countries like, say, Saudi Arabia—which I think of as very conservative in regard to women's roles?

MATTSON: I haven't been to Saudi Arabia, but I've met many, many Saudi Arabians. In fact, one of the first letters I received after having been elected president was from the Saudi Ambassador to the U.S. at that time, Prince Turki al-Faisal. He wrote a letter of congratulations to me, saying that it was a great thing for the global Muslim community to have a woman in this position. So it really is quite surprising to many people, I think, to see that the Muslim world is not as conservative as we think it is.

FIEDLER: What is the Islamic Society of North America? What does it do, and what's your role as president?

MATTSON: We serve multiple roles for the Muslim community. We aim to be a broad platform with a diversity of Muslim individuals, Islamic centers, schools, as well as other organizations. And then of course, there is our role trying to make life easier for Muslims in the United States and furthering the understanding of Islam.

FIEDLER: In your role as president, there must be a major challenge, because of course Islam has been under fire. It's been characterized as a violent religion, and there are all kinds of epithets aimed at it. How do you deal with these challenges as the president of that association?

MATTSON: You're absolutely right, Maureen, and sometimes it feels almost overwhelming. I mean, we represent only around 2 percent of the American population. And for us to try to reach out and make connections with others, so that we can alleviate these misconceptions, is very difficult. But the good news is that we aren't doing it on our own. We have many great partners in the interfaith community who have stood up for us, and who are pushing back against the hate speech. And that, I think, is probably the best news story of the past few years.

FIEDLER: Let's go back to you and your own life. You were not born Muslim. In fact you were raised by your parents as a Catholic. Why did you convert to Islam? What is it that you found in Islam to be so inspiring and compelling?

MATTSON: It is most interesting the way you phrase the question, Maureen, because according to Islamic theology everyone is born a Muslim. So Islamic theology believes that we're all born with this innate knowledge of and attraction to God. And then we're formed in a particular tradition by our parents and our society. So I was formed in the Catholic tradition, and I decided, around age fifteen, that the Catholic Church was not for me, and left the church.

FIEDLER: Was there some trigger?

MATTSON: No one trigger. It was a very deliberate decision on my part, that I did not have faith, that this wasn't for me anymore.

FIEDLER: So then, did you drift away from faith altogether for awhile?

MATTSON: Absolutely; I spent probably six or seven years with no faith, and was frankly not interested in it at all. I wasn't a seeker. I wasn't looking for something to replace my Catholic faith.

But then when I was older I was studying in Paris and I met West African Muslims who reflected this beautiful sense of confidence and generosity that was based in their faith. These weren't evangelical people, trying to tell me about their faith. But I felt the sense of attraction to them. And through them, I learned about Islam and began my own study. And it was really through reading the Qur'an that I started to rediscover these innate and early feelings of a connection with God that I had lost.

FIEDLER: Let's talk for a minute about the role of women in Islam. From your long study of Islamic theology, what should be the role of women in Islam?

MATTSON: Women are, like men, absolutely responsible for their own lives, responsible human beings, living ethically with their money, with their politics, independently accountable in front of God.

FIEDLER: Would you say that Islamic theology, properly understood, regards women and men as equals before God?

MATTSON: Very much so!

FIEDLER: Then what do you think when you look at the actual roles of women, in countries like say Saudi Arabia, or women under the Taliban in Afghanistan?

MATTSON: What's most important for us is to have a realistic understanding of women's lives in Muslim societies. And generally most Muslim women are doing relatively well, depending on their social or economic situation. Most of Muslim women's problems have to do with poverty, illiteracy, global warming, because most Muslims live in countries that are underdeveloped. So women, like men, are suffering because of these factors in their lives.

FIEDLER: But there are special circumstances; for example, the Taliban did not want women educated. In Saudi Arabia, women can't drive a vehicle.

MATTSON: If we look at the issue of the Taliban, we see that Afghanistan, with a population at least 99 percent Muslim, overwhelmingly rejected the Taliban's interpretation of Islam as it had to do with gender relations.

FIEDLER: I'm wondering, as a Catholic woman myself, how the roles of women compare in Islam and Christianity, or at least in Catholicism, because both of our faith traditions understand women and men as equals. But it doesn't come across that way in a lot of the roles that women play in each of these denominations. . . . Would you see it that way?

MATTSON: One thing I find very interesting is how within Islam and within Catholicism there is a struggle even about the portrayal of our history. There are those in our traditions who are in positions of authority who conveniently ignore the fact that women at various times in history have had much more prominent roles than they do now. So I think one of the things that we share is this struggle to recover our history, and to bring to daylight how women have been allowed, at various times, to participate much more fully within the leadership and life of the religious communities than they do now.

FIEDLER: Why do you wear the Islamic headscarf, or the *hijab*?

MATTSON: I cover my head because I believe it is a requirement for Muslim women according to my understanding of the Qur'an, and also the teachings of the Prophet Mohammed, which are the two main sources of Islamic norms.

FIEDLER: And I'm sure there are Muslim women who have given you an argument over that?

MATTSON: There are women and men who have different opinions about this. Certainly the vast majority of scholars, and the consensus virtually over the centuries, has been that it is a requirement for Muslim women. But of course, individuals have a right to make up their own minds. They have a right, according to the Qur'anic injunction, to live their religion as they like. And so I think the more important issue is, within the Muslim community, to what extent we are willing to accept the diversity of opinions that exists within Islam, not just about this issue, but many other issues, issues that perhaps are of even graver import.

FIEDLER: Islamic feminists like Amina Wadud and Asra Nomani believe that women can and indeed should be able to lead mixed-gender Friday prayers. I understand that leading women in prayer is not the issue, but *mixed-gender* Friday prayers is. And indeed Amina Wadud has done it. What's your view of that?

MATTSON: I've written an article on this subject that can be found on the Internet called *Can a Woman Be an Imam?* I believe, according to my methodology of interpreting Islamic law, that it is not permissible for a woman to lead a mixed-gender prayer. But Amina Wadud is a scholar; she's someone who has researched this issue. I respect her right to make her own legal judgment on this.

FIEDLER: Why do you *not* think women should lead mixed-gender prayers? It's often a role that involves preaching, and a woman like you, who's an Islamic scholar, has a great deal to offer.

MATTSON: I have preached in mosques before. I've stood in front of a mosque and preached to both men and women. But I would not do it on a Friday, and the reason is that the form of the prayer that we practice is the one that was taught by the Prophet Mohammed. And the Prophet Mohammed did not appoint a woman to a public congregation. He did allow a woman to lead the prayer in her household, so really the question is that of legal methodology. Can we extend the example of the household to the public congregation or not? So it's not something that I think is an unreasonable interpretation, as long as it's consistent with someone's legal methodology, but it's not something that I see as a compelling argument. It's perfectly possible that someday someone will come up with an argument, a very compelling argument, that would make me change my mind. But I haven't seen that argument yet.

FIEDLER: And finally, what do you think is the greatest challenge facing American Islam today?

MATTSON: I think our greatest challenge is simply being accepted for who we are. Muslims are constantly facing a caricature of themselves in the media, usually by politicians and others, and that's very difficult to counteract. And that's why we need the friendship and support of our brothers and sisters in the interfaith movement and other communities to help us push back against this unfair characterization of who we are, and to remove the barriers that keep us from doing what we want to do, which is to be helpful, responsible, contributing members of society.

Swami Krishna Priya Bognavati
First Woman Hindu Acharya in the U.S.

Hinduism is among the world's most ancient religious traditions, and its structures are quite informal. But there are recognized roles for teachers, gurus, swamis, and other revered leaders. One is *acharya*, a role found in Hinduism, Buddhism, and Jainism. It designates a guide or a teacher in religious matters, and the title is often affixed to the names of learned men. The first woman to achieve that role in the United States was Swami Krishna Priya Bognavati, and she joined me for a conversation on *Interfaith Voices* in July 2003. In the course of our conversation, she also talked about Ma Jaya Sati Bhagavati, a woman guru in the Hindu tradition. Both work at Kashi Ashram, an interfaith ashram in Sebastian, Florida.

MAUREEN FIEDLER: What is an acharya, and what is its significance in the Hindu tradition?

KRISHNA PRIA BOGNAVATI: "Acharya" simply means "respected teacher." It is someone who serves, who carries the lineage of our tradition, who helps people along their spiritual journey.

Fiedler: Is it something like a spiritual director? Would that be a Christian parallel?

Bognavati: I would say more like a minister. We have our guru, or our spiritual teacher, who I would say is the spiritual director of our community, Ma Jaya Sati Bhagavati. And basically I am someone who is an assistant, like a priest or a minister.

Fiedler: And the director of the Kashi Ashram, she is also a woman?

Bognavati: Yes she is, and she has forged an amazing path. She is our guru.

Fiedler: What's the difference between a guru and an acharya?

Bognavati: The guru is the catalyst for this community, the one helping guide people to become more aware and awake. Acharyas help Ma do her work.

Fiedler: So women have been gurus, but not acharyas. Why not?

Bognavati: It's very interesting, because I think Ma definitely forged a path, bringing Hinduism to the West in the early '70s, and she was one of the only female gurus in the West. She was really a pioneer for women in the United States. She's on the cutting edge. And so it makes perfect sense to me that she has initiated a woman into a role of acharya. But it is very unusual, and unique. But for me, being an acharya is about my commitment to my spiritual work, and my journey to experience God, and to serve humanity.

Fiedler: Generally speaking, does Hinduism treat women and men fairly equally, or are there real struggles?

Bognavati: It's a man's world in many religions. I think women have been suppressed for many, many, many years. And now it's time for the mother, for nurturing. It's about caring for humanity. And I think that's why women are so vital in religious and spiritual roles.

Fiedler: You are also a *sanyasi*, which would be the equivalent of a monastic, or what we would think of as a nun. Have you taken vows?

Bognavati: Yes, my vows are to serve and take care of others, to be kind and compassionate, to lead a life of service to God.

Fiedler: You are what would be called, I think, in Catholic monasticism someone who is of an active apostolic tradition, as opposed to a cloistered?

Bognavati: Exactly! I'm out there, hands-on. I teach yoga, I go out and do lectures. I am in the interfaith community, through the Parliament of World Religions, of which Ma is a trustee. We do a lot of interreligious, interfaith work. So we have to be out there. We're doing hands-on service with people with AIDS. We are serving the homeless and the poor. So it isn't about remaining in prayer. We need to do our spiritual practice and meditation—all of that is important in our teaching—but it is also about serving the community.

FIEDLER: What would you say is the core of your teaching as a spiritual guide for other people?

BOGNAVATI: I think the core of our message is service to humanity, and becoming an awake, aware, conscious individual in order to help others. Whether that is educating them, whether that is holding their hand while they're dying, or whether that is helping them find their true spiritual past, we serve them. We serve them whether they are Christian, Jewish, Muslim, and that's what Ma is so brilliant at. She's created Kashi Ashram, an interfaith community, that embraces all traditions.

FIEDLER: If people came to Kashi Ashram, what would they find there?*

BOGNAVATI: They would find an eighty-acre paradise. We have temples to all of the major religions; we have meditation; we have yoga. Ma's still actively teaching, and she offers something we call *darshan*, which is an opportunity to come and share in meditation in a large setting. We have the Kashi Center for Advanced Spiritual Studies, which runs all kinds of programs. We've had world-renowned interfaith leaders come and teach here. We have teaching about other traditions here, as well as the Hindu tradition. And people can then volunteer to go and feed the poor, and serve people with AIDS. So there are lots of opportunities here.

FIEDLER: And anyone who goes there would find his or her own faith respected?

BOGNAVATI: Absolutely. Because it's about the spirituality that each religion has at its core. And we're supposed to be living kindness and serving. And all we're doing is trying to help people find their way and their path. We are a very diverse a community, embracing people no matter what their race, color, creed, religion, or sexual orientation.

FIEDLER: I know that your guru has a particular interest in AIDS victims.

BOGNAVATI: Yes, we actually have been serving the AIDS community since the very beginning. We have a home here for babies with AIDS. We have done global work. We support an orphanage in Uganda with seven hundred children, orphaned primarily due to the AIDS epidemic.

FIEDLER: I have visited Yogaville, in southern Virginia, which is also an interfaith ashram founded out of the Hindu tradition. Is there something about Hinduism that makes it more open to interfaith experiences and opportunities?

BOGNAVATI: I know when Ma first started on her journey, she had an awakening through Christ, who told her to teach all ways. And Hinduism, for whatever reason, was the next step for her, because in its truest sense, it embraces all paths and all ways.

---

* www.kashi.org

Ishani Chowdhury

Director of Public Policy for the Hindu American Foundation

Women are leaders, not just in denominational structures, but in religious organizations as well. These include religious schools, universities, and hospitals, and major religious non-profit organizations. Ishani Chowdhury served as the director of public policy for the Hindu American Foundation, the largest human rights organization in the United States devoted to Hindu issues. It describes its mission as promoting "understanding, tolerance, and pluralism." There are about two million Hindus in the United States. I interviewed Ishani Chowdhury in December of 2006. Our conversation focused on misconceptions of Hinduism in the U.S.

MAUREEN FIEDLER: Hinduism is an ancient faith going back five thousand years at least. To whom, or what, does it trace its origins? Is there a single founder of Hinduism?

ISHANI CHOWDHURY: Unlike the Abrahamic religions that most of us are accustomed to, Eastern traditions, particularly Hinduism, do not have a single founder. It grew from a collection of books, sacred writings, and revealed scriptures. These scriptures, as many may know, are the Vedas, which are the most holy. And the succinct form, which many Americans may be familiar with, is the *Bhagavad Gita*, which translates to mean the Song of God. These capture the essence of the Hindu tradition.

FIEDLER: One of the most intriguing things to me about Hinduism is its teaching on pluralism and tolerance. It accepts all religious paths as legitimate. I once knew a great Hindu guru, Swami Satchidananda, who used to say it in this way: "Truth is one, paths are many." Could you say something about that outlook in Hinduism?

CHOWDHURY: Hindus believe that there are many forms and paths to God. There's no one single, collective, definite belief system that one can follow. Hindus themselves have accepted many paths and forms that have come to them, particularly in India. If you look at Indian history, the Jews are one of the oldest living people that have been living there since Nebuchadnezzar's time. Christians have been there since St. Thomas's time. The Muslims came around the seventh century AD, and Hindus, of course, have been there since time immemorial. India itself has given rise, not only to Hindus, but to the Jain tradition, to the Sikh tradition, and to the Buddhist tradition as well.

FIEDLER: Can you be a Hindu and something else at the same time?

CHOWDHURY: Hindus believe that you can be anything, as long as you love every being as you love yourself—the essential message, I'm sure, every religion preaches and hopes their adherents will follow.

FIEDLER: Let's talk about some common misperceptions of Hinduism.

Some commentators describe Hinduism as polytheistic, that is, they say Hindus believe in many gods. What's the truth about gods in Hinduism?

CHOWDHURY: Hindus worship one supreme God through many different names and forms. A very simple example is oneself. My mother may look at me as a daughter, my niece may look at me as an aunt, my grandmother may look at me as a grandchild, but I'm still the same person. People simply view me in different ways. And we view God the same way. Somebody may view God in a certain aspect, but God is essentially one Supreme Being.

FIEDLER: And in Hinduism, God can be named or portrayed as either male or female?

CHOWDHURY: God has no particular gender or qualification or specification. So God is depicted both as a man and a woman.

FIEDLER: Your website* says that all beings in Hinduism are considered divine. But this doesn't mean that all creatures are supreme beings to be worshiped, does it?

CHOWDHURY: No, there's a very sacred phrase—"the whole creation is of one family"—and I think that is what we're trying to stress. Every being, from the smallest micro-organism to a human, is the creation of God, and we have to live in harmony and love one another. That is the essential and eternal message of Hinduism.

FIEDLER: The Quakers have a great saying, which is, "there is that of God in every one." Is that close to what a Hindu might express?

CHOWDHURY: I think that is a perfect example of what a Hindu may profess. For example, many may believe that the simple gesture—holding palms together and bowing—means "Hello," but the essential message is, "I bow to the God within you." We look at everyone as a part and parcel and as a spark of God.

FIEDLER: A lot of people say Hindus worship cows. How do Hindus regard cows, or any animal for that matter?

CHOWDHURY: Although Hindus respect and honor the cow, they don't worship it in the same sense as we worship God. If you look at agrarian times, the cow was very important, because it provided milk, butter, and cheese. In this sense, the animal was considered particularly important. But we don't necessarily worship the cow, we just hold it in honor. And that's why traditionally Hindus do not eat beef.

FIEDLER: Some people criticize Hindus for idol worship. You see a lot of depictions of God and statues and pictures and so forth in Hindu temples. What's the truth of that?

CHOWDHURY: First of all we shouldn't be calling them idols, we should be calling them deities. It's . . . a symbolism of God. . . . a divine image. But

---

* To learn more about Hinduism, visit www.hafsite.org.

to say we worship idols is a little bit of a misnomer. If you go to a Catholic church, there are also many images. I could say that's idol worship as well, but it isn't. Images give you a visual representation, an ability to focus, and I think that they are essential.

FIEDLER: Another misconception is the meaning of the word *karma*. That's very popular in discourse today, because karma means luck or fate. How do Hindus understand the word "karma"?

CHOWDHURY: Karma, in its essence, means for every action there is a reaction to it. Whatever you sow, you reap. Hindus believe that karma is in every action that we do in everyday life. Everything that we do has a karmic reaction to it later on. Hindus believe the only way to break that cycle of karma is to not have any attachment to the end result. To act for the benefit of society, for the benefit of humanity.

FIEDLER: And the cycle of karma might come back to you in another life. Is that not right?

CHOWDHURY: Karma, we believe, means that for every action that we perform, we're going to get a reaction—maybe now, maybe twenty years from now, maybe another life from now. So the Hindus always believe we have to work for the benefit of society. Can we elevate our karma, elevate our good actions? And once we are able to do that, we become spirit souls and return to God.

FIEDLER: And how about the caste system in India, which many, I should say, are trying to dismantle. Does that have any basis in Hinduism?

CHOWDHURY: Hindu scriptures do not have what we call today a "caste." They have a system called *varna*. Varna is basically a person's qualities, or characteristics. Unfortunately, like the feudal system in the Middle Ages, it became warped. Something a father did, a son did, and his son did, and the next son did, and so on and so forth. Caste is not exclusive to the Hindu tradition. Christians and Muslims have castes in India. Open any newspaper's matrimonial section and you'll find a something-something Christian family is looking for a something-something bridegroom.

FIEDLER: India is a very rapidly developing society. The urban centers are becoming very economically developed. What effect is that having on Hinduism in India?

CHOWDHURY: I read a very interesting article a couple of weeks ago on the high tech boom that's happening in Bangalore, which is India's Silicon Valley. It said that young professionals leaving their jobs after very long days still run to the temple, have their moment of silence, and commune with the divine. So even though India has its stark contrasts, I think the thing that's holding it together is that it still believes in spirituality and the divine regardless of the fast pace of modern technology.

Fatima Zahra Salhi, Ilham Chafik, and Nezha Nassi

The Mourchidates of Morocco

Sometimes, new religious leadership roles for women sound like traditional female roles with a blessing attached: social service work, for example. But often, these roles represent a breakthrough, a first step to other significant roles down the road. Such was the case with women deacons in Christianity, a traditionally "helping" role that became the first step toward women priests and bishops in the Episcopal Church. And this may be the case for an entire new category of women leaders in Islam: the *mourchidates* of Morocco. This interview took place in May of 2009.

MAUREEN FIEDLER: Since 2006, Muslim women in Morocco have been trained and certified as mourchidates, a role in which they work alongside *imams*, the traditional male religious leaders in Islam, to promote equality, tolerance, and interfaith dialog. Three women mourchidates are currently visiting the United States. All of them work in Rabat, the capital of Morocco. Fatima Zahra Salhi provides spiritual and psychological counseling for people in hospitals who are critically ill. Nezha Nassi counsels and leads religious services for women in prison. And Ilham Chafik, who has a Ph.D. in Arabic language and literature, conducts workshops for the blind in Islam and in Qur'anic studies.

What does it mean to be a mourchidate, Nezha?

NEZHA NASSI: A mourchidate is a woman who works in society and seeks to provide services for the whole society. We work on different levels, in hospitals, in schools, and in prisons. And we provide services in education, in religious teaching, and in all other fields.

FIEDLER: What can you do as mourchidate that you could not do before, just as a normal Muslim woman, Ilham?

ILHAM CHAFIK: As a woman, my role traditionally was within my house with my children. Being a mourchidate officially gives me a chance to do outreach into society. I'm able to reach the sick in the hospital, the imprisoned, the psychologically disturbed, the children with special needs, at universities, and in the mosque, of course.

FIEDLER: What kind of training do you get to become a mourchidate, Nezha?

NASSI: It's very comprehensive. We spend twelve months training, which includes sociology, astronomy, geography, history, health, and religious studies.

FIEDLER: And what do you do day-by-day, Fatima?

FATIMA ZAHRA SALHI: I'm a mourchidate; I'm also married with a baby of seven months. So I'm a mother *and* a mourchidate, so that comes together. I try to be the leader at home, and a leader in society, of course.

FIEDLER: Do you do counseling?

SALHI: I work in the hospital . . . with children. So for example, if I'm at the children's hospital, we have workshops, like reading stories, reading the Qur'an, painting, or fieldtrips.

FIEDLER: Is this similar, Ilham, to what you do?

CHAFIK: My mornings are actually spent in meetings with my community members. We deal with the universities, charitable organizations, and orphanages.

FIEDLER: Nezha?

NASSI: In the mosques, I counsel people and I try to give them lessons, or lectures on morals. And in prisons, I do counseling on health issues, on psychological issues. I talk to them about sexually transmitted diseases. And I counsel women with breast cancer. Sometimes I do counseling for prisoners after they come out of prison, to try to integrate them into society, to get them jobs, education, whatever they need.

FIEDLER: What led you to seek the role of mourchidate, Fatima?

SALHI: I find in this role of mourchidate everything that is close to my heart and what I aspire to do as a woman. I was hoping to become a doctor, but now I find myself doing the same role in the hospitals, actually dealing with sick people. I was hoping to be in social service, and I found myself working as a social worker within the prisons. And I was hoping to become a teacher, and I found myself as a mourchidate, doing the same thing as teaching. Being a mourchidate gives me all the roles to play as a woman: religious scholar, teacher, doctor, and everything that would give me my identity as a woman.

FIEDLER: My understanding is that women are able to approach you with questions that are important in their lives that they might not ask a man, an imam. And I'm wondering what some of those questions are, Ilham?

CHAFIK: During Ramadan for example, women have questions about their periods, when they should fast, when they should not, when they are clean to fast again. Questions like that a man cannot answer; only a woman can.

FIEDLER: And I would assume these include questions about things like domestic violence, or sexuality, or sexually transmitted diseases, very intimate questions like that, Fatima?

SALHI: This is absolutely true. These questions actually dominate our work as mourchidates. We find ourselves in the middle of actually solving problems that deal with sexually transmitted diseases and intimate relationships between men and women, and girls and boys.

FIEDLER: What has been the reaction in the larger Moroccan society to your new role? Do they accept you, or is there opposition, Nezha?

NASSI: The role of mourchidate has really been accepted and has received positive reactions from society.

FIEDLER: You have no vocal opposition?

NASSI: Actually, on the contrary, our role has proven very important, and the fruits have already been seen in different fields.

FIEDLER: You work alongside imams, but you're not imams, and so you cannot conduct mixed-gender prayer services. I wonder, do you aspire ultimately to be imams, to conduct mixed-gender prayer services, Nezha?

NASSI: The meaning of "imam" actually, linguistically speaking, is to be a leader. And as a mourchidate, I feel that I'm already a leader. Just to give you an example, I'm actually the leader of the community prisons. So I'm very equal to a man. But to lead prayer is very explicit in Islam, and it's very explicit that a woman cannot by any means lead the prayer.

SALHI: So as mourchidates, we feel very equal to our male imam colleagues. We do not find that being an imam and directing prayer will give us any privilege. So we feel that to lead a prayer is another expertise, and for men, so let men do it.

FIEDLER: There are women, Muslim women in the United States—Amina Wadud comes to mind—who have, in fact, made the case that women can and should lead mixed-gender services, and have, in fact, done that in New York. Ilham?

CHAFIK: For us in Morocco, it's very clear. We follow the Maliki school of thought, which does not give women the right to lead prayer.

FIEDLER: Why would you say your work is important as mourchidates, for the people of Morocco?

CHAFIK: Our work has proven to have been extremely needed by society, especially women. Not necessarily only women, because we do deal also with boys, and girls, and men. But it's important for us to actually be approached by women, and asked questions, and be able to answer their questions.

~~~~~~

Starhawk
Leader of the Earth-Based Wiccan/Goddess Tradition

Some women religious leaders defy all categories. Such is Starhawk, a leader of the Wiccan, pagan, or earth-based religious tradition. There are no formal leadership positions in this group. Starhawk is not a "bishop" or a "rabbi" or even the president of something. She is an informal but widely respected leader in her tradition, the author of several books, and a sought-after speaker on Wicca. She is the closest one can come to a "denominational leader" in Wicca.

Maureen Fiedler: Those who study ancient religions agree that the cycles of nature were vitally important to primeval civilizations, and this spawned religions where people worshiped nature. One of those traditions grew among ancient Celtic peoples in the British Isles. It has been revived today in a belief system called Wicca, or sometimes Neo-paganism. One of the chief spokespersons for that tradition, which is growing in numbers, is the woman who goes by one name, Starhawk. She is the author of ten books, including *The Spiral Dance: A Rebirth of the Ancient Religion of the Great Goddess*, and *The Earth Path: Grounding Your Spirit in the Rhythms of Nature*. I had the opportunity to talk to Starhawk at a conference called Earth Spirit Rising, in Louisville, Kentucky, in June of 2007.

Starhawk, people sometimes apply negative terms to members of your tradition. What are some of these? How do you feel about them?

Starhawk: You can call me a pagan, you can call me a witch, I don't mind, because the root of the word "witch" really goes back to an old Anglo-Saxon root, "wic," which means to bend, or shape, or twist. And the witches were the wise women and men, who could bend or twist fate.

After Christianity came in, it didn't really destroy the pagan traditions in the old earth-centered traditions. And it wasn't until the sixteenth and seventeenth centuries that the church decided to make war on the old pagan traditions, very much in the way that the war on terrorism has served certain interests today. Having an enemy that you can make people fear is very convenient for maintaining power. And the sixteenth and seventeenth centuries were years of tremendous change and transition. The church was being challenged by Protestant reformation. There were peasant rebellions. The whole economic system was changing. And the people in power had a desperate need for control.

And so, it was useful to have an enemy that people could focus on, saying, "Your problem isn't the fact that the lord in the castle is taking all of your crops and leaving you to starve. Your problem is those bad witches down the street who are casting evil spells on your cow."

So they created a whole mythology of their own about devil worship and Satan worship and stuff that had nothing to do with the old religion. And probably millions of people were persecuted, and killed, and burned, and tortured in the name of that kind of fear. Those of us who identify as "witches" and "pagans" today have had to go on a long journey to actually overcome that fear, and claim those words again. For me it's important to use those words, because I think as long as we don't, they remain clubs someone can always use to beat us with. Once we claim that and explain them, it drains away the charge. And when it drains away that charge around the word "witch," it also drains away some of the fear that we have as women about speaking out and being powerful and assertive. It drains away some of the assumptions that any kind of knowledge that's not approved of by the authorities is somehow dangerous, and evil, and wrong.

And it gives us more freedom and more space.

FIEDLER: How does freedom from those assumptions shape your vision of the world?

STARHAWK: We need to re-envision the world and the earth itself as something sacred. Sacred, not in a sense that we bow down to it, but sacred in the sense that it's what we most deeply care about. It's what we care about beyond our immediate comfort or advantage, what we most deeply love. The root of the word "sacred" is the same as the root of the word "sacrifice." To sacrifice for something is to put aside your limited self-interest in the interest of something that's deeper, that's more important, that you more deeply love. From a pagan perspective, or Goddess-based perspective, we see the earth as alive, as a living being that all of us are part of. So in some sense we are in the earth; we are the divine; we all partake of that sacred deep creativity and love that's embodied in the living world. The world itself is the expression of the Goddess.

FIEDLER: How do you view the current ecological crisis?

STARHAWK: All of life is interconnected. And that belief raises certain ethical and moral imperatives. If we do believe that we're all interconnected, then we can't be destroying major pieces of ourselves and our ecosystem.

FIEDLER: And this includes all species?

STARHAWK: It includes all species; it includes all human beings. You know, that we can't write off whole groups of human beings and say they don't count, and their lives aren't worth anything, and we have license to kill them. We need to work on the basis of interconnectedness and say that we need to find ways to communicate and ways to celebrate that interconnectedness, and ways to cooperate, ways to work together.

FIEDLER: And so, you would oppose all war?

STARHAWK: I'm a Goddess-worshiper, but by birth I'm a Jew. My husband actually was the first draft-card burner in the Vietnam War.

He spent two years in federal prison for burning his draft card, and he's a devoted pacifist. And we always get into arguments, because he's very clear that he would never under any circumstances go to war or use a weapon. I say, "You know, I'm a Jew; if I were in Nazi Germany I'd like to think I would've joined the resistance." But I've been a lifelong practitioner of nonviolence, as a philosophy and also as a political strategy. And I strongly believe that we're obligated to work very hard to find a nonviolent solution before we ever give up, and to go to the default, which is violence and war and force.

FIEDLER: The Goddess Movement, which is both ecological and feminist, is unfamiliar to most of us. How would you describe it?

STARHAWK: You could think of the Goddess Movement as a way of re-balancing our conception of what's important and what's valuable in the world. It's looking at the sacred again, and choosing an image for the sacred that's a female image. People sometimes say, "Why not just be neutral?" And I always say, if you have ever been on a seesaw, and you're down on one end, you can't get back by standing in the middle, you have to go to the other end. And we've had five thousand years of male God images. And not only male images, but particular kinds of male images that identify power as aggression, as war, as domination. To challenge that in our minds, and our hearts, we also need to have images that see a different kind of power, the kind of power that is represented by women's ability to bring life into the world, the power of nurturing, the power of caring for something, the power of earth-giving. And when we do that, we also revalue the world. We revalue the life that comes into the world and those who bring life into the world.

FIEDLER: Belief in a goddess is very ancient, is it not?

STARHAWK: There are images of goddesses that go back twenty-five thousand to thirty thousand years to the caves in France, and in Austria and Eastern Europe. Some of the earliest human expressions of art are the sacred female body. And there were goddess cultures, certainly in Europe, that are really well documented from nine thousand and up to three thousand years before Christ. The earliest village cultures, the earliest beginnings of horticulture, and pottery, and weaving were in cultures where the religious images were goddesses, female figures, images of life, and of food, and of birth, and of sex. And those were the things that were considered sacred. There were not a lot of images of war. There were not weapons found, or human sacrifice, or any of that—that came later when there was a transition to war and conquest. Those became cultures that focused more on images of male gods, and God became re-conceived as the primary warrior, the king and war-leader. But in earlier times, the divine, the sacred, was conceived of as the earth, the mother, the Goddess.

FIEDLER: Does this tradition exclude men?

STARHAWK: In the Goddess tradition, it's not that we don't have any male images, because we also do see God as male. We say our religion is a religion of poetry, not of dogma. All the images we use are poetic images, and they're meant awaken certain emotions, and certain feelings, and certain energies. They're not descriptive images, or proscriptive images.

FIEDLER: How large is the Goddess Movement, and the Earth Spirituality Movement that surrounds that, as far as you know today?

STARHAWK: People always ask us how many Goddess-worshipers, how many witches there are, and the truth is nobody really knows, because we don't have a census for it, and there's no central registry. But I've heard estimates between five hundred thousand and two million in the United States. Our basic understandings go back to very ancient times. I don't think anyone would claim that our specific, exact rituals are exactly what they did five hundred years ago. But our understandings and our traditions have roots that go very deep, and probably go back to some of the earliest human expressions of religion.

FIEDLER: Like most other faith traditions, adherents of the Wicca tradition express their beliefs with rituals.

STARHAWK: We get together in different ways, in small groups mostly. But over the last ten, twenty years, we've also had larger and larger gatherings, as we felt safer to "come out of the broom closet." But often it'll be a very intimate ritual. We might gather and give everyone a chance to speak about what's going on in their lives, what they feel they need energy and support for, what they most care about at that moment. And then we'll sing or we'll chant, or we'll do a meditation, or we'll do a trance journey.

FIEDLER: What's a trance journey?

STARHAWK: A trance journey is like a guided imagery journey to raise energy, to focus attention and focus support on that person. And we also have ceremonies and rituals that celebrate the cycles of the seasons, the cycles of the moon. The full moon in particular is an important time.

And we have eight important holidays through the year that we celebrate. Halloween's probably the best known. In the Celtic cultures, it was the New Year, the end of the harvest, and the commencement of the new cycle. It was a time when people believed the ancestors were close by, since almost all the dead came back, and some people would light candles to guide them back.

There was a sense that death didn't sever the human community. Community continued beyond death. If you loved someone in life, you didn't stop loving them after death.

FIEDLER: Don't some popular Halloween images actually have a basis in ancient or current practice? Like dancing around a cauldron, for example?

FIEDLER: We do dance around the cauldron. But the cauldron might be a soup pot. It might be a place where we're brewing up herb tea, or it might be brewing something like compost tea you feed to the plants, to help heal the earth. It could be outdoors, it could be indoors. But the cauldron was simply what people used to cook in ancient times.

FIEDLER: When it comes to your major ethical concern, overcoming the ecological crisis in the world, how do you retain your hope and optimism?

STARHAWK: I think a lot of people are recognizing the depth of the ecological crisis we're in. And thanks to Al Gore and his movie *An Inconvenient Truth*, and thanks to a lot of people's work over the years, we're finally waking up and saying, "Oh yes, climate change is real."

The environment is not something we watch on the Discovery Channel. It is the ground of our lives. And I think a lot of people feel a tremendous amount of fear, conscious or unconscious, about what's going to happen, and often a sense of hopelessness or powerlessness. One of the things Al Gore said in his movie was that people go immediately from denial to despair, sometimes without stopping or doing anything useful in between. But guess what? I think we're also in a time of tremendous hope. There are solutions even for our grave environmental problems, and those solutions come from shifting our way of thinking, and really grasping that we are interconnected.

And when we make our interconnectedness the bottom line of everything we do, not only do we stop doing the things that are harmful, we awaken the creativity and resilience that exist within us as human beings. Once we start listening to nature, there are great forces that are working with us for the healing of the earth. And I am very optimistic. I think this is a tremendously exciting time to be alive. It's a moment we were called to make a huge transition in our way of thinking, and in our way of living, a transition that will ultimately land us in a world that is better, that is more just, that is happier, that's more beautiful.

Chapter 2
Women Leaders in Theological and Scriptural Scholarship

For centuries, theology and scripture studies were almost exclusively male domains. No more. For decades now, women have excelled in academic roles, publishing widely and often holding prestigious chairs at theological schools. These women have offered new insights into age-old problems and issues, and their work helped pave the way for women's acceptance in elected denominational leadership. I mention only a few here.

In the Christian tradition, scholars like Karen King and Elaine Pagels have highlighted the theological diversity of early Christian communities with their analyses of the so-called Gnostic gospels. Elisabeth Schüssler Fiorenza is an internationally recognized authority on the New Testament, and the author of many books of biblical scholarship. Rosemary Radford Ruether is a prolific theological author, focusing on feminist and environmental theology. Elizabeth Johnson tackled the overarching question of the gender of God. Feminist theologian Letty Russell and scripture scholar Phyllis Trible have been highly influential, as is evangelical theologian Virginia Ramey Mollenkott. Margaret Farley of Yale is a leading moral theologian. Systematic theologian Serene Jones was recently named president of the faculty at Union Theological Seminary in New York.

African-American women theologians such as Delores Williams and Emilie Townes have developed "womanist theology," and Latina theologians like Ada Maria Isasi-Diaz have created "*mujerista* theology."

Korean scholar Hyun Kyung Chung of Union Theological Seminary is known for a "liberation theology" for Asian women. Kwok Pui-Lan is a leader in post-colonial feminist Asian theology. Clara Sue Kidwell is a pioneer in Native American theology. Mary Evelyn Tucker is considered an authority in the field of theological ecology. Mary Hunt is a leading lesbian feminist theologian with wide-ranging interests often focused on theology in the public square.

Rita Nakashima Brock and Rebecca Ann Parker have challenged teachings commonly preached in Christianity, including the meaning of the crucifixion and the "doctrine of the atonement," the idea that God sent Jesus to die for the sins of humanity.

In the Islamic tradition, Fatima Mernissi of Morocco is known globally for her feminist approach to Islam. In the United States, scholars like Riffat Hassan, Amina Wadud, and Leila Ahmed have published numerous works on women in Islam. Aminah Beverly McCloud is a leading African-American scholar of Islam.

Azizah al-Hibri, Esq. is a leader in the all important field of Islamic law. She is a founder of Karamah: Muslim Women Lawyers for Human Rights, which seeks to overcome archaic interpretations of women's role in some Muslim communities and promote what they call "the egalitarian Qur'anic worldview of gender equity and humanity."

In the Muslim Middle East, Aisha al-Mannai is the first woman dean of the Shariah College at Qatar University. In Indonesia, Hajjah Maria Ulfah is considered one of the world's leading reciters of the Qur'an, a role normally filled by men.

Jewish scholars, like Blu Greenberg and Judith Plaskow, have focused on feminist re-interpretations of their tradition. Carolyn Sharp is an authority on the Hebrew scriptures. Amy-Jill Levine and Julie Galambush have offered distinctly Jewish insights on the Christian New Testament. Rabbi Andrea Weiss authored a women's commentary on the Torah.

In Buddhism, scholars like Upasika Kee Nanayon of Thailand and Sharon Salzberg from the United States have published several works on Buddhist theology and spiritual practice. Rita M. Gross has written on Buddhism after patriarchy. Pema Chodron is the author of several books on Buddhist life and practice, and has been interviewed by both Bill Moyers and Oprah Winfrey. Sandra Boucher is an authority on women in Buddhism.

In Hinduism, Rita Dasgupta Sherma serves as the chair of the Council for Hindu Studies and is one of the editors of *Hermeneutics and Hindu Thought: Toward a Fusion of Horizons*, a book that attempts to create a bridge between Hinduism and modern hermeneutics, or the study and interpretation of scriptural texts.

These names barely scratch the surface of women's achievements in theological academia. In this chapter, we meet a few of the women scholars who are pioneers in theology and scripture generally, and in the next chapter, we meet some of those who focus on feminist theology.

Dr. Amy-Jill Levine

on *The Misunderstood Jew:*
The Church and the Scandal of the Jewish Jesus

Dr. Amy-Jill Levine is Jewish, but focuses her scholarship on the New Testament, bringing a Jewish spotlight to the life of Jesus. Levine is a professor of New Testament studies at Vanderbilt University Divinity School in Nashville, Tennessee. She is the author of the book, *The Misunderstood Jew: The Church and the Scandal of the Jewish Jesus*. This conversation with her took place in January 2007.

Maureen Fiedler: Amy-Jill, as a child in North Dartmouth, Massachusetts, you dreamed of becoming pope. What pointed you to that dream?

Amy-Jill Levine: When I was a little girl, I came home from school one day and the only thing that was on TV was the funeral of Pope John XXIII, and I was looking for cartoons. I remember asking my mother why the cartoons weren't on. Who was this guy? Why is he so important that he's on every network? Back then, I think, that meant two different stations. And my mother said, "Oh, that was Pope John XXIII; he was good for the Jews." John XXIII was known for rescuing Jews during the Holocaust. And I somehow picked up the idea that he was in Rome, which to me meant you got to eat spaghetti. So I announced to my mother, "I want to be pope." My mother said to me, "But you can't be pope." And when I indignantly said, "Why not?" She said, "Because dear, you're not Italian."

Fiedler: You're not Italian; you're not Catholic. But you are Jewish.

Levine: Very much so.

Fiedler: And you have now explored the Jewish character of Jesus.

Levine: When I was a child, my parents told me that my Catholic friends, my Christian friends, thought that a Jewish man named Jesus was very important, that Jews and Christians worship the same God, and that we both thought the Ten Commandments were important. They also told me that our Bible was part of the Christian Bible. So I had always looked, at least early on, at Christianity as a cousin to Judaism.

And then one day—I was seven years old—this girl said to me on the school bus, "You killed our Lord." I couldn't put together how Christianity, which I had been taught was very much like Judaism, interested in loving God and loving neighbor, would teach horrible things about Jews or about me personally. This young girl had been taught that the Jews were responsible for the death of Jesus, and because I was the only Jew she knew, it must have been me. I started asking questions, and I came to realize very quickly that in order to understand Jesus fully, one has to recognize that Jesus is a Jew talking to other first-century Jews and that he died like many other first-century Jews did on a Roman cross.

FIEDLER: And where do you begin to tell Christians about the Jewish character of Jesus?

LEVINE: I tend not to start with any particular agenda. I'm much more interested in talking to my Christian friends and colleagues about where *they* begin with Jesus. What do they think about him? And then I take those aspects of the Jesus tradition that they find important, whether it's a message of social justice, or love of God and love of neighbor, or his death. And then I say, "You know, if you understood the Jewish context of this material, your appreciation of it will become even richer, even more fully developed."

FIEDLER: A common thing a lot of people say is that Christians read the Bible in the light of Christian teachings that developed much later. Do you think that's true?

LEVINE: Oh sure, because the stories we have of Jesus don't come to us unmediated. We have Matthew's view and Mark's view and John's view. It's hard sometimes to penetrate through the various layers of what we learned in Sunday school, or what the great figures of the church taught, to get all the way back to the Jesus who lies underneath the gospels. But I think it's an extremely worthwhile exercise in which to engage.

FIEDLER: Since you are one of the few Jews working in the United States who is a New Testament scholar, describe the problem that many Jews at the time may have had with Jesus, when he proclaimed himself to be the Son of God.

LEVINE: All Jews would have looked at themselves as children of God. We still do today. All people are children of God. The Gospel of Luke, in Jesus' genealogy, describes Adam as "son of God." Now, were Jesus to have proclaimed himself the messiah, which is simply a word meaning the "anointed one" or "God's anointed," he would be making a point that God had commissioned him for a particular mission. Where Jesus would have been provocative to the point where people would have said, "Wait a minute, I'm not sure I want to go this far," might have been his saying things like, "I am God's anointed one and through me comes about the Kingdom of God." That might have raised some questions, because others might have thought, "Well, how is it that you're bringing about the Kingdom and not somebody else?"

FIEDLER: Were there conditions on who would take the mantle of messiah?

LEVINE: Oh, it's a good question. There's no first-century checklist of what a messiah was or even what a messiah was supposed to do. Today there's a common sense that all Jews were waiting for this political messiah who would take up arms against Rome, and Jesus gets rejected because he preached love of God and love of neighbor. That's an unfortunate Christian stereotype. Some first-century Jews believed the messiah would be a priest, others an angelic figure, still others thought John the Baptist was the messiah; the Dead Sea Scrolls mention at least two messianic figures.

FIEDLER: And so there were literally competitors with the idea?

LEVINE: For those Jews who believed a messiah was coming—and by no means did all Jews believe in the messiah, then or now—one primary view was that the messiah and the messianic age would come together. In other words, it would be a package. We can see this in the Gospel of John when Jesus says to Martha, "Do you believe in the resurrection?" And Martha responds, "Yes, Lord, I believe in the resurrection on the last day." That's good Jewish belief in the messianic age. When the messiah comes, there's a general resurrection.

When Jesus died, his followers proclaimed him to be resurrected, but his followers weren't able to say, "And your parents will come back immediately, and you will be able to see your grandfather. And you will be able to see the wife whom you lost," because there was no general resurrection of the dead. There was no sign that the world had changed, and most Jews said, "We'll have to keep waiting."

FIEDLER: And so, Amy-Jill, there's been a real animosity since the beginning?

LEVINE: There's been first distrust and misunderstanding, and then ignorance, and from distrust, misunderstanding, and ignorance, you wind up with hate and then eventually you wind up with death.

FIEDLER: Now could you talk about some other Jewish traditions that really have been lost on Christianity?

LEVINE: A sense of the importance of the Jewish scriptures, what Christians would call the Old Testament, has been lost. I sometimes find in churches that Old Testament readings are just passed over, or considered antithetical to Jesus' message. I think it would be wonderful if the church recovered some of the love of the Old Testament, a term Jesus never would have used, of course.

How lovely if people went back and actually heard those words of the ancient prophets so you could hear Jesus echo them. When Jesus talks about the great commandment of love of God and love of neighbor, might it not be a good thing to know that love of God is actually a quotation from Deuteronomy and love of neighbor is a quotation of from—of all places—the book of Leviticus?

In interfaith dialogue, mistakes are rampant. For example, some say the Old Testament has a God of wrath and the New Testament has a God of love.

And on the Jewish side, I frequently find that in many synagogues, the Jewish default is Roman Catholicism. So Christianity is understood as the Roman Catholic tradition or it's understood as Jerry Falwell or a particular brand of popularized Evangelical conservative Christianity. And there's little sense of the incredible diversity within what we might call today the Body of Christ.

Rita Nakashima Brock and Rebecca Ann Parker

on *Saving Paradise: How Christianity Traded Love of this World for Crucifixion and Empire*

Two of the most provocative theologians today are Rita Nakashima Brock and Rebecca Ann Parker. They reexamine and reinterpret basic Christian tenets. In an earlier book, *Proverbs of Ashes: Violence, Redemptive Suffering, and the Search for What Saves Us*, they challenged the very notion of "redemptive suffering," or the "doctrine of the atonement," commonly taught in Christian theology. In their newest book, they challenge the very meaning of the cross and resurrection.

Rita Nakashima Brock is founding co-director of Faith Voices for the Common Good, an organization dedicated to educating the public about the values and concerns of religious leaders and organizations. She also works with The New Press in New York as senior editor in religion.

Rev. Rebecca Ann Parker is president and a professor of theology at Starr King School for the Ministry, the Unitarian Universalist school of the Graduate Theological Union in California. She is an ordained Methodist minister in dual fellowship with the Unitarian Universalist Association.

This conversation took place in December 2008.

Maureen Fiedler: When I picked up the new book *Saving Paradise*, I was stunned to learn that the crucifix, the image of a suffering, bloody, dying Jesus, so familiar today, was not a part of Christian art until the tenth century. For a whole millennium, the images of Jesus found in churches depicted a living, vibrant being, a shepherd, an infant, a youth, or a bearded elder, usually shown amid scenes of intense natural beauty. Why, I wondered, was there no crucifix? And why did it appear after a thousand years? And most important, what does such art tell us about the basic teachings and outlook of Christianity before and after the change?

Rebecca, why no crucifix for a thousand years? Did the early Christians have no interest in the suffering and death of Jesus?

REBECCA ANN PARKER: The early Christians worshiped the risen Christ because they believed the resurrection had reopened paradise in this world, on the earth. They lamented Jesus' crucifixion in rituals performed usually just once a year. So they didn't depict crucifixions because what mattered to them was the *life* of Jesus: his ministry, feeding the hungry, healing the sick, his teachings to appreciate the beauty of creation, his calling to people to create communities of care, and his resurrection over the power of death. Life is what mattered to them, not death.

FIEDLER: You both scoured the Mediterranean world for early Christian art. Can you describe an image of Jesus that you might commonly see during the first millennium?

RITA NAKASHIMA BROCK: One of our favorites in our book *Saving Paradise* is a church in Ravenna, Italy. In this particular image, Jesus looks like a teenager. He sits on a huge blue globe of the world so the earth is his throne and the sky sparkles golden like an Easter dawn behind him. He's flanked by heavenly beings, but the amazing thing is that the blue globe sits on a green bluff of paradise and the four rivers of paradise pour out from the bottom of the globe into the green meadows that surround the image at the bottom. I think one of the most marvelous details of this image is that Jesus is very plain looking. He has no imperial garb or high office images; he has a cap of curly hair. He doesn't have a beard. He wears simple sandals with bare feet. So he looks like a peasant almost, except for the robe he wears which is purple in nobility. And that is the one little detail that marks his sort of holy status.

PARKER: This beautiful young Jesus is seated in this beautiful world, green trees, and the rivers, sparkling skies, and this image of Jesus captures both the idea that the green meadows and blue waters of all the world are paradise here and now, and show that the risen Christ presides over the great feast of abundant life that Christians celebrated in the church.

BROCK: Some of my favorite images that are ubiquitous are little green weeping dolphins.

FIEDLER: Dolphins?

BROCK: Dolphins. Yes. They loved the dolphins in the first millennium.

FIEDLER: Some people would say, "Okay this is art. What difference do these images make? This is not theology after all. "

PARKER: The thing that we have to remember is that, for the first millennium, images are how Christians learned their theology. It's what they saw in the church, what they sang in their hymns, the movements and dances they did, the stories that were told, the poetic prayers. All these artful things are how they learned their theology. For fifteen hundred years, until the invention of the printing press, manuscripts were very expensive, very rare. Few people could read them. So art was the medium by which Christians learned their theology.

FIEDLER: You mentioned, of course, that these early Christians essentially had an image of paradise, not just in the hereafter, but in the here and now. I'm wondering, Rita, how can this be? As Christians, haven't we been taught that we have to suffer now so we can be happy in the hereafter?

BROCK: In the second millennium, Christianity taught that to some Christians, although the Eastern Orthodox churches maintained some of the older theology. But the early church believed that Genesis told the truth: God created paradise as a home for humanity on the earth in this life and that the serpent was actually there from the beginning. The fall didn't create the serpent, the temptations of the serpent were in the paradise garden itself. So paradise was not a utopia or perfect place, but a place of struggle, so that humanity could learn to discern the difference between good and evil and understand evil both inside ourselves and in an unjust world.

FIEDLER: Did early Christians also believe that paradise extended into the hereafter as well?

PARKER: Yes. their notion was that when you die, you moved to a realm of paradise very close to where the living were, not far away in some distant galaxy or high above the clouds. The dead lived in another realm of earthly paradise where they were protected from evil and could be at peace. But they could return to the realm of the living through the veil that separated the living from the dead, and offer assistance to the living. So when Christians gathered for worship, they believed that their ancestors, the saints, those who had gone before, the communion of saints, came and assembled with them, invisible but tangible, connecting the living and the dead.

BROCK: We describe it as like working your whole life in Minnesota or New York or some place like that, and then getting to retire to Florida, but flying back home and visiting people.

FIEDLER: Now, of course, their notion of paradise on earth included some struggle, right? I keep thinking about poor people during the first thousand years. They lived a pretty miserable existence, and a lot of them were Christian. So their notion of paradise wasn't that all things were just super swell?

PARKER: That's right. In fact, the notion that this world has been created by God as a good and abundant garden to support life for all was precisely the notion of paradise needed by the poor, and the struggling and the oppressed, because its message was that God wants abundant life for all of us and has provided for all of us. So injustice, human cruelty, the travesties of empire and its greed might separate people from the gifts of life they were meant to have. So this was a world of promising affirmation for the poor and the suffering. And Christians were to assume that these good gifts of life were provided for everyone to be shared by everyone. That meant resisting unjust structures that withheld the gifts of life from people and it meant working to alleviate suffering and create communities of compassion and care. In this way, the church was understood to be paradise in this world.

BROCK: And the church had a whole welfare system across geographical boundaries, sharing goods in common. If one church was in trouble in one region, the other churches that weren't in trouble would help them. And so they saw the dire suffering of the world as a call to alleviate it, not as a holy thing they were supposed to endure.

FIEDLER: Now someone listening to this business of paradise on earth who knows a bit about the gospels might remember Jesus' words to Pontius Pilate, "My kingdom is not of this world." Isn't Jesus saying that his realm, normally thought of as paradise, is in another life? Not here?

PARKER: No. He's saying that this world means the powers of this world, the structures of this world. It's like Jesus was saying, "My kingdom is not of Wall Street. My kingdom is something else."

FIEDLER: "My realm is not the Roman Empire, Pontius Pilate." Is that what he was saying?

PARKER: That's what he was saying. My kingdom is not the social systems that leave some people hungry and give other people wealth, or that torture terrorized people.

FIEDLER: I must say that when I read that part in your book, I had an "ah ha" moment, in the interpretation of that particular passage.

BROCK: His other world is a world touched by heaven, not touched by Rome.

FIEDLER: In the tenth and eleventh centuries, the crucifix appears as a prominent image of Jesus, and as time goes on it gets bloodier and bloodier. Why the change?

PARKER: To answer that question, we had to look at northern Europe in the ninth century because that's where the image appears, among the Saxon people who were forcibly converted to Christianity by the violence of Charlemagne's empire. The image was first produced by victims of Christian violence, and they may have identified with the crucified Christ and seen themselves as like Jesus, tormented and tortured by an unjust empire.

But very shortly, the empire that did this violence started to say that this violence was holy. They started to say that Jesus' death saved sinners from their sins, and they started to say that the Eucharist was a reenactment of the crucifixion of Jesus. That was a new theology of the communion meal because the older theology of communion was a celebration of the feast of life presided over by the risen Christ. But once the communion meal began to be seen as the reenactment of the killing of Jesus, there was this whole tragic turn towards a crucifixion-centered Christianity.

BROCK: One of the key pieces of that was once the priest "killed" Jesus, then the communicants consumed his corpse. And in doing so, if they had not repented of all their sins, they would eat and drink damnation and be in hell forever. So the Eucharist turned from being a feast of life and joy and a celebration of Christian life in paradise into this moment of intense terror—that you might have forgotten a sin that you didn't confess, and then if you ate accidentally, you would be doomed forever. And so the Eucharist became a terrorization process, a way of trying to control populations. And then it became a kind of empire-propaganda liturgy.

FIEDLER: And you say in the book that the appearance of the crucifix ultimately made a difference in the teachings of Christianity about the use of violence.

PARKER: For most of the first centuries of Christianity, Christians completely rejected the use of violence. But once the image of Jesus' death started to become a sacred image, you have this switch in theology to the idea that Jesus' death saved people. Christianity loses its grasp on nonviolence and the church starts to teach that soldiers who kill are doing so for God, for Christ. And soldiers who are killed have offered themselves to be sacrificed like Jesus was. So you start to have a notion of "holy war" in the late eleventh century. And then the Crusades begin. And the church begins to teach that if you go off on a crusade and kill Muslims, Jews, or heretical Christians, you do so for God, and you will be rewarded with paradise in the afterlife.

FIEDLER: So it would be true to say that this crucifixion imagery actually fed anti-Semitism and racism in the policies of the Christian monarchs of the day?

PARKER: That's correct.

FIEDLER: Now, the crucifix itself is different in different places. It can be quite graphic and bloody, for example in Spain and Latin America. And of course, Catholics and Orthodox tend to use the crucifix, but many Protestant churches typically use just a plain bare cross. Why the differences here?

BROCK: When I was growing as a Protestant, I was taught that in the Protestant tradition, it's really the cross of Resurrection which is actually how the early church tended to use the image of the cross. But this is actually not exactly true. The reason that Protestants tend not to use crucifixion images is that Protestants are just hostile to visual images. Iconoclastic Protestantism was trying to wipe out everything visual and make people listen to the sermon and the word and to read the Bible and do nothing else but that, as a source for their faith. A lot of churches even broke their stained glass windows because they didn't like the darkness, and they couldn't read their Bibles.

FIEDLER: What difference does a crucifix image rather than the living, vibrant Jesus image make in the lives of ordinary Christians today?

PARKER: One of the things I learned when I was a pastor, working day in and day out with Christians in a church context, was how often people interpret their own experiences of suffering through the lenses of their theology. So when someone's theology teaches that Jesus' suffering and death was God's will and was a good thing and brought about redemption, Christians who are victims of sexual abuse or violence, or men who served in war, try to believe that their suffering is also a good thing, or that they deserved it. Or they believe that God wanted them to experience this pain, and that if they just endure faithfully they will have a reward sometime in the future.

And this has tragic results in the lives of people because it means that people are interpreting their suffering as good, like Jesus' suffering. It restrains them from trying to alleviate suffering or resist the causes of suffering.

If Christian theology teaches that life is good, that God wants us to thrive and have abundant life and share the gifts of life, then when suffering comes, our first instinct is *not* to say, "Oh, God willed this and I must endure this." Our first instinct is to say to ourselves and to one another: "How can we alleviate this suffering; how can we help one another?" And if suffering has come because of injustice, we tend to ask, "How do we counter this injustice, say no to it and work for real justice and for abundant life for all people?"

FIEDLER: So that's why you characterize the reform movements in nineteenth-century America, like the struggle against slavery, the struggle for women's suffrage, for worker's rights, and in our own time for civil rights, as in some sense, a struggle to say that suffering is not desirable, and to regain that sense of an earthly paradise that you talked about?

BROCK: Yes, we believe that, as partial as some of these movements were, and as often uncoordinated as they were, they all affirm in some sense that Christian life has to be lived in this world as a call to make a better world, to work for justice, to love beauty, to love each other. This is, if not the whole of Christian salvation, a crucial piece of it.

FIEDLER: Finally, how can Christians today go about regaining paradise as the early Christians understood it?

PARKER: I think we regain paradise here and now when we focus our spiritual lives first of all on the beauty and goodness around us that is present every day. And then, we need to have a love for life and an appreciation for beauty and goodness as the foundation of our ethical commitments, so that we work for a better world out of love for this world.

BROCK: Another aspect of this is that the medieval focus on suffering and the death of Jesus tended to valorize victimhood and see holiness in being vulnerable and powerless. And I think that the early church was much more sophisticated about how it understood power. We should respect the fact that we have the power to help and to think about being wise in the moral uses of power. We shouldn't be afraid of power or avoid power, or think that having power is always a bad thing.

PARKER: And the phrase we like is actually from the great historian of the early church, Peter Brown, who says, "Early Christianity was a *this-worldly, life-affirming, optimistic faith.*"

FIEDLER: And that's what you would like to see return?

PARKER and **BROCK:** Yes.

~~~~~~

Dr. Elaine Pagels

on *Beyond Belief: The Secret Gospel of Thomas*

Dr. Elaine Pagels is one of the leading scholars of the so-called "Gnostic gospels," the accounts of Jesus' life and times that were *not* included in the canonical New Testament. Her book, *Beyond Belief: The Secret Gospel of Thomas*, spent six weeks on the *New York Times* best seller list. In it, she delves deeply into one of these suppressed gospels, the Gospel of Thomas. She is the Harrington Spear Paine Professor of Religion at Princeton University. This interview took place in July 2003.

MAUREEN FIEDLER: Elaine, most Christians have heard of Matthew, Mark, Luke, and John. But they might say, "What is with this Gospel of *Thomas*?" What are we talking about?

DR. ELAINE PAGELS: That's what I would have said too. I went to graduate school some time ago because I wanted to understand something about how Christianity started, and I was amazed to find that my professors had many gospels in their file cabinets that I had never heard of. They had the Gospel of Philip, the Gospel of Thomas, the Gospel of Peter— and it turns out that these were found in 1945 in Upper Egypt. It was a very surprising discovery—although people knew there were many other gospels written in the early Christian churches. We didn't know what they said because they'd all been destroyed thousands of years ago—or so we thought.

These gospels were discovered because they were part of a library of Christian monks in one of the oldest monasteries in Egypt. The archbishop came and told the monks to destroy the "illegitimate secret books," as he called them, and keep twenty-seven of them. The twenty-seven he said to keep are what we call the New Testament. The others that he wanted destroyed were apparently put into a jar and hidden where they were recently found.

FIEDLER: So we have these because of some disobedient monks.

PAGELS: Exactly.

FIEDLER: Who was this archbishop and when did this happen?

PAGELS: It happened in the year 367, about thirty years after being a Christian became legal. We knew that there were many gospels in the early movement, as I said, but we just didn't know what they said, because the bishops and church leaders had destroyed what they called illegitimate secret writings, even though some of them are pretty early. The Gospel of Thomas, people now think, may go back to the first century, certainly the early second century. It's probably about as early as the others.

FIEDLER: Why were they suppressed?

PAGELS: I've been thinking about it a long time. In my first book, *The Gnostic Gospels*, I suggested that it had to do with a bishop incensed that these texts did not support his authority. I now think that there may be some truth in that, but the Gospel of Thomas also expresses a different view of Jesus, which did not become what we call the orthodox view.

FIEDLER: For example, what view of Jesus would be in the Gospel of Thomas but not, say, in the Gospel of John?

PAGELS: The Gospel of John promotes a view of Jesus that is not shared by Matthew, Mark, and Luke. The Gospel of John sees Jesus as a divine being who came down from heaven and that one has to believe in him to be saved. Actually Paul says something very similar.

The Gospel of Thomas suggests that he is, so to speak, the divine light that comes from God, but that that same light is not only in Jesus but actually in every person. Instead of being exclusive to Jesus, the idea is that the divine source can shine in any person. It's more like a Buddhist teaching, or a Jewish or Christian mystical teaching. Because every person is made in the divine image, there is hidden deep within us a capacity both for knowing God and for understanding truth.

FIEDLER: In your newest book, *Beyond Belief*, you take a look at the early Christian centuries and you really say that this was not one great big wonderful unified faith community where everybody lived in harmony.

There were serious struggles and there was great diversity, and these various gospels exemplify that struggle. Can you say more about that?

PAGELS: Yes, that's right, and it isn't just that this is a naïve view that we have. Actually, the view that the ancient church was single-minded, and that all spoke in agreement and so forth, is promoted in the book of Acts from the very beginnings of Christian orthodoxy. But when you begin to look at the sources, you see that the story is much more complicated and much more interesting on that.

FIEDLER: Can you give some examples?

PAGELS: We find for example that the Gospel of Thomas, which pictures Jesus as the voice that comes from God to speak the truth, speaks somewhat differently from the way that he does in the Gospel of John, say. Instead of saying you must believe in me and be saved, he says you must come to know who *you* truly are, that you are made in God's image, and discover access to God.

The Gospel of Mary shows that questions about women in the early Christian movements were very much alive. They weren't invented in the twentieth or twenty-first centuries. Questions like: "Can women teach, can they preach, can they be disciples?" and so forth go very far back. When I went to graduate school, I was looking for something simpler, a simple golden age of early Christianity when everything was clear and unanimous. What I found was something much more complicated, much messier, and completely fascinating. I found a very human story of different groups and different interpretations of the message of Jesus and that's what the history of Christianity actually turns out to be.

FIEDLER: And that's certainly the way it is today.

PAGELS: You know, it's true. Most of us would think, if you take the range from Russian Orthodox to Baptist and Presbyterian and Methodist, Episcopal, Roman Catholic, that there's a huge range of Christians today. There is, of course, but when you go back to the first century there's even more variety. The reason for that is that all those denominations we mentioned agree on the books of the New Testament and all of them agree on certain basic things about Jesus, like Jesus is the son of God. But in the earliest communities, even those points of agreement were not unanimously shared. And leaders of the church were actually very much concerned to simplify a message that could be unanimously shared and practiced. So they not only simplified the message, which is totally understandable and probably necessary, they said you can't believe anything besides this. You must believe this and you must believe it the way we teach you.

That happened largely, I think, because Christianity was an illegal movement. You could be tortured, arrested, and executed for the faith, so the leaders were trying to simply keep the movement surviving, and they did that by deciding on a basic common denominator of beliefs and saying everybody must agree with this.

FIEDLER: Now what are some aspects of the life of Christ found in those Gnostic gospels that would surprise the average traditional Christian?

PAGELS: First, the Gospel of Thomas claims that there are secret sayings which Jesus taught. It says that Jesus not only taught what he taught to everybody, as in the Sermon on the Mount, but that he also spoke privately and secretly to his disciples and might have said things in somewhat a different way in private. That's something that might surprise them. Also, Mary Magdalene and other women were actually disciples as well as the ones that we know from the New Testament. That might also be surprising.

FIEDLER: They were disciples on a par with what we think of as the twelve apostles?

PAGELS: Apparently that's something that was argued about among Jesus' followers after his death. Are they on a par or not? The Gospel of Mary shows you that this was a very live argument. Peter said no and Mary said yes. Predictably, they were at odds. And also another important question is who can say whether what you preach, what you teach, is inspired or not. "Who speaks for God?" may be the primary question in these early sources.

FIEDLER: Would you say the gospels that were admitted to the New Testament favored a system that led to a more hierarchical church structure?

PAGELS: Indeed. The gospels that we have—Matthew, Mark, and Luke—all picture Peter as the greatest disciple and these are gospels that were favored by the church that began in Rome, with the names of Peter and Paul as the great apostles. So there were apparently different groups claiming different traditions and it is the Peter traditions, combined with the Paul traditions, that largely survived. The Gospel of John actually comes from quite a different tradition, and if you look at John carefully, you see that it does not view Peter as the greatest leader of the church; he's actually second to John himself.

FIEDLER: How did the Gospel of John make it then?

PAGELS: It probably did because it nevertheless acknowledges Peter as a leader and because it basically said that Jesus is God.

But there are very different perspectives in those early years. Some viewpoints won out and simply declared the others heretical. I think that's unfortunate because it cuts us off from a very wide range of early Christian sources that might enrich our understanding and, in fact, our spiritual lot.

FIEDLER: Let me ask you a different kind of question. It's very rare that a book that is so theological is on the *New York Times* best seller list for so many weeks. What is it about your book? I certainly know it's very well written. But is there something about the book, or perhaps the times in which we live, that make it especially popular?

PAGELS: It's an interesting question. I would guess there are two things. One is that so many people who are Christians, who are familiar with Christian tradition, are asking questions about their relationship to those traditions and how we understand them. How do we relate to them? How do we love them? What do we love about them, and what do we *not* love about them? Second, I did something in this book which I've never done before, which was to speak partly in the first person. So I tried to invite the reader in by saying, "These are how certain issues engaged me, and this is what I want to share with you."

~~~~~~

Dr. Karen King

on The Nag Hammadi Library and *The Gospel of Judas*

Dr. Karen King is another scholar of the so-called "Gnostic gospels"—the "gospels that did not make the cut" for the New Testament. Many were discovered in the so-called "Nag Hammadi library" of Egypt, a place which has proved to be a treasure trove for serious scholars of the early centuries of Christianity. Dr. Karen King is the Winn Professor of Ecclesiastical History at Harvard Divinity School. This interview from February 2005 discusses the significance of the Nag Hammadi library.

MAUREEN FIEDLER: What was Nag Hammadi, and what was found there?

KAREN KING: Nag Hammadi is a place in middle Egypt. It's the location of a village near a place where a cache of papyrus books were hidden in a jar. They were found in 1945, and inside were over forty new works, mostly written by Christians in the second and third centuries. And these texts are showing us that Christianity was much, much more diverse than we ever expected.

FIEDLER: These Nag Hammadi findings are often described as Gnostic texts. What is Gnosticism? And what was its role in early Christianity?

KING: To put it briefly, Gnosticism was one of the losers in the early Christian battle for orthodoxy. The term itself was actually invented in the seventeenth century, and the scholars actually divide early Christianity into three kinds—Orthodoxy, Jewish-Christianity, and Gnosticism. What this shows is not only the way that scholars understand early Christianity, but it also shows the way early Christians were struggling over a wide range of issues: how to understand who Jesus was, what his teachings meant, the significance of his death and resurrection, the role of women and slaves, and so on and so forth.

FIEDLER: How has the discovery of the Nag Hammadi library influenced our reading of the gospels we know and indeed our view of Jesus Christ? What's new there?

KING: I have to emphasize that we have over forty different texts. They show a wide range of perspectives. Some of them, for example, the Gospel of Thomas, make the *teachings* of Jesus absolutely central to salvation. And there's no teaching there about the death and resurrection. It's his teachings that bring salvation.

This is true for another text that actually wasn't discovered in Nag Hammadi, but was also discovered in Egypt, called the Gospel of Mary. It too communicates Jesus' teachings as being the central significance for salvation. Of course, the teachings of Jesus are also very central to the four canonical gospels, but when we get to the later church with something like the Nicene Creed, it actually doesn't ask Christians to affirm anything about Jesus' teachings, but places emphasis on the death and resurrection. And so, in a way, some traditions have made the death and resurrection really the central event of salvation, and these texts don't see that as important.

FIEDLER: And was there some kind of a struggle in early Christianity between those who held those various perspectives?

KING: Oh yes, definitely. In the Gospel of Mary, Jesus says not to trust those who say, "look over here or look over there; the savior is coming." You should look *within* for the Son of Man. That's an interpretation of Jesus' teachings about the Kingdom that focuses on the Kingdom within. It's very different from the Gospel of Mark, which talks about the Son of Man coming on the clouds of heaven at the end of time.

FIEDLER: You mentioned the Gospel of Mary a couple of times and I know that some of the writings in the Nag Hammadi library deal with the feminine principle of God, the Divine Sophia. What do they suggest about women, or perhaps the role of Mary, that might be different from what is commonly thought today?

KING: It's a complicated question, partly because, for early Christians, scriptures were not the New Testament gospels. They were writing them. The scriptures were the Jewish scriptures and the figure of wisdom, Sophia, is very prominent in many of the texts, especially in the literature of Proverbs and Psalms.

What happens in early Christianity generally is that we see Jesus himself identified with the wisdom figure as the power of God, with God's wisdom actually at work in creation.

FIEDLER: And wisdom is Sophia, right?

KING: Yes, and wisdom in Greek is translated *Sophia*, and it's gendered feminine. And so it is an identification of Jesus with this feminine figure. We see too in these texts the centrality of God in masculine terms, but also in feminine terms. And we see Mary Magdalene portrayed as one of the most important apostles of Jesus.

FIEDLER: And there's a lot of controversy around Mary Magdalene today, as to whom she really was, and who, in the course of Christian history, was turned into a prostitute.

KING: No one thinks that Mary Magdalene was historically a prostitute.

FIEDLER: This all begs the question, when you have the Gospel of Thomas, the Gospel of Philip, the Gospel of Mary, along with Matthew, Mark, Luke, and John: who decided that Matthew, Mark, Luke, and John were the canonical gospels?

KING: It's a very difficult question to answer. What we know is that certain gospels began to be used by communities. And those were the communities that carried on the Christian faith at the time when Constantine was converted. We don't actually have any kind of synod when people sat down, stacked all the gospels on one side and yelled "This one's in!" and "That one's out!" It was really a very long process. It's not until the fourth century that we have a list of the texts that are in the New Testament. It really isn't until the invention of the printing press that we get all of the texts that that we now call the New Testament together under one cover in the order in which they are today. It was a very long process.

FIEDLER: Now what would you say to the average listener, who reads the Bible reflectively, perhaps prayerfully? Would you suggest that a serious Christian go and read the Nag Hammadi texts which are available in translation?

KING: I certainly would. I think one of the things that happens is that, because the gospels have been passed down to us for so many years, we think we already know what they mean.

The amazing thing to me is that for 1500 years nobody noticed that there's nothing in the New Testament that said Mary Magdalene was a prostitute. Why didn't we do that? It's because tradition has been telling us that she was. So every time we read Mary Magdalene, we said, "Oh, she's a prostitute." We read it in. So I think that one of the things that these texts can do immediately is help people begin to see them fresh and read them anew and really read and understand what's there.

I think they help people see too that we have four gospels, not one. We have four different interpretations. We have many versions of Jesus' parables.

When someone says that the Bible should be read literally, that is very different from the understanding in antiquity. Origin, for example, one of the main biblical interpreters in the early church, said that heretics made the mistake of reading scripture literally instead of looking for its spiritual meaning. One needs to be able to read it at the grammatical level and the historical level, the spiritual level and for its contemporary meaning. And perhaps, people need to learn how to do all four of those things.

The Gospel of Judas

I interviewed Karen King again in 2007 to talk about *The Gospel of Judas*, one of the Gnostic gospels in the Nag Hammadi library. Elaine Pagels and Karen King published an analysis of that text in a book called *Reading Judas: The Gospel of Judas and the Shaping of Christianity*.

MAUREEN FIEDLER: You say that the Gospel of Judas wasn't written by Judas.

KAREN KING: It's true. The Gospel of Judas is ascribed to Judas but we don't know who wrote it, any more than we know who wrote the gospels of Matthew, Mark, Luke, and John in the New Testament.

FIEDLER: You say that you and Dr. Pagels were jarred when you first read the Gospel of Judas. How so?

KING: It's not what you would call a warm and fuzzy gospel. It has a lot of violence in it. It accuses the twelve disciples of being killers of their own wives and children and fornicating—of being immoral people. It's anti-Jewish, and homophobic. It is really not the kind of gospel that seems particularly appealing. And we tried to understand why the author of this gospel seemed so angry.

Its portrayal of Judas himself is quite different from the one we are used to, which is a picture of Judas as the betrayer, the bad guy, the one who took money, and the one who either killed himself through suicide or actually had his guts spilled out.

But in the end of the Gospel of John, Jesus himself tells Judas to go and do what he has to do. It's a small step then to move to the place where the Gospel of Judas has gone, namely that Judas understood what his role was. Jesus told him what he would be doing, and Judas was the one who helped Jesus carry out God's plan.

But what we found much, much more striking was an incredibly negative attitude toward the twelve disciples.

FIEDLER: How is that manifest?

KING: It begins when Jesus laughs at them in a mocking way when he finds them practicing the Eucharist and praying and practicing piety. And then again the twelve disciples have a dream. It's a really horrible dream where they see twelve priests at the temple slaughtering people and doing all kinds of immoral and sinful acts. And they're stunned by this and they come to Jesus to interpret the dream for them. And Jesus shockingly says: *you* are the priests at the altar. You are the ones who are leading people astray like these animals that are being brought to slaughter.

FIEDLER: Do you have any idea what the purpose of telling that story would be?

KING: We thought long and hard about this. The important thing, I think, is to see this, not as a story set at the time of Jesus and his disciples, but set a hundred years later in the midst of Christian persecutions. And there, what role did the twelve play? At a point in the history of Christianity, the bishops of the church are calling upon apostolic succession. That is, they were claiming that their authority came from the twelve who were appointed by Jesus. And so by attacking the twelve, it's basically a way to attack and undermine the authority of the bishops in the age in which the Gospel of Judas was written, which is sometime in the middle or late second century.

FIEDLER: And one of the disputes in early Christianity that is revealed is the dispute over how to respond to the Roman persecution.

KING: That's right. The text seems really angry about Jesus' death being interpreted as a sacrifice. And we asked ourselves why. What is the problem with sacrifice? Well, in the second century, Christians are being put to death because they refuse to sacrifice. They will not sacrifice to the gods of the Romans and were considered traitors. Christians believe such sacrifice to be idolatry.

But what the Gospel of Judas is claiming is that the leaders of the Christians are bringing sacrifice right back into the center of Christian worship, by understanding Jesus' death as a sacrifice for sins, by understanding martyrs as sacrifices pleasing to God, by saying that God wants their death as sacrifices, and also by celebrating the common Christian meal, the Eucharist, as a sacrificial meal.

This contradiction seems to be one of the major theological points that the Gospel of Judas really is arguing against.

FIEDLER: You also mentioned what today goes under the name of the doctrine of the atonement, the idea that Jesus' death atoned for our sins. You say that whoever wrote the Gospel of Judas was questioning what kind of a God would let his son die so violent of a death. Do you want to talk about that?

KING: The document of the atonement has a rich theological heritage over many centuries. But the Gospel of Judas seems to object most strongly to this notion that God willed Jesus' death and the suffering of martyrs and believers. For the first time, we're seeing that people who were arguing about martyrdom were not merely cowards who ran away. They were people who had serious theological issues, and these voices that were critical of religious violence, critical of seeing God as desiring this, have been silenced.

FIEDLER: In a sense, what we've had until the last few decades is simply the writings of those who won the disputes, the winners.

KING: That's right. And these are alternative voices that we haven't heard before. People may choose to throw them back on the trash heap, but they are extremely important to us. First of all, historically they give us a much fuller picture of Christianity. But they also provide important possibilities for contemporary kinds of theological reflection. Can we talk about dying for God? Does God desire that? What does it mean when we say, "This is what God wants"?

And because Christianity has developed in so many different places and so many different kinds of ways, the question is always: has the tradition ever been truly unified? And the answer to that, historically at least, is no. There have always been multiple possibilities inside the tradition and Christians have selected out of their tradition what they were going to live out and how they were going to live it.

FIEDLER: At the end you say you wouldn't want this book in the canon of the New Testament. But on the other hand you wouldn't assign it to the trash heap of history either. So how should a believer read this book?

KING: Look at it critically. Look at what it offers us. Look at what it offers us by way of a correction, if you will. I think one of the deepest points of this text is precisely the insistence that our deepest connection with God is a spiritual connection. At the same time these texts are also very anti-Jewish in that they portray the Jews as being responsible for sacrifice at the altar and for the death of Jesus. There is no mention of the Romans who are the ones who historically, truly put Jesus to death. And the text is homophobic. It clearly describes homosexuality as idolatrous sinfulness, much the way we see in Paul's letter to the Romans. And that for me is very problematic.

~~~~~~

Dr. Julie Galambush on

The Reluctant Parting: How the New Testament's Jewish Writers Created a Christian Book

Dr. Julie Galambush is a former Baptist who converted to Judaism. Her studies led her to confront a question that has troubled many Jews and Christians for centuries: Why the long-perceived anti-Semitism in the New Testament? She says: these are not Christians talking about Jews, but Jews talking about other Jews with whom they disagreed on a basic question: circumcision.

Her book is called *The Reluctant Parting: How the New Testament's Jewish Writers Created a Christian Book*. Julie Galambush is an associate professor of religious studies at the College of William and Mary. I interviewed her in March 2006.

MAUREEN FIEDLER: First of all, Julie, did the followers of Jesus see themselves as the founders of the new religion?

JULIE GALAMBUSH: Certainly not. Jesus' followers were apocalyptic Jews, of which there were many in the first century. But Jesus' followers did believe that Jesus was the Messiah. So the Messiah had come; the end of the world would not. Under those circumstances, namely that every hope of the Jewish people had now been fulfilled in Jesus, founding a different religion would have been the last thing on their minds.

FIEDLER: And yet we read it that way today because . . .

GALAMBUSH: A break happened between the followers of Jesus and the rest of the Jewish community. In fact a new religion, a religion made up almost exclusively of non-Jews, was formed, and within a century or so quite a bit of hostility grew up between the two religions. So these religions have a very long history of seeing each other not only as different but as opposed to each other.

FIEDLER: You make the case that first-century Judaism was very complex and that the New Testament actually portrays three kinds of Jews: Jews who rejected Jesus, those who accepted Jesus as Messiah, and Jews who accepted Jesus as Messiah on different terms than the New Testament offers. And then, of course, add to the mix the Gentiles, and the Gentile converts around the Mediterranean world. What significance did all of this have in the writing of the New Testament? Were some of these New Testament writers having an in-house fight, if you will, with some of these other groups?

GALAMBUSH: Absolutely. This is a very good question and it's a complicated one because it asks us to look at the New Testament as a result of the interaction of groups whose existence we've completely forgotten. First of all, probably all the authors of the New Testament were ethnically Jewish, but many of the intended readers were not Jews.

Several books were intended for Jewish communities, that is, Jewish communities that followed Jesus: Matthew, Hebrews, James, and probably Revelation. And in these the author argues for the sake of the community that this group is authentically Jewish. They want to reassure the followers that they haven't somehow abandoned the rest of the Jewish community by following Jesus as Messiah. Probably most New Testament books were written by Jews for non-Jews, welcoming them to the family, if you will.

FIEDLER: But what about the *Jewish* family?

GALAMBUSH: The Jewish family absolutely—these authors still understand themselves as part of Jewish communities. And so, these authors often have two tasks. One, they want to convey Jewish values to these non-Jewish converts. They want to teach these people Jewish sexual mores, Jewish rules of survival in a non-Jewish world. They have a whole world of Jewish lore and customs, and particularly ethical values that they want to pass on to these pagan converts. The second thing they want to make sure is that non-Jewish converts do Christianity—if I can call it Christianity—*their* way. Some believe that Gentile converts are actually converts to Judaism, and therefore had to be circumcised. Others believed that the converts should be welcomed in as Gentiles and that the community should stay mixed: the Jewish community that welcomes all nations, and on that basis they allow converts who are not circumcised.

But here's the key, the trick to reading the New Testament. The New Testament is written by a group who do *not* circumcise converts. That means often when you're reading the New Testament book, what you're seeing is not an argument against Jews, but *an in-house argument between Jewish followers of Jesus.* And so the New Testament authors are arguing very hard to keep these Gentile converts from going over to the circumcising side of things. They want to convince them that they can be full members without circumcision.

FIEDLER: If we understand that parts of the Jesus movement are arguing with other parts of the Jesus movement, both *within* Judaism, we still have lots of statements in the New Testament that are read later on as anti-Semitic. The most famous of course is, "His blood be upon ourselves and our children!" Or St. Paul's statement in 1 Thessalonians, where he says that "the Jews killed both the Lord Jesus and the Prophets." Have these been totally misinterpreted? And if so, how should we read them?

GALAMBUSH: It's so easy to say that they've been totally misinterpreted and certainly they have. But I think it always takes awhile to buy into a very different reading of the New Testament. It's a book that Christians have a long heritage of reading in certain ways, so it's hard to re-believe that a radically different interpretation is accurate. But I'll go ahead and try to convince you on both of those quotations if you want.

FIEDLER: Or try explaining the overall question of the vilification of Jews by biblical authors who are apparently Jewish authors. They're not talking about all Jews, obviously.

GALAMBUSH: They're definitely not talking about all Jews. Jesus' followers are sectarians, and so they want to claim that their way of being Jewish is the right way of being Jewish. And therefore, they're going to put down Jews whom they perceive as being critical of their way of being Jewish. That's the simplest way in which you see the New Testament authors criticizing Jews.

But usually the much more virulent form of invective against Jews is actually the argument that's happening within the Jesus movement itself. Those members of the movement who circumcise are furious with those who don't circumcise and so you see Paul saying things like, "those who are trying to circumcise you have cut themselves off from the gospel." He likes these puns. And indeed, he says, "I wish they would just go and castrate themselves." These horrible circumcisers that Paul is mad at are not what we would call "Jews." The circumcisers, the evil circumcisers, are members of the Jesus movement who want to do this Christianity thing in a way slightly different from the way Paul wants to.

FIEDLER: So much of what we interpret as anti-Semitic today is really Jews talking about other Jews?

GALAMBUSH: Absolutely. All the authors of the New Testament are Jewish and still see themselves as Jewish. All the New Testament, in fact, is Jews criticizing other Jews. And I think that's hard, not only for Christians to see, but also for Jews to see.

FIEDLER: Don't you wish that the New Testament could have been understood this way, before we got into pogroms, before the Holocaust, before all of the oppression of Jews down through the centuries?

GALAMBUSH: It's hard to imagine what our religious history would be like if we had been able to remember that this was intended as a Jewish book. It's a very painful thing.

FIEDLER: Now in other statements in the New Testament, in the letters of Paul, for example, there's the suggestion that Judaism is somehow not a complete religion, that Christianity has superseded it, or completed it, or improved it somehow. Why would Jews write that?

GALAMBUSH: I think anyone who belongs to a new sect of an old religion considers their sect to be an improvement on what the religion has been so far. A lot of what you see in the New Testament are things like Paul's references to Christ as the end of the law, meaning that in Jesus the law has been abolished. But I don't think that's what Paul means. The Greeks would tell us it means completion or a goal of something. In this case, what Paul is saying is that the Messiah represents the goal or completion of the law of the Torah.

FIEDLER: That's good Jewish teaching.

GALAMBUSH: Exactly. That's what takes us back to the question about whether these folks think they're practicing a new religion. Jews understood the Messiah to be the fulfillment of Jewish history and therefore he's also the fulfillment of the law.

FIEDLER: Many of our listeners would like to be intelligent readers of the New Testament. What advice would you give to them about biblical interpretation?

GALAMBUSH: I think the first thing to remember in reading any ancient text is that the text really *is* ancient. It wasn't written with us or the norms of our culture in mind. And of course we come to the Bible with these cultural assumptions. So I think it's very important to let reading the Bible be difficult. Let the ancient texts have their own authority and historical context.

When one sits down to read the Bible, it's definitely worthwhile to be conscious of what your goal is in reading. Am I reading this for personal devotion? Am I reading it for ethical direction? Do I want to understand the original readings of these texts in their ancient context? These are very different goals, and I think we often have this illusion that if we sit down and study the Bible, we're going to get them all at once. Some believe, for example, that whatever it meant in the first century it should mean in the twenty-first. I think that sets us up for a lot of trouble, because I'm not convinced that what the first-century authors needed for their congregations is necessarily what a modern reader needs. And then I wish readers could be more fearless.

FIEDLER: How do you mean that?

GALAMBUSH: I think we come to the Bible generally with such a feeling that it's a holy book, a special book, a perfect book, that we're afraid to get mad at it. We're afraid to be disappointed by it, angered by it, or we can't disagree with it, for example. I think it's not unlike some human relationships where we're so afraid that the relationship will break that we can't quite be ourselves. I think we do that with the Bible a lot. God is greater than our hearts. And for me fearlessness is probably the most important virtue in a Bible reader.

FIEDLER: And finally, talk briefly about your own story. How did you go from being a Baptist minister to being a Jew?

GALAMBUSH: I went from being a Baptist minister to being a Hebrew Bible scholar and a professor. I had always been one of those Christians who was attracted to Judaism, who sort of wished we still kept the festivals and such. And so, I think I was in love with Judaism. And it wasn't until after I had been married to an old college friend for a few years, who is Jewish, that I decided to convert. I didn't convert to get married, but to live as a mother to my Jewish step-daughters. We can say I was led, as it were, to become a Jew.

FIEDLER: And you're totally comfortable in Judaism today?

GALAMBUSH: There are few things in life for which I am more grateful. It's been wonderful.

Chapter 3
Women in Feminist Theology

Feminist theology looks at faith traditions or traditional teachings through the lens of women's experiences, offering new, and sometimes startling, insights. These scholars have resurrected traditions of equality and justice that had not been applied to women until the present. They re-interpreted scriptural stories, parables, and teachings. Many have reclaimed a lost past in which women played a greater role than had been told in traditional histories.

Dr. Mary Hunt and Dr. Judith Plaskow
on Christian and Jewish Feminist Theology

We begin with an introductory overview of feminist theology in the Judeo-Christian tradition: my interview with two of the best known feminist theologians in the United States. Dr. Judith Plaskow is a pioneer in Jewish feminist theology. She is a professor of religious studies at Manhattan College in New York. Dr. Mary Hunt is a nationally recognized leader in Christian feminist theology, and serves as co-director of WATER, the Women's Alliance for Theology Ethics and Ritual. She comes from the Catholic tradition. This interview took place in June 2009.

MAUREEN FIEDLER: First, why feminist theology at all? What is wrong with the traditional theologies that demanded that new perspective, Mary?

DR. MARY HUNT: The first thing is that the way in which we live in the post-modern world calls for equality of men and women. And if you think of religion as one of the ways in which we inform our consciousness as a society, the fact that religions focus their divinities on male figures, and that we live in a society of discrimination against women, we had to find the connection. And so it was out of that discrimination that feminist theology arose. It also arose out of what I would call spiritual dissonance, the distance between what people feel and what they believe, what they believe in political terms and educational terms, and what they experience religiously.

FIEDLER: And is the same true with the Jewish tradition, Judith?

DR. JUDITH PLASKOW: It is, in many ways. If you look at what the situation was forty years ago, women were second-class citizens in every branch of Judaism, even the liberal branches.

FIEDLER: When would you date the beginning of this modern feminist theological movement, Mary?

HUNT: A lot of people put it in the late 1890s, when the women who were working for suffrage began to understand the relationship between the way in which the Divine was understood and women's lack of rights in the world. And so a lot of people date it to 1898, when the *Women's Bible* came out. It was a collection of essays written about different parts of scripture from the perspectives of women. Now, these were not women who were highly trained theologically, or who read Greek and Hebrew. These were ordinary women working in the Suffrage Movement. So from the very beginning there was a connection between religion and politics. And women who were working in the Suffrage Movement understood that if the Divine was not understood in feminine terms, then women could not expect to have any kind of power in the society.

FIEDLER: But the very contemporary movement would date from what, the '70s or the '80s?

PLASKOW: I would say from late '68, '69, and '70. That's when the new work really began.

FIEDLER: And Judith, you wrote a book called *Standing Again at Sinai*. What is feminist theology in the Jewish tradition?

PLASKOW: My feminist theology is an attempt to rethink the central categories of Jewish thought: Torah, God, and Israel. And so I raised the question: what would Jewish tradition look like if we approach it from a feminist perspective?

FIEDLER: And what *would* it look like?

PLASKOW: The most important part of the book is where I talk about the transformation of Torah. Torah is understood in the narrow sense as the five books of Moses, and in the broad sense as the whole history of commentary. And you have, in the Jewish tradition, really three thousand years of conversation around that text, in which women have not been included.

So I ask: what does it mean to begin to recover women's Torah? For example, I was just teaching a text the other day that goes back to the giving of the law at Mount Sinai. And there's a wonderful poem by Merle Feld that talks about how all the women were at the back of the crowd, gathering about the mountain, because they were carrying the children, and they were pulling them along. And therefore we don't have the whole record of that event in what's come down to us. So we ask: how do we recover the whole record?

FIEDLER: Mary, in the Christian tradition, how would you define feminist theology?

HUNT: I think it's very similar: the effort on the part of women to bring women's experiences where they have never been before. Women have obviously been part of the tradition from the beginning, but never had a voice. And they did not have the power to make decisions in the shaping of the tradition—everything from how church history is understood, to the ethical questions, to the interpretations of scripture. And it certainly includes what we would call systematic theology, looking again at God and the world in human relations, and asking, "How do we understand these things?" And that's not based on what white men think, but on how women, people of color, and those who have been marginalized because of poverty and discrimination think.

FIEDLER: Why do you think the word "feminism" is so scary?

PLASKOW: I see in my students today a tremendous fear of the word "feminism." It's associated with excluding men and man-hating, and they're terrified of being seen as people who are somehow in opposition to men.

FIEDLER: Mary, what's your experience on that?

HUNT: I think Madison Avenue and other media have done an enormously effective job at demonizing feminism, when, in fact, the very women who are in positions in some of those places that shape our consciousness around issues like feminism wouldn't be there if their mothers and grandmothers hadn't raised these issues.

So if the word "feminism" is a problem, I'm not willing to give it up, because it represents a rich history. But if the word is a problem, I would rather put my energies into saying, let's talk about equality, and let's talk about the ways in which thinking of the Divine in more than male terms will help us to imagine, and move constructively from our imaginations to a different world. That's the approach. I won't spend a lot of time arguing over the word. But I think it still needs to be used for its historical and political value.

As long as it's a problem, let's keep using it.

FIEDLER: How do you deal with a traditional religious woman who doesn't want new interpretations of scripture or new theological approaches?

Who's even offended that somebody would try that? Judith, do you ever run into that?

PLASKOW: It's interesting to me that there's a tremendous amount of movement and excitement within Orthodoxy around feminist issues. But I'm not denying for a moment that there are traditional women who are put off by it.

FIEDLER: And Orthodoxy would be the most conservative of the major Jewish traditions?

PLASKOW: It is the most traditional of the Jewish denominations. But women have especially struggled to gain access to learning the Jewish text, and interpreting Jewish text for themselves. And there's been a tremendous blossoming of women's Torah study and women's Torah interpretations. And there's excitement about women teaching women, so I'm not sure that you'd meet many women who'd say, "I don't want new interpretations."

FIEDLER: Mary, in the Christian tradition, there are certainly some conservative Catholic women and conservative Evangelical women who would make objections. What do you say to them?

HUNT: There are two things. One—I would say some of the most exciting work is being done by some Evangelical feminists, people like Letha Dawson Scanzoni and Virginia Ramey Mollenkott. The other thing I think is a real problem is the question of letting women make choices. We who are feminists don't say to people who aren't, "you have to be." But *we're* often told *we* shouldn't be. And so that's really, to me, the rub. Feminist interpretations are as valid as any other, and yet there are those who say, "But you're not really a Catholic," or "You're not really a Jew."

That's the problem. We don't turn the tables and say, "If you're not a feminist, you're not a Christian or a Jew."

FIEDLER: And then what about Eve, the quintessential second-class citizen? Why do you think that interpretation has stuck, Judith?

PLASKOW: Eve does not play as important a role in the Jewish tradition as she does in the Christian tradition. She's not that central theologically. The rabbis raise the question, "Did Adam have a first wife?" Because after all, Genesis 1 says God created man and woman in God's image. And Genesis 2 says that God created Eve from Adam's rib. So the rabbis ask, did Adam have a first wife? And they answered yes, he did. Lilith was created first. She was created equal to Adam, because they were both created from the dust of the ground.

FIEDLER: And is this a commonly accepted teaching in Judaism?

PLASKOW: It depends what you mean by commonly accepted. Midrash plays with the text; it expands the text. It raises questions about gaps and contradictions in the text, and fills them in. It's not doctrine.

FIEDLER: As we all know, in traditional scriptural translations God is pictured as a male. Why is it important to call God "she" as well as "he," from a feminist perspective, Judith?

PLASKOW: I think that goes back to Genesis 1, and the notion that God created human beings in God's image. And I think that for women to fully experience ourselves in the image of God, there needs to be female as well as male imagery. That's what makes it real.

HUNT: The issue I think, is really who gets to do the naming. Back to the Greeks—Heraclitus said that if dogs, and cats, and cows, and pigs had gods and goddesses, they'd look like dogs, and cats, and cows, and pigs! So the real issue here is when people begin to name what's divine for them, they tend to go for the questions of power. So it's not just the maleness, Maureen. The bigger issue is not just father, but Lord, Ruler, King. The power issues are really important. The notion of the Divine as Father, Lord, Ruler, King is not unrelated to the fact that Fathers, Lords and Rulers and Kings are at the top of the heap in society.

FIEDLER: As opposed to Mother, Nurturer, or Friend.

HUNT: Mother, Nurturer, or Friend, and perhaps natural images.

PLASKOW: Source of Life.

HUNT: Source of Life, Ground of Being—loads of ways to go. But the fundamental issue is who gets to say. And it's lots of people. That's the chorus issue; lots of people in the chorus have a say, rather than the one soprano who gets to sing.

PLASKOW: And I think that question, "Who gets to say?", is the fundamental question that runs through all of feminist theology. Who gets to create the future of the tradition?

FIEDLER: There's long been a tendency to identify women with their bodies, as opposed to their minds or their spirits. How does that come into feminist thinking, Judith?

PLASKOW: Within Judaism, there's been an attempt to proudly reclaim women's embodied experience with a host of new ceremonies and rituals for the important moments in women's lives. For example, the Jewish tradition has hundreds of blessings for every aspect of experience. But there's never been a blessing for childbirth. There's never been a blessing for nursing or for weaning, and feminists have created a host of new rituals for these experiences.

HUNT: Christian women do this too, which is really exciting. For example, in Catholicism, there are not just seven sacraments. (In fact, for girls, we say there are only six to start with, because they can't be ordained.) But there are loads of ways of sacramentalizing, of lifting everyday experiences, to public expression.

FIEDLER: Of course, as we all know Judaism and Christianity have, until very recent times, relegated women to inferior roles within their denominations. And they justified that theologically. Even today, in Orthodox Judaism, women are still not counted in the minion, which is a ten-person quorum necessary for some rituals. And of course in Catholicism, and the Orthodox Church, and in conservative Evangelical Christianity, women cannot be clergy. Are you making any inroads here?

PLASKOW: In Judaism, the transformation is so enormous that it's almost hard for me to remember what my experience was growing up as a girl in the Reform Movement. There was lip service to equality, but women did not participate. There were not even bat mitzvahs. Today, there are hundreds of women rabbis in all the Jewish denominations except Orthodoxy. But even as we speak, a yeshiva is being started to train women as rabbis in the Orthodox community, although they may not be given that title for awhile. So there's been enormous change.

HUNT: I think that's true in Christianity as well, with the notable exceptions of the Roman Catholic Church, Seventh Day Adventists, and some types of Lutherans and so forth. Having said that, the questions for me are not just the numbers, but the ministry as currently conceived could be considered a recipe for women's jobs in patriarchy: the long hours and endless nurture, the low pay, the endless availability.

I'm interested in how the structures change because women come in. And so I think the feminist question here is more important, at least in Christianity. Where you *do* have larger numbers coming into Lutheran, Presbyterian, and Methodist churches, does it really change the structures of those churches? It certainly changes the aesthetic, which I like. It certainly improves the quality of ministry. But it doesn't really make *structural* changes. And this is the problem that we as Catholics have around ordination. To get women ordained and not make structural changes, I think, would be a disaster. So it's a mixed bag on the Christian side in my view.

FIEDLER: Okay—what about feminist theology in the pews? Does this kind of perspective ever get preached, Judith? Or is it still trickling?

PLASKOW: Yes, it's still trickling, and to me the next front line is curriculum transformation. These kinds of issues need to be integrated into curricula from kindergarten through seminary. And that's happening in only a few places.

HUNT: We're doing feminist ministry training through WATER, the Women's Alliance for Theology Ethics and Ritual, where I work. And it's really rudimentary, but we find that many women go through seminary and they're shipped off to a small place in rural God-knows-where, and people have never heard of this. They're isolated, they say, "My gosh, this is what I want to do, but I'm going to lose my job if I start talking about God in inclusive language, much less beginning to preach from a feminist perspective on certain texts. I'll be out on my ear." So this is a very difficult problem, and we're at the very beginning.

FIEDLER: And so wherein lies the future of feminist theology, then? What is the major frontier, Judith?

PLASKOW: I see the major frontier as linking feminist issues to other social justice issues, beginning to talk about racism, and poverty, and issues of war and peace, as Jewish feminists. I think we're just starting to ask those questions.

HUNT: I would say we need to embrace those issues without losing the particularity of the issues that started feminist work in religion, like the questions of reproductive health and sexuality, and gender questions.

But we need to begin to put them together. And I'm very excited. I think there are young women who are going to be all over this question in years to come, if we can help provide the support that makes it possible for them to have careers in this work, and do their work from the feminist perspective.

FIEDLER: And so to become a full part of the theological conversation in Judaism and Christianity?

HUNT: Without apology, absolutely.

Dr. Rosemary Radford Ruether
on *Goddesses and the Divine Feminine*

Rosemary Radford Ruether is regarded as one of the greatest Christian feminist theologians of our time, with numerous published works of scholarship. Although she is a Catholic, her theological interests stretch far beyond Catholic—or even Christian—theology. In this interview, she reviews ancient and contemporary goddess traditions, which she described in her book, *Goddesses and the Divine Feminine: A Western Religious History*. She is currently retired, but at the time of this interview in November 2005, she was the Carpenter Professor of Feminist Theology at the Graduate Theological Union in Berkeley, California.

MAUREEN FIEDLER: First, Rosemary, why in contemporary religious thought do we generally conceive of God as masculine and not feminine?

ROSEMARY RUETHER: Basically, the problem with that statement is that it's not true. People of the Abrahamic faiths—Judaism, Christianity, and Islam—generally see God as masculine, but they are only a part of the religions of the world. Hinduism, Buddhism, Confucianism—and that's perhaps half of the world—all have Goddess figures.

FIEDLER: So in fact there is a goddess tradition or a divine feminine tradition that's alive and well in the world today.

Your book is a marvelous history. You begin by taking on the scholars who say that the prehistoric world, the time before written records, was matriarchal. You believe that these very ancient societies were really much more complex than that.

RUETHER: I think the problem is the confusion of the term "matriarchy," which means rule by women, or rule by the mother, with "matrilineal" or "matrilocal," or other kinds of societies which have female descent, or where the male joins into the female family. There's no evidence there ever were matriarchal societies, in which women rule. But there's a lot of evidence of descent-through-the-mother societies where the male joins the female clan, so there was both male and female symbolism. In other words, all of the evidence from early society is that males and females have their place in the divine pantone.

FIEDLER: We know that's also true of places like Egypt, the Fertile Crescent, Greece, and Rome. In those societies what were the roles of the goddesses, and did they affect the status of women in any way?

RUETHER: What modern feminists who are seeking goddess figures always fail to understand is that the basic model for gods and goddesses in historical antiquity was the aristocracy. Gods and goddesses represented the ruling class, and the ruling class was male and female. So unless you factor in the class, you simply make ridiculous mistakes about Goddesses as empowering all women.

FIEDLER: And so they did more to reinforce the established aristocratic order than they did for any gender division.

RUETHER: They support those roles of women in the aristocracy but that doesn't mean they support women in general.

FIEDLER: In your book you deal with both Jewish and Christian history, and you contend that these patriarchal societies did not in fact bury the divine feminine but resurrected it periodically for male purposes. You mention, for example, the figure of Wisdom in the Hebrew scriptures. Do you want to talk about that?

RUETHER: First of all, let's be clear that these ancient Egyptian and Canaanite and Babylonian societies were patriarchal. It's not as though patriarchy starts with the Jews, which is a fundamentally anti-Semitic idea. In early Hebrew society, in fact, the goddess wife of the Canaanite god really continued to be venerated by the Hebrews and only gradually disappears by about the sixth century before Christ. But then you have this whole reappearance of the female image of the divine in Wisdom. And that really becomes the central female image for the divine in both Judaism and Christianity. Now, Wisdom ideas can be used simply as mediators between male leaders and a male God and not necessarily empower women, or Wisdom can be sympathetic to women in a more empowering way. So you find Wisdom used in different ways.

FIEDLER: In Christianity, but especially in Catholicism, the role of Mary the Mother of Jesus has long intrigued feminist scholars and I know it has intrigued you. Is Mary in any sense a "goddess figure"?

RUETHER: Yes and no. Effectively, there can be a Mariology which becomes the center of peoples' spirituality—men and women. You can see this in the dominating role of the Virgin of Guadalupe, which for many people is really the center of their spirituality and of course, she's been referred to as the Goddess of the Americas. But at the same time, Mary has been shaped by a patriarchal theology and spirituality to represent mainly the submission and passivity of women. So Mary can be very central, but also can communicate a very submissive role to women.

FIEDLER: But she's also been talked about by feminists in a more revolutionary, egalitarian role for women, has she not?

RUETHER: She has been, but that's a reinterpretation. The dominant Mariology that has been shaped by the Catholic Church has made her symbolize a submissive kind of femininity that complements and buttresses male power.

FIEDLER: Is there any sense in which Our Lady of Guadalupe took the place of a more ancient Aztec goddess?

RUETHER: That's a common interpretation, but also the assumption is that somehow these Aztec goddesses represented a matriarchal society. Aztec societies were warrior, patriarchal societies.

FIEDLER: In one chapter, you say that the Protestant goddess is Wisdom. What do you mean by that?

RUETHER: The Protestant tradition in the sixteenth century pretty much marginalized Mariology and female saints. But we do see revivals of Wisdom spirituality, mainly in mystical traditions, like among Shakers or Pietists, but it's obviously not the mainstream.

FIEDLER: Of course there are contemporary goddess movements today. Who are the goddess worshipers today? And what's their significance?

RUETHER: A number of communities of women and men feel that the dominant patriarchal theology has not only enforced subordination of women but also fostered violence, militarism, destruction of the earth. They believe we have to find an alternative that is much more female-centered, and empowering, not only of women, but also of a different relationship to the earth. So essentially you have a new goddess religion drawing on ancient images, but being reinterpreted in the contemporary context.

FIEDLER: In the end of the book, you contend that men as well as women need the Goddess. Why is that?

RUETHER: The term "need" is somewhat ambiguous because I think men have always used the Goddess. They have used goddesses or Mariology to enforce their own power, not to empower women. But that's very different from saying that we "need" goddesses to overthrow male hierarchy, which is a whole other question.

FIEDLER: But *do* we need the divine feminine to balance the divine masculine?

RUETHER: I don't like divine-feminine, divine-masculine because it assumes stereotypes of maleness and femaleness. I think we need whole humans, and we need to have a variety of images of the divine male and female but also images of bread, water, fire, and air that can symbolize the fullness of life.

Dr. Rosemary Radford Ruether
and Dr. Delores Williams
on Feminist and Womanist Theologies

Dr. Delores Williams is a leading "womanist" theologian, reexamining Christian teachings from the perspective of African-American Women. She is the Paul Tillich Professor of Theology and Culture at Union Theological Seminary in New York, and she is the author of *Sisters in the Wilderness: The Challenge of Womanist God-Talk*. In March 2004, I interviewed her together with Dr. Rosemary Ruether on feminist and womanist theologies.

MAUREEN FIEDLER: First, Rosemary, approximately when do you date the beginning of feminist theology?

ROSEMARY RUETHER: I would date it to the fourteenth century. But that's my perspective as a historian, because there were women who were doing this kind of critical reflection from the late Middle Ages. In recent waves, you can say roughly about 1968 was the beginning of a new wave of feminism, and with that, a number of women were beginning to do reflection on the theological aspect or the religious aspect. But it's important to realize that a number of the women who began in '68 were already in the Civil Rights Movement. And so they embarked on this not only from a religious perspective, but also from a perspective that integrated class and race issues.

FIEDLER: What was inadequate about older theology that required a feminist approach?

RUETHER: It was sexist, racist, and homophobic and classist and imperialist —just for starters.

FIEDLER: Okay! And therefore feminist theology did what?

RUETHER: What feminist theology did, and what all of the critical theologies did—liberation theology, black theology, and so on—was to reveal these limitations. Traditional theology had been done by ruling class or dominant white men who were oblivious to their own social context and who incorporated attitudes that not only ignored everybody else in the world but actually validated this kind of ruling-class power.

FIEDLER: Can you give me just one example of that kind of thinking?

RUETHER: You have to start with a critique of the Bible and the historical tradition which said directly things like: women are misbegotten males; they're not full human beings, therefore they can't represent Christ; they can't be ordained, and so on. So feminist theology started out by critiquing that kind of tradition and the way it continued to be enunciated and supported into the late twentieth century.

FIEDLER: Was there anything in your life that led you to become a feminist theologian?

RUETHER: My mother and her friends were feminists. I grew up in a community of older women who were very independent and self-affirming.

FIEDLER: Delores, when do you date the beginning of womanist theology and how would you describe it?

DELORES WILLIAMS: I would date womanist theology from about 1980. Alice Walker, of course, coined the term "womanist." Alice Walker did a book called *In Search of Our Mothers' Gardens: Womanist Prose*, and she had a full definition of womanist in there. We who are in theology and religious studies have made some adjustments to that definition, but we basically hold fast to some of the insights and definitions she provided. So I would define a "womanist" as a black feminist who lifted up other critiques of women's oppressions, and has been lifted up by some of our Anglo-feminist sisters.

FIEDLER: What would some of those critiques be, Delores?

WILLIAMS: One of those critiques was, of course, the racial critique. The other was the survival and quality of life critique. In womanist theology, race, gender, and class simultaneously provide a critical lens through which to critique woman's oppression in the United States and abroad.

FIEDLER: How did you become a womanist theologian?

WILLIAMS: I was a feminist first and I still believe in feminist presuppositions, but I became a womanist as a result of seeing what Alice Walker was describing as the condition of African-American women. It seemed to fit us because it unearthed certain kinds of female traditions that have been buried beneath the cultural spiral of black life and had not seen the light of day. Alice Walker began to lift up such images as woman liberator and named some issues that we had forgotten and were not mentioned by male liberation theologians.

FIEDLER: Was there anything in your own life and background that led you to this?

WILLIAMS: You know, I think most of our mothers were feminists and womanists before they even knew they were, and they provided us with certain kinds of philosophies of life that caused us to develop as women. My sister and I had one of those philosophies of life where it was said, "You're on your own as a woman. You have to make it for yourself."

FIEDLER: Rosemary, was Jesus a feminist?

RUETHER: I think that the use of "feminist" is an anachronism. It's importing modern categories of gender analysis two thousand years ago. So I wouldn't use that language. I would say that he was a Jewish prophet and his message was primarily in terms of good news for the poor, but he did have a particular sensitivity to the most marginalized women who were the poorest of the poor.

FIEDLER: Do the scriptures support a feminist approach? There are many Evangelical Christians who would say, "Hey, scripture and feminism are antithetical." What would you say to that?

RUETHER: I think the scripture is a mixed bag. That is to say, it has elements in it which support oppressive hierarchies and it has elements in it that are prophetic and seek to overturn oppressive hierarchies and validate the full humanity of all people. I think you have to recognize the ambiguity of scripture.

FIEDLER: Delores, what would you say is the central message of womanist theology?

WILLIAMS: The central message of womanist theology goes to the race, class, and gender critique. But I wouldn't say there's one message because there are many of us. We write from different points of view, but one of the central issues in some of the work, and especially mine, would be the wilderness tradition, following the Exodus in which the Hebrews were trying to make a people. African-Americans are constantly in this process of making and keeping together people. That is the central issue for us: community building and community construction, and holding it together.

FIEDLER: I know that both of you have also been involved in linking feminist or womanist theology to a concern for the earth and to creation spirituality. It's called, I believe, eco-feminist theology. Rosemary Ruether, can you talk about that connection? How is the concern for the earth linked with a concern for women?

RUETHER: I think the term eco-feminism, which was coined in the late '70s, recognizes certain kinds of ideological patterns in which domination of women, domination of slaves, and domination of the earth are really all linked together. They're part of a kind of ideology in which ruling class men see all of these categories of women, working classes, slave people, and the earth as property and as tools to be employed. Eco-feminism and eco-justice movements essentially unpack the way in which these kinds of oppressions have been linked and then they seek to find ways of transforming both our relationship as humans to each other and our relationship to the Earth.

FIEDLER: And Delores, do you see it pretty much the same way?

WILLIAMS: I've recently done an article that looks at some of the eco-feminist ideas in relation to what has happened to the earth and what has happened to black women's bodies in the nineteenth century: the rape of the land, the rape of women, the exploitation of people, and the exploitation of the land.

FIEDLER: What are the frontiers of your respective theological traditions? Where does feminist theology go from here, Rosemary?

RUETHER: I've always been interested in the interface of class, race, and gender. By the early '70s, I was also linking this with the oppression of the earth, with women-based theologies around the world. It's the kind of work that's being done in Africa and Latin America and Asia, and increasingly across religions. I believe that networking across many different contexts is the cutting edge of feminist theology.

FIEDLER: Delores, what do you see as the frontiers in womanist theology?

WILLIAMS: One of the major frontiers is actually in the field of medicine, where AIDS and other diseases are growing at such a rapid rate. We want to pay attention to women's bodies, to ways in which black women and women of color can savor their bodies and find the resources to take care of and safeguard their health. So, we are raising questions about how the Christian theology can support caring for our bodies and our communities in this health crisis.

Dr. Amina Wadud

on *Inside the Gender Jihad*

Many women are Qur'anic scholars in Islam. Dr. Amina Wadud is one such scholar, and she has developed new interpretations of that sacred text that support the rights of women.

When I interviewed her in August 2006, she was an associate professor of Islamic studies at Virginia Commonwealth University. She is the woman who jolted the world of Islam when she led Friday prayers for a mixed-gender group in New York City in 2005, and before that, preached at Friday prayers in Cape Town, South Africa. Her latest book is called *Inside the Gender Jihad: Women's Reform in Islam.*

MAUREEN FIEDLER: Professor Wadud, you weren't always a Muslim. How did you become a Muslim and then how did you grow to be a Muslim feminist or, as you say, a pro-faith, pro-feminist woman?

AMINA WADUD: I think an emphasis on faith is something that I was raised with from childhood, because my father was a Methodist minister, and I consider my father my first spiritual mentor. And among the lessons I that I learned from him is a tremendous sense of love and justice, and I began to explore other faith traditions. I lived a year as a Buddhist in an ashram and I still incorporate mediation into my personal worship. Stepping into the field of Islam helped me to understand how all the faiths are connected and gave me a sense of the permanence of the sacred in all things. When the order of the sacred that extends to the universe is disrupted, there is disharmony, there is discord, and there is injustice. And so it is on the basis of my faith that I struggle within my faith in order to improve conditions for women and men.

FIEDLER: And one of the injustices you perceive is the treatment of women within the Islamic tradition?

WADUD: Yes, there has been a very long history of women's marginalization, women's silence, women's subjugation, and in more recent years, violence toward women and exploitation of women, sometimes in the name of the Islam. I'm trying to help women feel the fullness of their faith and at the same time the fullness of their beings as representatives and agents of God.

FIEDLER: As you and I both know, most interpretations of Islam, at least in the contemporary scene, have emphasized or justified male dominance, but in your book you say that these traditional ideas are often based on misunderstandings or on selective use of the sacred text. Can you give us an example or two of the distortions and then how you deal with them?

WADUD: One of the most contentious ones that I deal with is the notion that God is male. The Arabic language divides all things into masculine and feminine. The tendency to use the male form for God is often taken by Arabic-speaking and non-Arabic-speaking people as being a *literal* indication that God is male. But the Qur'an clearly removes God from similitude to humans in that way. Humans are male and female, but God is above that. At the same time, another aspect that helps to promote the idea of gender justice is that the Qur'an is emphatic that all things are created from the first pair. Therefore, being male or being female is equally essential to what it means to be human and any priority or privilege given to one or the other is in fact again a corruption or distortion of the essential message of the text.

FIEDLER: How is that message received in the Muslim communities of which you are a part?

WADUD: Certainly there is a lot of enthusiasm from some corners and there is a lot of opposition from others. I have to contend with both aspects of it, but mostly because my work is directed towards women's self-empowerment. I am trying to work to help women understand more about their faith, to self-affirm with regard to their faith, to interrogate the sources in order to be able to find the messages of hope and transcendence available to them. And then, I encourage them to take those messages into their homes and into their villages, into their cities, and into their jobs, with the full awareness of their responsibilities before God.

FIEDLER: Traditionally, women have not been imams, or prayer leaders in Islam. What's the barrier, theologically or Qur'anically?

WADUD: There is no Qur'anic barrier to it. The theology that was formulated in social, cultural, and historical circumstances certainly privileged men over women. And therefore the idea of men leading prayer in mixed settings was given precedence rather than sharing that role with women. But women have been leaders among other women; it's just a question of what happens in a mixed setting. Perhaps the practices that restricted women, since they do not have Qur'anic mandates, need to be changed and the spectrum needs to be broadened to be more inclusive of women.

FIEDLER: Are imams ordained or consecrated in some kind of formal way as rabbis or priests or ministers are in Judaism or Christianity?

WADUD: No. The imam is the one that stands in front, and because the formal ritual prayer has different bodily postures, the imam is the first one to make that movement and then to call for the rest of the congregation to follow. Because the postures include bowing from the waist in full prostration, some have felt a kind of decorum is lost when women are in the front. I am arguing against these ideas, trying to encourage people to understand that all forms of worship are supposed to be concentrations on God, not concentrations on anything or anyone, and therefore a knowledgeable woman is eligible to lead prayer. So I'm reestablishing the principle in Islam: the one who has the most knowledge with regard to the tradition is the one who should lead.

FIEDLER: And of course right now in the United States most congregations and mosques separate the men and women, do they not?

WADUD: The practices within the communities in the United States have tended to move more and more conservatively toward a tendency to separate women and men. Some even build an inferior space for women within their structures. I find it interesting that that is happening in the United States, while in other parts of the world, say for example in Egypt, they're actually moving to have greater space accessibility for women.

FIEDLER: I've talked to women who've made the *hajj*, and they say that when you go to the great mosque in Mecca, men and women pray together there.

WADUD: That's right. We call that the Meccan Prayer and we use that as an example of the requirement to be able to participate in the ritual with women in front, women behind, women next to you. But at the same time, you focus on God.

FIEDLER: In both Cape Town, South Africa and in New York, you dared to do what imams do: preach and/or lead the Friday prayers, and I believe it was a mixed-gender group in both cases. Can you talk about that experience?

WADUD: I was first introduced to the idea of women leading informal rituals in South Africa in 1994. But subsequent to that time, I gave it a great deal of scholarly deliberation and a great deal of spiritual meditation, and I came to the place we've talked about before. I came to understand that the practice of prayer is significant in our faith, and the marginalization of women in leadership has been acculturated over time but is not essential to maintaining the integrity of the faith or of the ritual. And so, after many years of deliberation, I invoked all my experience and now I've done it. In fact, I have done it frequently and hopefully others will also be able to do it.

FIEDLER: You are, of course, an African-American woman in Islam. How would you say that African-Americans or African women Muslims are treated in what is largely an Arab or Asian world of Islam?

WADUD: I think certain racist tendencies still run amok in certain parts of the Muslim world. So it's especially important for me as an African-American woman to self-identify with my black origins and to assert, as the Qur'an has asserted, my rights to full integrity and honor on the basis of my agency and on the basis of my heart.

FIEDLER: And just to clarify, you are not part of the Nation of Islam?

WADUD: That's correct, I've never been a member of the Nation of Islam, even though I recognize it as important in the American Islamic context.

FIEDLER: People can recognize you easily as a Muslim woman because you wear the *hijab*, or the headscarf, but many Muslim women who are feminists don't wear it. Why do you choose to wear it?

WADUD: I wear hijab by choice. I actually covered my hair before I was Muslim and I began to wear long clothes before I was Muslim because I wanted to retake the integrity of my body that my slave ancestors were not given the right to choose. Women on the auction block, even Muslim women, were brought to this country and stripped naked. So a certain kind of bodily integrity had inclined me towards certain forms of modest dress. The hijab in particular is a sign of identity with Muslim women worldwide.

FIEDLER: And yet you would leave it up to a woman to choose, or choose not, to cover?

WADUD: I do not consider the hijab a fundamental principal of faith, nor do I consider it to be the only expression of modesty. I advocate wearing the hijab only by choice. In these days, sometimes I don't wear the hijab.

FIEDLER: And finally, at one point in the book you say, and I'm quoting, "One cannot stand on the sidelines in the face of injustice and still be recognized fully as Muslim." Is this why, at the most basic level, you continue to struggle against what seem to be enormous odds in seeking to improve women's status in Islam?

WADUD: Yes, I think we are responsible for our actions and that responsibility has a divine component to it. We will in fact be judged, and that judgment is a way in which the cosmic order comes back into balance. And so, for example, I cannot use styrofoam cups knowing that they are non-biodegradable. I am adamant about all aspects of taking care of this planet. Everything to me reflects how important it is that we in fact stand up, down to the smallest thing, as an agent of God on the earth. I cannot stand in the face of any injustice and not feel a responsibility to stand against it.

Dr. Elizabeth Johnson
on *She Who Is: The Mystery of God in Feminist Theological Discourse*

In the world of Judeo-Christian scripture scholarship, Dr. Elizabeth Johnson took on perhaps the most controversial feminist question of all: "Is God male?" She is a distinguished professor of theology at Fordham University in New York, and the award-winning author of several books. Her most famous is *She Who Is: The Mystery of God in Feminist Theological Discourse.* This interview took place in May 2003.

MAUREEN FIEDLER: There are many people who would be shocked even by the thought of naming God in female terms. What would you say to someone like that?

ELIZABETH JOHNSON: I would say, "Yes, it's right to be shocked." Once you start thinking about it, the male imagination has gripped our own imaginations to the point where anything else is inconceivable. It's been taken for granted that God is male because the language which we've experienced all through the tradition, almost universally, has addressed God with names taken from the male world, like Lord and Father and King. And so without reflecting on it, we assume that we're addressing a male person. So as soon as the idea comes up that we can address God differently, there is a shock, because suddenly what we took for granted isn't necessarily for granted any more.

FIEDLER: Where do you yourself start, Dr. Johnson? Is God male or female or both?

JOHNSON: How about—start with neither. God is spirit, neither male nor female, but as we read in the book of Genesis, God creates male and female together in the divine image and likeness. Therefore, God is imaged by both male and female, and can be addressed as male or female.

FIEDLER: So what we're really talking about in our discourse about God is not the essence of God, but rather how we image this spirit we call God?

JOHNSON: Yes, because God's the creator of the universe and can never be captured in words or images or names. We are finite and God is infinite. God always goes beyond what we can say or imagine.

FIEDLER: Why is this question important? I've certainly heard lots of people say that "Look, language is just words." What difference does it make whether we address God as male or female?

JOHNSON: Words have power. The way we use words is the way we conceive the world to be. If you just want to look at the English language in recent years, virtually every politician worth his or her salt now refers to the *men and women* in uniform, the *women and men* in this department or that department. We no longer take for granted that "man" generically refers to everyone.

FIEDLER: And we know certainly the injury that racist language can do to somebody.

JOHNSON: I was just going to make that same analogy. Words structure our world. They are powerful, they let us know who's in and who's out, what's valued and what's not valued. And so, using male words for the human race is less and less acceptable.

FIEDLER: You say in your book that we court idolatry when we address God only in male terms. Is that carrying it a little far?

JOHNSON: Not at all. Because when we use only male terms, we forget that they're only metaphors. We make them literal. Literal words do not speak about the true God because we reduce God to our size when we do that. So it's like making the Golden Calf and bowing down and adoring it. When we do that, we're forgetting who the true God is.

Let me hasten to say, I am not opposed to using male names for God, but my criticism is against using them *exclusively*, precisely because they lead to idolatry as well as to oppression.

FIEDLER: And so you might be likely to say, "Our Father, our Mother who art in heaven"?

JOHNSON: Right, our Father, Mother, Maker who art in heaven.

FIEDLER: What does this do to the female psyche when she uses male names over and over again?

JOHNSON: It puts the female psyche at a distance from God because if God is only male, women cannot intuitively grasp themselves in the image of God. In order to do that, we women have to abstract ourselves from our bodies and our sexuality and our way of being in the world as human beings. So it deprives women of spiritual power.

FIEDLER: I've interviewed Christians and pastors who will say, "Look, Jesus called God Father himself, and Jesus had a choice." They point out that he was very progressive in his attitudes toward women, but that he did not call God by a female name and so therefore we have to follow suit. How do you answer that?

JOHNSON: Jesus called God Father but he called God many other things as well. I like to say that he had a veritable symphony of ways of talking about God. Just think of his parables. And he didn't hesitate to use female images in some of those parables for God.

FIEDLER: There is the woman in search of the lost coin, and, I believe, the mother hen.

JOHNSON: Exactly, and also the woman kneading the leaven into the dough as a symbol of God's working justice into the world. I should point out too that in Luke 15, the woman looking for her lost coin comes after the parable of the Good Shepherd, the man looking for his lost sheep, and they both begin and end the same way. Both of them are images of God the redeemer.

FIEDLER: In your book you talk about other female images of God in the Judeo-Christian scriptures, and one is Sophia in the Hebrew scriptures. Can you say more about that?

JOHNSON: This is a female figure of power and might. And there's great debate among scholars about what this figure signifies and if, in some instances, she signifies a messenger sent from God. But in other passages, she clearly signifies God herself. In the Book of Proverbs she says, "Whoever finds me, finds life." The gospel writer who wrote John's Gospel took those words and put them in the mouth of Jesus. "Whoever finds me, finds life," is a divine saying. If you go to the Book of Wisdom, which is not considered part of the regular books of the Bible by Protestant and Jewish believers, but is considered so by Roman Catholic and Orthodox believers, you have there a Sophia who creates the world, a Sophia who leads the people in the Exodus. She is more powerful than evil; against her, evil does not prevail. In other words, she is God.

FIEDLER: Some people, when they look at the traditional Christian Godhead—which is Creator, Jesus, and the Spirit—sometimes attribute female qualities to the Spirit. How do you feel about that?

JOHNSON: If you're coming to this question cold, the Father is locked in with a male image and Jesus is obviously a male human being. The Spirit has always been more ambiguous. So you could start there. And the scriptures show the Spirit using female metaphors in a number of places, for example, the dove signifies the Spirit, the hovering mother bird. One can go with that some distance but I would never want to stop there, because that's still two to one.

FIEDLER: You mention Jesus himself. I assume that in your view it's perfectly fine to use male pronouns or titles for Jesus.

JOHNSON: I think it would be rather foolish not to, because he was a male.

FIEDLER: There are some feminists who have problems with that.

JOHNSON: I think if you're talking about the historical person, he's a male. If you want to go forward in faith and talk about Christ, then the whole thing expands again, because the whole body of Christ includes all genders, all races, all ages. So the Body of Christ is more than male.

FIEDLER: So therefore the Resurrected Christ, if you will, is not time-bound or bound to a single set of human characteristics.

JOHNSON: Right; whoever drinks of the one spirit is one in Christ Jesus. There's no more Jew or Greek, slave or free, male or female.

FIEDLER: Would you encourage some creative nouns as applied to God?

JOHNSON: One area that I've been working in lately are the cosmic nouns that even go beyond female gender.

FIEDLER: Such as?

JOHNSON: Such as Cloud, Wind, Light, Rainbow, Fire, Rock. They're all biblical images of God and they really do get us out of the human-centered language we have for God into something more inclusive of the earth.

FIEDLER: You make a wonderful case for the desirability of using inclusive language, but it's very difficult in actual houses of worship to encourage people to change. How is it going to change at the practical level? What's going on out there?

JOHNSON: There are a few things I think that have taken us a couple steps forward. One is the *Inclusive Language Lectionary*.

FIEDLER: And that's the *Inclusive Language Lectionary* by Priests for Equality, I believe.

JOHNSON: Right. But a lot depends on the preacher and the one who presides at the service in worship. As women move into those positions and as men are more sensitive to this issue and have hearts that love justice, they too begin to use language in ways that open it up.

Kathleen Schmidt is an ordained priest in the Episcopal Church, serving in Vancouver. Over the course of several years she and her parish worked out the prayers for each season of the year so that they would be inclusive, and still trinitarian. She published her work in a three-volume set called *Seasons of the Divine Feminine*. You know, it's possible to change if you don't hit people over the head with this, and instead say gently, "Look this is even in scripture, let's do it this way." It works if there's a lot of love in the end.

Dr. Rena Pederson

on *The Lost Apostle: Searching for the Truth about Junia*

Every once in a while, a scripture scholar probes the life and meaning of a woman who has been obscure in the scriptures. Dr. Rena Pederson found Junia in Paul's letter to the Romans.

Dr. Pederson is a journalist who served as editorial page editor at *The Dallas Morning News* for sixteen years. She also served on the prestigious Pulitzer Prize board for nine years, and has been a finalist for the Pulitzer Prize herself. She is currently director of communications for the American College of Education and helps to establish American colleges worldwide. She is the author of a new book called *The Lost Apostle: Searching for the Truth about Junia*. I interviewed her in January 2007.

MAUREEN FIEDLER: Rena, how in the world did you get interested in what would look to some people like an obscure woman of the first century?

RENA PEDERSON: I was speaking to a women's book club, and we were discussing how the stories of women of faith are not played up, not spotlighted in any of the three great monotheistic religions: Christianity, Judaism, and Islam. And a woman of the group raised her hand and said, "Yes, like Junia." And we looked her and I said, "Who, who is Junia?" And she said, "Junia. She's mentioned in scripture as one of the apostles, but we don't know her name today, because her name was subsequently changed to a man's name and her story was lost." I was so intrigued, because I'd never heard of her before. I think it must've been the Nancy Drew in me. I went home and started looking up everything I could find about Junia. I looked in commentaries, looked in books about women of the New Testament, and sure enough, once I started looking, I found mention after mention about Junia.

FIEDLER: Who was Junia and what does Paul say about her?

PEDERSON: We don't have much about her, but at the end of Romans, Paul's great masterpiece, Paul singles out some people for particular praise, and a lot of them are women. And he singles out Junia and Andronicus in Romans 16:7. We know when their names are linked that they were probably husband and wife. He says that they were kinspeople, which means they were probably Jewish. He said that they were Christians before he was, which means that they were probably in the very earliest circle of Christians. And he says that they were thrown in prison with him. So they obviously had come to the attention of the authorities. So they were leaders.

FIEDLER: In a movement today, we would call them activists.

PEDERSON: Probably so. Now intriguingly, Paul goes on to say that they were noteworthy among the Apostles. That's what makes Junia so special, because she's the only woman named in the scripture as an apostle.

FIEDLER: She wasn't number thirteen, after the original twelve? What does the word "apostle" mean there?

PEDERSON: Not apostle with a capital "A," you're right—not one of the twelve. She was an apostle with a small "a," which means that she was a leading missionary. She was prominent enough in her preaching, and teaching, and work with Andronicus in proclaiming the church that Paul praised her. She was not only an apostle, but she was noteworthy among apostles. And indeed once you look in the writings of the early church, there were quite a few early commentators who praised Junia.

FIEDLER: So if you traveled in Christian circles in that first century, her name was a name you would likely know?

PEDERSON: Obviously, because if you look at the earliest translations in Greek, they all used the feminine form.

FIEDLER: But you just mentioned that over the centuries her name was changed by some biblical translators into a man's name. Why did this happen?

PEDERSON: That was a great part of the whodunit. Apparently, up to the thirteenth century, the reference was a woman's name. And the first instance where we see it changed to a man's name was in commentaries by a fellow named Giles of Rome. He was an archbishop of Rome, a leading intellectual in the late Middle Ages, very influential for his time, an advisor to Pope Boniface. He changed this couple into a description of two old men. And it stuck for centuries.

FIEDLER: And is that just because he couldn't imagine that a woman could be an apostle?

PEDERSON: That's right. By the Middle Ages, the church had become more hierarchical, and women had been reduced to the margins of the church. The early church started in house churches, meeting in homes. Women were dominant in the home; that was their domain, literally. Men were active in the public square; women lived in the private square. And so women were influential in the early house churches, because women could determine who crossed over the threshold into their domain.

FIEDLER: Perhaps they presided over what we might call the Eucharist today.

PEDERSON: Right, although it wasn't as formalized. The church got increasingly standardized and formalized as it moved out of the home into the public square. Christians moved from house churches into basilicas. And when they did, they became more hierarchical and more like the culture around them.

FIEDLER: Isn't it possible, given the patriarchy of the age in which the scriptures were written, that there might be historical figures, women leaders, who've been lost forever?

PEDERSON: Oh yes! I ran across other stories of women whose names were changed, or women described as being prominent members of the church, and mention of their roles would be taken out. I want to take care to point out that this is not feminist revisionism. It's a matter of justice as well as faith to go back and restore those names, and restore that missing history.

FIEDLER: In the course of his letter, Paul talks about women prophesying, about their being leaders in the church, and spreading the good news. On the other hand, we also know that Paul said women should be silent in church, be subject to their husbands, and keep their heads covered. One message doesn't seem to square with the other. How should we read what are often called "problem passages" in Paul?

PEDERSON: We have to re-examine that debate over some of those scriptures to see what Paul did in practice, and compare that with some of the scriptures that were later attributed to him.

There were a lot of scholars who aren't so sure that some of those verses that you mentioned were actually written by Paul. We do know that in practice he worked with women, and that he praised women for their work for the church. For example, he sends his letter to the Romans with Phoebe, and praises her, and says that she was a deacon in the church and that they should trust her. So what Paul did in practice sometimes contrasts with the "problem passages." And so perhaps we should look at them and see if they're truly scriptural, or if they're part of a cultural bias at that time that still exists in many parts of the world.

FIEDLER: In other words, some of our cultural biases can creep into scripture.

PEDERSON: Absolutely! For example, the verses that condone slavery.

We can say, "That was part of a cultural bias at the time. We have moved on." But we have to ask ourselves what's going on when we're willing to understand the scriptures regarding slavery in the context of their times, but not willing to re-look at the ones regarding women.

FIEDLER: The overarching question that some people might be asking is, why should we care about Junia? Why is she significant?

PEDERSON: She's very relevant today, and we've come such a long way. We have a woman as Speaker of the House; we have women being considered to run for president, and yet many cultural biases against women remain. And we still see them in the headlines. There was a story last summer where a woman, Mary Lambert, who taught Sunday school for fifty years in upstate New York, was fired by the minister because he said there were scriptures that said women shouldn't teach. There was a big front page article in the *New York Times* last fall about the stained glass ceiling. There are record numbers of women going into theology schools, going into the field to preach and teach, but they're also leaving in record numbers because of frustration, because they bump up against the stained glass ceiling when they are relegated to smaller churches at a sustenance wage, or they're given only assistant positions.

FIEDLER: And what does all this say, in your view, to Christian denominations today that refuse to ordain women or that do not permit them to preach?

PEDERSON: We find that all over the country, where women have been ordained, that the church is not diminished at all, the only difference is there are women standing next to men doing the work of faith. I hope that other denominations that don't ordain women will look at some of the new scholarship coming to light about the roles of women in the early church, from Mary Magdalene, to Prisca, to Junia, and that they revisit their views on ordination, and give women the full place they certainly deserve.

Dr. Phyllis Trible

on *Hagar, Sarah, and Their Children*

Dr. Phyllis Trible is one of the leading scripture scholars in mainstream Protestant Christianity. For decades, she has used her knowledge and insights to illuminate the roles of women in the Bible. I interviewed her in July 2006 about a book she edited with another highly respected scripture scholar, Dr. Lettie Russell. It is called: *Hagar, Sarah, and Their Children: Jewish, Christian, and Muslim Perspectives*, and it offers perspectives on the wives of Abraham: Hagar and Sarah. Dr. Phyllis Trible is a professor of biblical studies at Wake Forest University Divinity School.

MAUREEN FIEDLER: In the Hebrew scriptures, Sarah is the first wife of Abraham, but because she is barren, she suggests to Abraham to take Hagar as his second wife in order to bear a child for him, correct?

PHYLLIS TRIBLE: That's correct. And you immediately see the contrast between the two women. Sarah is the old woman; she is barren, but she is the first wife, and she holds the power. And it is her suggestion that Abraham take her maid, Hagar, an inferior, but one who is fertile. The contrast between the two women is set up immediately with Sarah having the power and Hagar having none.

FIEDLER: And each has a son. Hagar has the son Ishmael and Sarah has the son Isaac.

Later, Sarah banishes Hagar and her son to the wilderness where, except for God, they would've died?

TRIBLE: Abraham sent them forth with very meager provisions. And the Angel of the Lord comes to their rescue.

FIEDLER: You note that Abraham is used as a symbol of unity, but that his wives have actually been used to sow discord among the Abrahamic faiths. Are these women understood differently in Judaism, Christianity, and Islam?

TRIBLE: Yes they are. Sarah, in Judaism, is understood as the mother of Jews, the founding maternal figure. Hagar is pretty much dismissed in Judaism. Hagar, strangely enough, becomes the mother of Islam, and Sarah is embraced as the founding mother of Christianity. And in Islam, though Sarah is treated with respect, she is there only tangentially.

FIEDLER: And of course, the stories of these women don't end with what's in the scriptures. There is a wealth of post-biblical commentary in all three faiths. But there's no unity here, either. These women have been used symbolically to sow discord among groups.

TRIBLE: That's the telling phrase, they've been used, and they have been used to sow discord.

FIEDLER: In the present day, you tie this story to the Israeli/Palestinian struggle. How do you do that?

TRIBLE: In the Bible, all the relationships in the family get resolved one way or another, except for the relationship between Hagar and Sarah. Hagar and Sarah are never reconciled. And their story is one of conflict, and jealousy, and envy, and rivalry, and malice. And that continues to this day, in the Israeli/Palestinian conflict. The children of Hagar and the children of Sarah are still locked in conflict. And it does not help to say we all have the same father, Abraham. The mothers are where the struggle resides.

FIEDLER: You make the point in the book that both of these women, but perhaps especially Hagar, represent the voices of all marginalized peoples.

Trible: Yes indeed. There are a host of unusual things about Hagar. She is the first person in the Bible to flee from oppression. Now that's quite a model. She is the first runaway slave. She's the first person visited by a messenger of God, which is really striking, because you might think that the messenger had to first visit Abraham, or some other man, or at least a Hebrew—but no, it's Hagar. She is the first woman to receive an annunciation. So she becomes a model for similar scenes later in the Bible. And she is the only woman in the Bible to receive a divine promise of descendants.

And there are even more striking things. She's the first surrogate mother. She's the only person in the Bible who dares to name God. Other people call upon the name of God, but she names God. And she's the first woman in the ancestor stories to bear a child. It goes on and on and on. She's the first to be a divorced wife. She's the first single parent, and she's the first person to weep. So you see all these links between her and contemporary issues. Sarah was also marginalized. In that, both women of these women were trapped within patriarchy.

And patriarchy has basically two places for women: the pedestal or the pit. That is: put a woman on a pedestal, as for example the Virgin Mary; or call a woman a prostitute, or a whore, as for example, Mary Magdalene. I think Sarah and Hagar represent those opposites within patriarchy.

Fiedler: And so is that why it's important to pull apart, if you will, the pieces of patriarchy, to learn about, and to learn from, women in scripture?

Trible: Most surely. It's a feminist perspective that gives us the freedom, and the knowledge, and insight to do this kind of thing, and thereby to recover dimensions of the biblical text that have been buried for centuries. And also to expand our understanding of the Bible as a diverse book, not as a book speaking with one single voice. It speaks with many voices, and voices that counter one another.

Chapter 4
Religious Feminist Activists

Every movement for justice, inside and outside faith traditions, has not only scholars and thinkers, but activists, those who build organizations, talk to the media, run conferences, create symbolic events, demonstrate, and commit civil—or, in this case—ecclesial disobedience.

The women leaders in this chapter have challenged the status quo in their respective traditions, much as the Hebrew prophets challenged the Jewish establishment of their day. Some are theologians or scripture scholars; some are not. But in the process of offering public witness, they have provoked a great deal of thinking about the roles of women in the world of religion.

Their lives recall other women activists over centuries who were "firsts" in their respective traditions. To name just a few:

- In the thirteenth century, Mugai Nyodai, a Japanese Buddhist nun, became the first Zen Buddhist abbess.
- In 1660, Margaret Fell, a Quaker, published a booklet, revolutionary for that time, arguing for gender equality and a woman's right to speak in a house of worship.
- In 1853, Antoinette Brown Blackwell was ordained in the Congregational Church, but her ordination was not recognized, and she later became a Unitarian minister.
- In 1860, Olympia Brown was ordained a Universalist minister, and later became a Unitarian.
- In 1866, Helenor Alter Davisson became the first woman ordained a minister in any Methodist denomination, and in 1880, Anna Howard Shaw was the first woman ordained in the Methodist Protestant Church.
- In 1875, Mary Baker Eddy launched the Church of Christ, Scientist, giving it a formal charter in 1879.
- In 1911, Ann Allebach was the first Mennonite woman ordained.
- In 1935, Regina Jonas of East Berlin, Germany was the first woman ever ordained a rabbi. She was of the Reform tradition.
- In 1956, Margaret Towner was ordained as the first woman minister in the Presbyterian Church (U.S.A.).

- In 1972, Sally Priesand became the first woman ordained a rabbi in the United States. She is part of the Reform tradition.
- In 1974, the famous "Philadelphia Eleven" were ordained to the priesthood in the Episcopal Church before church laws were changed to permit ordination. In 1976, the church recognized these ordinations, and approved women as both priests and bishops.
- In 1974, Sandy Eisenberg Sasso became the first woman rabbi ordained in the Jewish Reconstructionist tradition.
- From 1976 to 1988, Buddhist nun Tenzin Palmo became the first Western woman in the Tibetan tradition to spend twelve years in seclusion in a cave in the Himalayas. As a result, in February 2008, she was given the rare title of *Jetsunma*, which means Venerable Master.
- In 1985, Amy Eilberg became the first female rabbi in the Conservative Jewish tradition.
- In 1988, Barbara Harris became the first woman bishop in the Episcopal Church.
- In 1995, Amina Wadud became the first woman to preach at a Friday Muslim prayer service in Cape Town, South Africa, and in 2005, she became the first woman to lead the entire Friday prayer (*salat*) in New York City.
- In 2002, seven women were ordained Roman Catholic priests in a service held on a boat in the River Danube. (The Vatican does not recognize these ordinations.)*

In this chapter, we meet some of the women whose lives helped crack the stained glass ceiling in recent times in several faith traditions.

Rabbi Eveline Goodman-Thau
First Woman Orthodox Rabbi

Many faith traditions still exclude women from formal ministerial roles. This is true for the Roman Catholic and Orthodox Christian traditions, Southern Baptists, several conservative evangelical groups in Christianity, the Church of Jesus Christ of the Latter Day Saints (Mormons), Muslims, and Orthodox Jews. But women are challenging that status quo.

In September 2003, I met Rabbi Eveline Goodman-Thau at a conference in Spain, and interviewed her about her ordination to the Orthodox rabbinate in Israel. She believes she's called and ordained, but many do not accept her role at the moment.

MAUREEN FIEDLER: Eveline Goodman-Thau is a Jewish woman whose life spanned the years from the Holocaust to the contemporary struggles

---

* An extensive listing can be found at the website of Ontario Consultants on Religious Tolerance: http://www.religioustolerance.org/femclrg13.htm.

in the Middle East. She was born into Orthodox Judaism, which does not permit women rabbis. Yet her feminism led her to challenge that exclusion. I met Eveline at the 2nd European Women's Synod in Barcelona, Spain in August 2003, where she was a keynote speaker. . . . She shared with me the story of her life, and her challenge to Orthodox Judaism.

Eveline, you say your "miracle journey" began at the age of four; how so?

EVELINE GOODMAN-THAU: I fled from Vienna at age four and came to Holland with my parents. We were on the last train out of Vienna on December 31, 1938, because on that day our passports were expiring.

FIEDLER: And you were one of a handful of Jewish survivors in the Netherlands?

GOODMAN-THAU: Yes. Before the war there were a hundred and thirty thousand Jews in Holland and only eight thousand survived. It's a miracle when you survive.

FIEDLER: When Israel was founded, you moved there, but don't you really have your feet planted in both Europe and Israel?

GOODMAN-THAU: Yes. When I went to Israel, I realized that I was in two places. So when my children grew up, I decided I must go back to Europe and teach there. And that's what I've been doing for the last twenty years. I have an apartment in Berlin and I conduct Jewish studies there. I was first the vice president of the European Society of Women in Theological Research. Then I founded, together with others, Associations for Jewish Studies in Germany and in Holland. After the opening of Eastern Europe, I helped found a Jewish Studies Association there.

You know, the great challenge in a united Europe is to leave aside centuries of Christian domination, and value all the great Abrahamic faiths: Christianity, Judaism, and Islam. This is a kind of spiritual reparation, learning from the past, having historical consciousness.

FIEDLER: In Israel, you married, and had five children, and you say all are active in the peace movement in Israel. Talk about your daughter, the doctor.

GOODMAN-THAU: Her first job was in a clinic in East Jerusalem and we said, "Oh, it's so dangerous," and she said, "Oh Mommy, the police station is next door and I want to treat Arab babies." And she learned Arabic and she took her kids to all their parties and she said, "I want them to know that life on the other side is the same."

FIEDLER: And your son is in the Israeli military, but how is his perspective unique?

GOODMAN-THAU: I'll give you an example. He told me once, "I was on the bus from Jericho to Jerusalem and, at a certain stop, an old Arab entered the bus with his wife and I got up and I gave my seat to the Arab woman. Everybody on the bus thought I was crazy, including her husband." He will, of course, defend his country when it's necessary, but he will not lose his human values.

FIEDLER: You say you heard the call to become a rabbi at a conference of Reformed Judaism in Germany. What happened?

GOODMAN-THAU: I was asked to preach, and I love to preach. I just open up the Bible and talk. After I preached, a person came up to me at the conference and said, "We're looking for a rabbi in Vienna, and we would like you as our rabbi." I said, "My God, I always wanted to be a rabbi," but I said it only as a joke because the one profession I think I would really be good at is being a rabbi because I have this preaching thing. But I'm Orthodox.

FIEDLER: But you took it seriously enough to search in Israel for a courageous Orthodox rabbi to ordain you. What happened?

GOODMAN-THAU: I went to Orthodox rabbis behind the scenes because I didn't want to make a fool of myself. After all, I am not young; I will be seventy next year, and I have a large family. I have a brother in Jerusalem who's fairly religious and I didn't want to shame him. But I wanted this in a serious way, so I asked rabbis. Several said, "Do it, but don't quote me on that." One referred me to an Orthodox rabbi who said he would give me ordination. I knew this rabbi for many years and we studied for six months. At the end, he said okay, and we did the ordination ceremony.

FIEDLER: Was this a public ceremony?

GOODMAN-THAU: No. It was a private ceremony but there is a document where it says Eveline Goodman-Thau came to me and I ordained her a rabbi; it's all in Hebrew.

FIEDLER: Are you the only woman in the quest for the Orthodox rabbinate?

GOODMAN-THAU: There are some others, but they are underground. Actually, I am not the first Orthodox woman ordained; I am the first woman who said *openly*, "I am ordained," and I am the first woman rabbi of Austria.

I am not recognized, but that does not disturb me. There are a number of women in Orthodoxy who are preparing for ordination in Jerusalem. So it's only a matter of time now. The problem lies not in the tradition, but in the attitudes of society.

FIEDLER: As we both know, Orthodox Judaism is decentralized. There is no Jewish Vatican to forbid such ordinations. So do other Orthodox rabbis recognize your ordination?

GOODMAN-THAU: Not publicly. The chief rabbi of Vienna had studied with the rabbi who ordained me, and he said, "Your credentials are tops. You're okay; but you know I can't recognize you." I was not recognized by the Orthodox or by the Reform Movement. Even the Reform women don't like me very much.

FIEDLER: Why?

GOODMAN-THAU: Because they believe that private ordinations are breaking down the system.

FIEDLER: After ordination, you served a Reformed community in Vienna, Austria, but that lasted only one year. Why?

GOODMAN-THAU: I was too Orthodox for them. But I was true to myself, and I was true to the tradition. I actually called myself trans-denominational. I am not for denominations.

FIEDLER: Can you share just a bit of your theology supporting women as rabbis?

GOODMAN-THAU: The woman is the one who stands in the Bible between man and God. She is the medium of recognition; she makes the bridge to God, and she names her sons according to her relationship to God.

FIEDLER: And so you moved on from Vienna to form an international Jewish women's community, a kind of floating synagogue that spans more than one continent. Can you describe that?

GOODMAN-THAU: It's called the Mother of All Living, because my name is Eve. It is a floating community. It is in Vienna, in Berlin, in Jerusalem— wherever women come together with me or without me. It is founded by women for women, but men are welcome.

FIEDLER: Eveline Goodman-Thau is one of those rare but remarkable religious free spirits who interpret a tradition so it makes sense for them, who listen for a call, and who forge new spiritual paths wherever they might lead. Her critics may not approve, but at age seventy, Eveline is still on the frontiers of her beloved Orthodox Judaism, beckoning, challenging, calling forth, and loving every minute of it.

Aisha Taylor

Former Executive Director, Women's Ordination Conference on the Archeological Evidence for Women's Leadership

Aisha Taylor was executive director of the Women's Ordination Conference when I interviewed her in July 2007. She was an activist leader of the women's movement in Roman Catholicism, with a wide-ranging knowledge of first-century archeology. In 2007, she reviewed new archeological evidence showing that women's leadership in Christianity was a fact of life in the early centuries of the church.

MAUREEN FIEDLER: A few years ago when I was in Rome, I visited the Church of Saint Praxedes. There, above a doorway, is a mosaic picturing the heads of four women, one of whom has the word *Episcopa* written above her head. For the record, "Episcop*us*" (masculine) or "Episcop*a*" (feminine) means bishop. But did a woman actually serve as a bishop in the early centuries of the church? This mosaic is but one of several works of art on catacomb walls and elsewhere in Rome that suggest that women led celebrations of the Eucharist, held leadership positions, and generally filled roles forbidden to women today by the Catholic and Orthodox churches, and in some Protestant denominations. Aisha, can you give us some overall idea of the type of iconography found in various sites in Rome that suggests women's leadership?

AISHA TAYLOR: There are iconography pieces all throughout the Mediterranean as well, and they are not only mosaics and frescos. They are also inscriptions on tombs and artwork. They are on catacomb walls and on church walls, in very holy places. One of these is in the Catacombs of Priscilla. It's a second-century fresco and it pictures a woman presiding at Eucharist, which is a role reserved specifically for priests, and only for priests. Another example is the fourth-century inscription on a tombstone in Jerusalem where it says in Greek, "Here lies the minister and bride of Christ, Sophia the Deacon, a second Phoebe." This is also important in that it relates to the biblical person of Phoebe, a New Testament woman, who Paul references as a deacon. And the other important thing about that is the word for deacon, *diakonos*, is the word that's used for Paul's ministry as well. So it really shows an egalitarian form of ministry in the early church. These two women had the same ministry as Paul.

FIEDLER: When did feminist scholars first become aware of this art?

TAYLOR: They've been doing work in this area for about twenty years. One of the scholars is Dorothy Irvin. And she is an archeologist with a pontifical doctorate in Catholic theology. She's been working for twenty years as an active archeologist and she has found many of these works all around the Mediterranean. In 2003 she started publishing her work in a calendar to get it out to more people. Another feminist scholar is Uta Eisen. In 2000, she published her book *Women Officeholders in Early Christianity: Epigraphical and Literary Studies*, which is an exhaustive study of that subject.

FIEDLER: If these icons say what Catholic feminists hope they say—and they're not without their ambiguities in some cases—why are they significant?

TAYLOR: They're significant because they would say that there's a tradition of Catholic women holding offices in the church, a tradition of Catholic women priests, women bishops, women deacons, and that's important to us as Catholics because tradition is extremely important. It's what links us to Jesus and his earliest disciples. It would set a precedent for women priests. It's not the lynch pin in the case for women's ordination, but it would be important.

FIEDLER: An article in the *National Catholic Reporter*, which is generally favorable to the idea of women priests, indicates that there's not unanimity among scholars on how to interpret all of this evidence. For example, Episcopa Theodora is pictured next to Mary of Nazareth and two women saints. Some people say this is a type of female apostolic succession, and others say that the artist just wanted to associate her with holy women. And then there's Philip Rousseau at Catholic University who says the evidence is suggestive but not plentiful enough to clinch the argument. How really definitive is this evidence?

TAYLOR: I think the evidence is very convincing and one of the reasons is because of the large number of archaeological finds around the Mediterranean. In almost every major Christian community in the early church, you'll find images of women as priests, bishops, or deacons. And that's convincing evidence. The other pieces that are important are the inscriptions on tombstones. People wanted future generations to remember these women as leaders in the church. They put them in the holiest places they could: in churches and on tombstones.

FIEDLER: However ambiguous some scholars find this evidence, there seems to be a scholarly consensus that women were at least deacons in the early church, deacon being the first order of the priesthood before one is ordained a priest. Do we have any idea how widespread women deacons were in the early church?

TAYLOR: We do know that in the first nine centuries in many places in the church, women were serving in ordained deacon roles. The scholarly evidence shows that there are sixty-one inscriptions and forty-one literary references to women deacons in the church.

One of the foremost scholars on women's ordination is John Wijngaards. He was a former Roman Catholic priest and he actually left the priesthood over the issue of women's ordination. In 2006 he published his book *Women Deacons in the Early Church*, so the evidence is getting out there. U.S. Catholics in particular are learning about the evidence for woman deacons.

FIEDLER: But the offices of deacon, priest, and bishop in the early church were not identical to those that we know today. It wasn't like these women went to formal seminaries, took theology courses, and went through some formal ordination ceremony. How were these roles different?

TAYLOR: They were very different. Until the Roman Empire made Christianity the state religion, the Catholic Church was much looser and less hierarchical. But, despite increasing hierarchy, these inscriptions and the mosaics and frescos were found all the way up until the Middle Ages. So we could say that these women were serving in the more standardized roles of deacon, priest, and even bishop in the later centuries. Earlier you mentioned Bishop Theodora. That's a ninth-century mosaic, well after the Romanization of the Christian Church.

FIEDLER: There was a huge debate about that at the time, was there not? I can recall that the scholar Rosemary Ruether suggests that perhaps women were trying to hold on to some of those roles, but there was a lot of objection found in the writings of popes at the time.

TAYLOR: And that provides further evidence that these women were actually serving in these roles because the popes were saying, "Oh, women aren't supposed to be doing this." We actually have that evidence.

FIEDLER: Another scholar that's quoted in the *National Catholic Reporter*, Janet Tulik, says that women also wielded influence in the early church depending on their wealth. Some women are reputed to have bankrolled, if you will, parts of the early Christian movement. What do we know about that?

TAYLOR: The biblical evidence in this regard is strong. Luke, chapter 8, verses 1–5, talks about how Mary Magdalene—who is a popular figure these days—Joanna and Susanna, and many other women supported Jesus' ministry in Galilee with their own resources. Also in Paul's letter to the Romans, he commends twenty-nine leaders, ten of whom are women. So it's reasonable to assume that if ten of these leaders were women, that they were supporting their house churches with their own resources.

FIEDLER: With all this archaeological evidence coming to light, is there any sign that the male leaders of either the Catholic or the Orthodox churches are moved by the evidence?

TAYLOR: It's hard to tell what moves the leaders of these churches, but one of the things that we see specifically in the Roman Catholic Church is that there is some support within the hierarchy. In a movement that began in 2002, Roman Catholic bishops who claim apostolic succession ordained seven women into the priesthood along the Danube River between Germany and Austria. Since then, many women have been ordained, and the leaders of this movement say that at least five Roman Catholic bishops in good standing with the Vatican support them and are working with them to make this grow.

FIEDLER: But this is going on behind the scenes.

TAYLOR: Exactly. Nobody knows the identity of these men.

FIEDLER: And the official position of the Vatican is that these are irregular, and indeed, even invalid ordinations. But is the movement for women's ordination taking on a new life and a new face with this?

TAYLOR: It is. And the same is true with the Orthodox. There's a sister organization called the Women's Orthodox Ministries and Education Network. They're very similar to the Women's Ordination Conference in that they dialogue to get women ordained into the Orthodox Church. An article in a mid-1988 issue of the *Greek American* contained a transcript of a call-in radio program that included a question from a listener, who asked Orthodox bishop Harvey Done about women's ordination. He replied, "The Orthodox Church does not know anything of the institution of priestesses, but it does know about the institution of deaconesses." He also mentioned that such a post existed until the eleventh or twelfth century, and that there is currently active discussion about women's ordination in the Orthodox Church.

FIEDLER: The women that have actually been ordained, what kind of ministry are they engaged in? Are they celebrating the Eucharist, for example?

TAYLOR: Yes, they are. And this is something that is very exciting about what's going on right now. Among the women who have been ordained in the U.S., almost all of them have formed vibrant communities. One formed by Jane Via in San Diego has over a hundred members and it's a full-service church. It has baptisms, and weddings, and obviously weekly mass. So very exciting things are happening from San Diego to Boston. Communities are forming and Catholics are accepting these women as priests.

FIEDLER: So they're building kind of mini-parishes?

TAYLOR: Exactly. But they're staying in the church. That's something that they cling to very strongly. They are Roman Catholics; they're building Roman Catholic communities that are more inclusive.

FIEDLER: Therefore, just to make a clear distinction, they regard themselves as Roman Catholic priests although the hierarchy does not.

TAYLOR: You name a major distinction that Catholics make in the light of the Second Vatican Council. We believe that *we* are the church. The church isn't identified only as the hierarchy.

FIEDLER: Is the hope that change will come as more and more Catholics see women in these roles, and thus someday the Vatican will come along and bless it?

TAYLOR: Yes, and that's how women in the Episcopal Church did it. They were ordained in irregular ordinations and then they were later accepted into the fold. Another really important piece of this issue though is that the women aren't working only for women to be ordained into this system. We're trying to create a renewed and inclusive church, so that when women are ordained into it, it is a more participatory, more inclusive structure.

FIEDLER: So you're out to change the very structure of the church, if you will.

TAYLOR: Exactly, but to keep it in line with the model of Jesus.

FIEDLER: I trust you don't have a great deal of hope that Benedict XVI is going to approve the ordination of women. But as you look into the future, what do you see? Do you have hope?

TAYLOR: I do have hope because I see Catholic women and men working to change the church. They're staying in the church to change it. They're saying, "I am Roman Catholic. I am a follower of Jesus and I know that the church can be better than this and it will be."

FIEDLER: What do the polls show about Catholics and women ordination?

TAYLOR: The most recent Gallup survey said that 64 percent of U.S. Catholics support women's ordination, and the number's much higher when asked only about the deaconate, which is supported by 71 percent of U.S. Catholics.

The Reverend Andrea Johnson
Roman Catholic Woman Bishop

Aisha Taylor talked about a new movement in the Roman Catholic Church in which women have actually been ordained as deacons, priests, and bishops. Here's how it happened: women who felt called to ordination located a bona fide Catholic bishop who would ordain (secretly) some as women priests, and a couple of women bishops. These women bishops were then empowered to pass the priesthood on to others. The identity of this male bishop or bishops will not be revealed under after his/their deaths. This plan became public with the first ordinations of Roman Catholic women on a boat on the Danube River in 2002, when seven women were ordained. Later, some women became bishops, and began ordaining other women. In April 2008, I interviewed one of those women priests, Rev. Andrea Johnson. Since this interview, Andrea has become a bishop in the movement.

ANDREA JOHNSON: I am reminded that blessed Pope John the XXIII, at the opening of the Second Vatican Council, told us that the church is not a museum. It is much less about the preservation of the past, than it is about moving forward.

MAUREEN FIEDLER: Andrea, who ordained you, and is your priesthood recognized by the Vatican?

JOHNSON: I was ordained on July 14, 2007 by Bishop Patricia Fresen, who lives in Munich, Germany. The Vatican does not recognize it as a valid ordination.

FIEDLER: And can a woman like Patricia Fresen call herself a Roman Catholic bishop?

JOHNSON: Patricia Fresen is one of several women bishops who were ordained priests and bishops by male Roman Catholic bishops who are in good standing with the Vatican. The ordinations were done in secret by male bishops who, I believe, were tired of the non-discussion of this issue, and are determined to do something about it.

FIEDLER: We don't have any idea who they are.

JOHNSON: Some in the movement, and I cannot say who, know who they are. Most of the women in the movement do not know. At some point, when those bishops are deceased, I believe, their names, which are held in a vault, will be made public.

FIEDLER: And this is done out of the Catholic theological belief that the priesthood is passed on, from bishop to priest, and then those priests in turn can be consecrated bishops. And thus you could get a Patricia Fresen as a bishop.

JOHNSON: Exactly.

FIEDLER: The Vatican, as we both know, is adamantly opposed to the ordination of women. And it has said in documents that women cannot image Jesus, because Jesus was a man, that there is no tradition for women priests in the history of the church, that Jesus didn't ordain any women, or have them among his twelve apostles. How do you respond to that?

JOHNSON: First of all, I think it's important to say that the argument that women cannot image Jesus is a rather new one. And we find it rather a strange argument, because it isn't Jesus that Christians image. The image is the Risen Christ who is beyond gender, so, as baptized persons, it isn't a matter of imaging a male person. It's a matter of a spiritual likeness to the risen Christ.

FIEDLER: And what about tradition, what about Jesus and the twelve apostles?

JOHNSON: Leonardo da Vinci notwithstanding, there's no evidence that the twelve apostles were ordained by Jesus as priests. The priesthood as we know it evolved over many centuries. The beginnings of it as an institution were many, many decades after Jesus. And so we can't really liken ordination to the gathering of the twelve.

FIEDLER: And you're referring there, of course, to da Vinci's painting of the Last Supper, which shows Jesus and twelve men. Do you think there were only men at a meal where there was food to be prepared?

JOHNSON: I don't think so at all.

FIEDLER: Isn't it likely that it was, in fact, a seder meal?

JOHNSON: It most probably was a seder meal. And it's not usual at all for men to celebrate a seder meal alone.

But as far as the statement that there is no tradition for women priests, there's good evidence from archeology and iconography, in areas of what is now the former Yugoslavia, and southern Italy, that there were women presbyters, leaders of Christian communities in those places, in the early centuries. And a presbyter is what we would call a priest today.

FIEDLER: How do Catholics in the U.S. feel about women's ordination? What do the polls show?

JOHNSON: Everything that I have seen over the last twenty-five years shows that anywhere from 65 to 75 percent of the people in the U.S.A. believe that women ought to be ordained as priests. And, there are even higher percentages of faithful Catholics who are very concerned about the crisis of the priest shortage. And for this reason, they are taking a harder look at a married priesthood and women priests.

FIEDLER: You were ordained under the aegis of a group known as Roman Catholic Women Priests. What does that group demand of priestly candidates? Do they have to have the same theological training as men do in seminaries?

JOHNSON: The short answer is yes. Women who wish to discern a path toward ordination with Roman Catholic Women Priests have to show themselves to be persons of a mature faith, of psychological soundness and health. They have to be people who have a high level of integrity, and ethics, and of course, they have to have adequate theological preparation and spiritual formation over several years.

FIEDLER: How many women have been ordained? And how many are waiting in the wings?

JOHNSON: Worldwide there are fifty women who are priests or bishops. Most of our bishops are in Europe. But as of April 9, we have a new North American woman bishop, Dana Reynolds.

FIEDLER: How many women are waiting to be ordained?

JOHNSON: I would say over a hundred are in formation.

FIEDLER: That's a fairly large number for what the Vatican has labeled as an illegitimate group.

JOHNSON: The growth is exponential, and more and more people are coming in contact with this directly.

FIEDLER: If you get ordained this way, no parish is going to hire you. No bishop is going to appoint you to be a pastor. What ministries do you engage in?

JOHNSON: Many of the women have communities, small faith communities to which they belonged prior to ordination. These are communities that gather for prayer, for scripture study, for spirituality. They were recognized by these communities as leaders, and put forth by these communities for priesthood. These women lead the Eucharist in these communities, and the communities are growing.

FIEDLER: What are some of the ministries they have engaged in?

JOHNSON: We have people who are in prison ministry, people who minister to the homeless, people who are long-time hospital and hospice chaplains, retreat leaders, and spiritual directors.

FIEDLER: And finally, will this ever happen officially?

JOHNSON: I am certain that women will be officially ordained in the church. The question is, when and how. We in Roman Catholic Women Priests know that the church is called not just to admit women to ordination, but to much more. The church is called to renew its entire concept of ministry—to conform to the vision of Jesus, which is an inclusive model, a discipleship of equals.

~~~~~~~~~~~~~~~~

Rabbi Susan Talve

Central Reform Congregation, St. Louis, Missouri

Rabbi Susan Talve is one of the first twenty-five women ordained a rabbi in the Reform Movement of Judaism, and she is the founder of the Central Reform Congregation in the city of St. Louis, a center of activity for peace, dialogue, and social justice. In 2008, she opened her synagogue to the irregular ordinations of women in the Roman Catholic Women Priests movement. As a result, she was threatened with a cutoff in relations by the Archdiocese of St. Louis, but stood her ground. I was not surprised, because I had interviewed Rabbi Susan Talve in April 2003.

MAUREEN FIEDLER: Rabbi Talve, you trace the roots of your religious feminism, not only to the women's movement, but also to early Catholic influences. How so?

SUSAN TALVE: I was shaped by a generation of women who were very influenced by Catholic sisters, sisters who were the first doctors and principals I knew. The principal of the school next to mine was a woman, and I noticed. I also saw a big statue of a woman in the Catholic Church. I thought that was very cool. Of course, I wasn't theologically aware enough to understand Mary's role, but I was taught to believe that women in positions of power and authority could really make a difference in the world, and bring balance to the world.

FIEDLER: Can you share that story from your childhood about the time your family visited Rome?

TALVE: I was in my early twenties on a family trip. We were in Rome and it was the eve of Yom Kippur, one of the holiest nights on the Jewish calendar. And there we were in Rome. But that morning was the canonization of Elizabeth Seton. My mother made us get up at three a.m. so that we could stand near the front in St. Peter's Square. Never mind that we would have to go to the synagogue that night. The most important thing was that her daughters were going to stand in the front row in St. Peters Square to see this American woman made a saint. I will never forget what it looked like to see a huge tapestry of that beautiful American woman, Elizabeth Seton, who had done so much for children, for education, for the liberation of both boys' and girls' minds in this country. Next to this huge tapestry the cardinals seemed small. Even the pope was tiny next to her. All of them were looking up at this big beautiful American woman.

FIEDLER: Rabbi Talve, you are concerned with women's rights, but you are also deeply involved in the inner city of St. Louis. Can you talk about your work for racial justice in St. Louis?

TALVE: This synagogue was founded only eighteen years ago on the premise that St. Louis city needed a Jewish presence. We decided to be part of one of the greatest challenges to this community. We wanted to challenge racism and the segregation that exists here, and so we located the synagogue in the city. The benefits have been overwhelming. For example, in this racist city where Jews of color often have to choose between being black or Jewish, we're actually able to provide a safe place. We did the same for the gay and lesbian community, and for people with interfaith families who want an authentically Jewish place to raise their children, but who don't want to be told what religion they should practice. We're trying to apply the same model now to Jews of color.

FIEDLER: I notice a group of people here who are mentally challenged, using the synagogue for recreation. What other work goes on here?

TALVE: We make space for people who don't have any place else to go. We have a food pantry here and we provide other services. Because of our location, a lot of homeless people find us, and we try to do more than give out band-aids; we help them find long-term solutions. We also have a coat closet. It invites you to put things there if you don't need them anymore, and also it allows people to walk in the door anonymously and take what they need without having to ask. Hospitality means letting people have dignity.

FIEDLER: Interfaith work is an important dimension of your ministry. Can you describe that memorable service you had on September 11, 2001?

TALVE: September 11 was a Hebrew school day for us, but instead of having Hebrew school from four to six, we decided to have a service so that everyone could come to the synagogue to pray, to mourn, and to process what had gone on that day. As we began the service, I looked to the back of the room, and saw the Muslim imam Dr. Waheed Rana. I asked him to join me, saying, "Dr. Rana, what an honor that you're here." And we led the service together. We were also joined by Rupert Lovely, a Unitarian minister.

FIEDLER: Rabbi Talve, you say you are a Jew who is pro-Israel and pro-Palestine. What do you mean by that?

TALVE: I love Israel, and I would love to see a just solution for the Palestinian people. I'm hoping that that's going to be a two-state solution. But the building of more settlements in the occupied territories has really been a mistake. And I would love to see that end.

FIEDLER: Rabbi Talve, you are also opposed to the U.S. war in Iraq, and you see it through a feminist lens. What do you see when you look at this war?

TALVE: I don't mean to blame it on the men. It's women too, but I do feel like these wars are often like games that little boys play, and I think we have to bring a deeper wisdom to finding solutions for oppression other than wars. The toys are too dangerous. The toys have gotten too deadly. We're all going to suffer, and some great mother has to say, "Enough, enough!"

~~~~~~

Asra Nomani

on *Standing Alone in Mecca*

In most mosques, women are relegated to the rear, or sometimes to a separate room, at the time of Friday prayer. Asra Nomani boldly challenged that segregation the day she walked into her mosque in Morgantown, West Virginia, and knelt down in front with the men to pray. As a result, she is often regarded as something of a feminist iconoclast in the Muslim community. She is the author of *Standing Alone in Mecca: An American Woman's Struggle for the Soul of Islam*. In 2003 Asra Nomani made the hajj, the pilgrimage to Mecca that every able-bodied Muslim is required to make once in a lifetime. Asra Nomani is a feminist inspired by the great Muslim women from the days of the Prophet Mohammed.

Asra Nomani currently teaches journalism at Georgetown University in Washington, DC, and co-directs the Pearl Project at Georgetown, a faculty-student investigative-reporting project studying the kidnapping and murder of *Wall Street Journal* reporter Daniel Pearl in 2002 in Pakistan. I interviewed her in May 2005.

MAUREEN FIEDLER: Asra, I was fascinated by the fact that your inspiration to make the hajj came not from a Muslim but from a Buddhist, the Dalai Lama. Both of you were at a Hindu festival when this happened. Can you talk about that?

ASRA NOMANI: I saw the Dalai Lama, giggling as he often does at press conferences, and he said, "Read the text of each other's religion and do the pilgrimages of each other's religions." And it dawned on me at that moment that I was there in the midst of the Hindu pilgrimage. I had climbed the Himalayas for the Buddhist pilgrimage, but I'd never done my own pilgrimage as a Muslim.

FIEDLER: And so you made the Hajj. What is its significance for Muslims?

NOMANI: It is a journey into the birthplace of our religion. Mecca is a place where the Prophet Mohammed was born. It was in a cave outside of Mecca that the Prophet received the revelations that are now written in the Qur'an. It is where it is said that Abraham built the symbolic house of God. We're supposed to go to Mecca as a journey into the most pure and beautiful place of our religion. There we surrender to the beauty of the divine.

FIEDLER: But in embarking on this journey you encountered many obstacles. Mecca is in Saudi Arabia after all, and you were a woman planning to make the pilgrimage on your own.

NOMANI: You know, you'd think that the heart of Islam would be open to anyone and everyone. But as a woman, the rules are that I have to go with a chaperone, and it has to be my father, my husband, my brother, or my son. So for me it was my father. I was a woman who journeyed from Morgantown to Chicago to Thailand to Tokyo on my own, but as a woman, I couldn't go the most sacred place in my religion by myself.

FIEDLER: Were there other obstacles?

NOMANI: The greatest obstacle was fear. It was fear of the kind of Islam that is perpetuated in this world from Saudi Arabia: Wahabi Islam, the most puritanical and strictest interpretation of the law in Islam. That means that a woman has to be completely veiled, that no strand of her hair can show, that a woman cannot drive a car, that she must go in public with a male escort. And the laws are strict about people of other faiths.

FIEDLER: You point out in the book that a non-Muslim can't even ride into Mecca on a bus. Is that only at the hajj or is that at any time?

NOMANI: At any time. And I found that quite sad. I had learned so much about Hinduism and Buddhism by walking beside pilgrims and I cast aside so many stereotypes and misunderstandings that I had about these faiths. I thought that if we could burst open the doors of our Muslim world, at our most sacred place, to people of other faiths, we could do much together.

FIEDLER: But there was another risk. You had a son out of wedlock and you brought him with you, but you were scared to death.

NOMANI: Yes. In Saudi Arabia, they punish a woman who has a baby out of wedlock. You are subject to a hundred lashes if you are single, and stoning to death if you happen to be married.

FIEDLER: Today you are not wearing the hijab or the veil, but you did wear that in Saudi Arabia, right?

NOMANI: I could not have entered Saudi Arabia without my hair covered.

FIEDLER: But once you got into the Hajj, which is I believe a five-day experience, you were totally enveloped and inspired by the great women of early Islam.

NOMANI: We all talk about being sons and daughters of Abraham, but there are two great women in that equation. Christians and Jews are sons and daughters of Sarah, and Muslims are sons and daughters of Hagar, who was abandoned in the desert outside Mecca thousands of years ago. She ran in desperation between two hills called *Safa* and *Marwah*, searching for water for her baby, Ishmael. Every year, Muslims follow in her footsteps. We literally go between those two hills in a ritual called struggle. And I recognize that it was the power of this single mother of Islam from whom we received our faith because she was strong.

And centuries later, the Prophet Mohammed came from that tribe, bringing the revelations. But somehow we've forgotten the power of Hagar. And in Saudi Arabia today I, a woman, am not allowed to run. I have to walk because they say that I am too tempting and distracting to my male pilgrims if I should run. So, we are denied even the physical act of this great woman. Her full power and her full experience are what we have to reclaim.

FIEDLER: And I'm sure there are women of many other faith traditions who can identify with your struggle.

NOMANI: Yes, because this is not just a struggle for women in Islam. This is a struggle for women everywhere. We're sadly denied the same status as men—as spiritual equals—and yet we're all supposed to believe that the divine force of this universe is one of social justice and equity and equality. So we need to practice what all the great religions have preached at their heart. Discrimination, sexism, bigotry, and racism are not a part of that equation. We can't allow our religions to be corrupted by the power and control of a few.

FIEDLER: In your case of course, the inspiration you got from the Hajj led you to walk into that male-only space in your mosque in Morgantown, West Virginia. But most recently you have also led mixed-gender prayers, unheard of in most mosques anywhere in the world. This was at Brandeis University in Boston. Aren't you something of an iconoclast?

NOMANI: I am an iconoclast of the status quo, but I believe that I am united in spirit with so many pioneers who believed in a just world, and that in fact no religion that keeps women shut up and stuck in a corner can really claim to be spiritual.

FIEDLER: You were also a reporter with the *Wall Street Journal*, and in that job you met Danny Pearl, who was killed by radical Muslim extremists in Pakistan. Danny was Jewish, something that many thought was a factor in causing his murder. Talk about your friendship and what his death meant to you.

NOMANI: It's really poignant for me to be in Washington because this is where Danny and I built our friendship. And we were also both connected on this mission to try to bridge our worlds. And so that is how we ended up in Pakistan. He was working for the *Wall Street Journal* and I was working for *Salon Magazine*. Danny sacrificed his life, and it's his face that I see whenever I face intimidation and abuse from people who'd rather have me silenced. In some parts of my Muslim community they want to condemn me for being a friend of a Jew, but I know that we have to overcome all of that intimidation that separates us as human beings.

FIEDLER: It strikes me as I read your book, as I listen to you talk, that the problems women of faith face in many religious traditions are incredibly similar. For example, women's sexuality tends to be threatening. Women are denied power and decision-making; women are denied full equality or access to that which is sacred. Have you engaged in any interfaith dialogue with women of other traditions?

NOMANI: What's so beautiful is that for every letter I receive from Muslims, I receive letters from Catholic women and men, Jewish women and men, Hindu women and men, Buddhist women and men. We're united as people of conscience to include everyone and value all people as spiritual equals.

FIEDLER: And finally, how do you see the future of women in Islam?

NOMANI: I believe that progress is inevitable, that the forces of darkness cannot always define this world, and that we are going to redefine our Muslim world and we're going to do it together. Each one of our faiths is facing the same forces, and we have to stand up to them if we're going to allow this world to exist.

Daisy Khan

Executive Director of ASMA,
the American Society for Muslim Advancement
and Muslim Women Organizing for Empowerment

In any movement, some activists organize people who will take up the cause, change their own lives, and spread the word. In that spirit, Muslim women activists are attempting to empower Muslim women worldwide. One is Daisy Khan, the executive director of ASMA, the American Society for Muslim Advancement. I interviewed her in December 2006.

MAUREEN FIEDLER: In mid-November 2006 a group of Muslim women leaders gathered in New York to form WIISE, the Women's Islamic Initiative in Spirituality and Equity. Its purpose is to empower Muslim women to play a greater role in their societies worldwide.

Daisy, how did this idea originate, and how long has it been in the planning stages?

DAISY KHAN: Even though 9-11 was a catastrophic event, it shed light on the Muslim community in more ways than one. We began to see images of women who were repressed, leaving a very strong perception in America that Muslim women are repressed throughout the world. Some of us who are not repressed felt a need to step up to the plate and to amplify women voices, so the germ of the idea of WIISE really began after 9-11. Since then, it's taken us almost five years to come together and create this coalition of women.

FIEDLER: This was a global conference?

KHAN: It was a global conference because we did not want it to appear that it was American-centric.

The issues are global issues, so we recruited from all over the world. We wanted to learn from the struggles of other women. We learned from Sister Joan Chittister that there are struggles in Catholicism that are very similar to Muslim issues. We learned from Devorah Zlochower that even though some Jewish scholars in Orthodox Judaism have a very high status, they still don't have the status of rabbi. The Muslim women felt relieved from the pressure of feeling that they were the only faith community that was struggling.

FIEDLER: How would you describe the overall vision for this movement?

KHAN: Traditionally women have been engaged in political realms. As you know, five Muslim women have been heads of state. But in the world of religion, Muslim women—even though they are extremely articulate scholars—have, for some reason, not stepped up to take leadership roles in the debate around religion.

FIEDLER: Would you call this an Islamic feminist movement, or is that not the proper term for this?

KHAN: If you look at what feminism means in terms of empowering women, then one could call it a feminist movement. But I would call it more a Muslim women's reclamation movement. We are reclaiming our faith. We're asserting our rights within Islam.

FIEDLER: In your public statements you talk about an international shura council of Muslim women that you want to establish. What is a shura council and what will its function be?

KHAN: A shura council is a consultative council that is part of Islamic law. The shura council will function as a body that will draw out a consensus on certain issues. We want to tackle issues like honor killings, rape laws, women's leadership in general, and other issues that keep coming up.

FIEDLER: One of them that came up recently is the veil. In Europe right now the *niqab*, or the face veil, has become a major source of controversy. What's the feeling among Muslim women?

KHAN: Muslim women know that at the deepest level the veil represents a sense of piety or a sense of modesty, but when it becomes a major issue of debate, it becomes a political issue and people start asserting their religious identity by putting on more veils and putting on *niqabs* (face veils). I think we have to turn that debate around to bigger issues going on in the world.

At our conference, we specifically did not have the veil issue as a central subject for debate. But it did come up and provoked one of the most heated debates, so there needs to be an internal debate within the Muslim community.

FIEDLER: What about the segregation of men and women in mosques or the possibility of women leading Friday prayers? Were they a part of what you discussed?

KHAN: It did come up because we brought together women from different ideologies. What is happening right now is that you're seeing the emergence of very confident Western Muslim women who are reinterpreting the Qur'an in their own way. And they feel confident enough to make certain statements about their own potential to become leaders. I don't think all of the women are ready for that just yet. There is going to be a debate among Muslim women whether this is something that they are ready to tackle.

FIEDLER: This is like the debates over the ordination of women in many Christian and Jewish communities.

KHAN: This is one of the things that we discussed with Devorah, our Orthodox Jewish speaker, and she said, "Because we were excluded from certain leadership roles, we created a scholarly leadership role." And this is why our group, WIISE, gives authority to women in the areas of scholarship and jurisprudence. Islam is a religion of law, and seeks social justice. If you can make change within the framework of Islamic law, you can create a significant shift in society.

FIEDLER: What kinds of projects do you hope to initiate to empower Muslim women?

KHAN: The first thing that we have to do is to create a campaign where we begin to educate people about their rights. Muslim women don't even know their own rights. The second thing that we want to embark on is to begin to produce our own jurists, Muslim women jurists. Our goal right now is ten jurists.

FIEDLER: How are you going to overcome the resistance of many Muslim men who maintain that women's inferior status is somehow the true Islam? There are a lot of Muslim women who, I'm sure, think that as well.

KHAN: It's a question of how you position it. Most Muslims do not react very well to feminist arguments or human rights arguments because they see them as an imposition from the West. Where we are able to articulate our position using the framework of Islam, we should be able to create a significant shift.

FIEDLER: Who funds this?

KHAN: Most of the funding for the launch of this initiative came from the goodness of a lot of American foundations, like the Ford Foundation, Rockefeller Brothers, and the Booth Foundation. They see the benefit of what we're doing and they understand that to advance society you have to advance women.

FIEDLER: And how are you going fund it going forward? Is this going to be a membership organization?

KHAN: Now, because of the global initiative, we are looking at sources of funding that would keep this an independent entity. Perhaps other women's groups can support WIISE, perhaps some business women might be able to support this independently. Right now we're looking at it globally. In fact, I was just in Turkey a couple of days ago. I was speaking to a number of women there who are exploring ways to fund it. We want this to be a globally funded initiative. In fact, one of the things that we talked about at our conference was the development of a global Muslim women's fund.*

---

* For more information visit www.asmasociety.org.

Chapter 5
Women Leaders in Spirituality

"Spirituality" is that character or quality that makes it possible for a person to transcend the barriers of worldliness, caste, creed, and sensuality, and realize her or his connection with the "truth," whatever the ultimate truth is for that person. It usually involves prayer, contemplation, and a host of practices in various traditions, from meditation, to fasting, to yoga, to the rosary. Ideally, a strong spirituality embues a person's life so profoundly that it infuses every thought and action.

At one level, women have always been leaders in spirituality because it does not require appointment or election to a position, the founding of a monastic order, or writing books. Ordinary people of both genders can be, and have been, exemplars in spirituality in the sense that they lead outstanding lives, and share—in multiple ways—their sense of the sacred in their lives, with others. Many women mystics, saints, and monastics from the past have long been recognized leaders. It is possible to name only a few of them here.

In Catholicism, for example, Hildegard of Bingen, Clare of Assisi, Teresa of Avila, Catherine of Siena, and Julian of Norwich are acclaimed as mystics. In the Protestant tradition, Jane Addams of Hull House is a nineteenth-century model, and women like Ann Lamott and Barbara Brown Taylor are creating new models of spirituality in contemporary times. So are the Benedictine women at Holy Wisdom Monastery in Madison, Wisconsin, where they are developing an ecumenical form of monasticism.

In Judaism, where Orthodox women have traditionally been barred from mystical practice, Perle Besserman has opened up a contemporary woman's approach to meditation and Kabbalah, or Jewish mysticism. Scholars like Ellen M. Umansky and Dianne Ashton are uncovering centuries of Jewish women's spirituality. Rabbi Tirzah Firestone is nationally known for re-integrating the feminine wisdom tradition into Judaism. And Rabbi Rachel

Cowan leads the Institute for Jewish Spirituality with a program that includes yoga as well as contemplative practice.

In Islam, Fatimah, daughter of the Prophet Mohammed, is often recognized as the first Muslim mystic. In the eighth century, Rabi'a al-Adawiyya first spoke of her relationship with God as the Beloved, a term now associated with Sufism, the mystical tradition in Islam. In the fifteenth century, Aisha of Damascus was a well-known mystic. In the contemporary Muslim world, Egyptian scholars Aliaa Rafea and Aisha Rafea are both theologians and leading spiritual writers, with a feminist perspective.

Hindus revere many women through the centuries for their spirituality. Among them are Akka Mahadevi, a twelfth-century woman saint and an early advocate of women's emancipation, and Mirabai, a sixteenth-century saint and mystic. Today, Mātā Amritanandamayī Devi, commonly known as "Amma" or the "hugging saint," promotes humanitarian activities as she attracts thousands to come and get a hug from her. And a woman in Germany named "Mother Meera" also bestows her blessing, known as *darshan*, widely and publicly.

In Buddhism, women like Tenzin Palmo, Pema Chodron, and Sharon Salzberg are spiritual guides for thousands. Susan Murcott and Sallie Tisdale are bringing to light the long history of Buddhist women known for their mysticism and spirituality.

Leaders in spirituality today typically publish books, give retreats, speak at conferences, and sometimes counsel individuals. Women are full participants in this field. Even though some traditions relegate them to an official secondary status, women provide an unofficial but influential leadership with best-selling books on spirituality, lectures, and lives worthy of emulation.

~~~~~~

Sr. Joan Chittister, OSB

on *Called to Question: A Spiritual Memoir*

In the Catholic world, an undisputed leader in spirituality is Sr. Joan Chittister, a Benedictine nun from Erie, Pennsylvania. She is the author of more than forty books, and is everywhere on the global speaking circuit, dealing with spirituality, social justice, peace, and the rights of women. She is the former prioress of her Benedictine Community in Erie, and the former president of the Leadership Conference of Women Religious. She is also a regular columnist for the *National Catholic Reporter*. Among her most recent books is her memoir, entitled *Called to Question: A Spiritual Memoir*. Joan is a friend of long standing. This interview focuses on her autobiography; it was conducted in June 2006.

MAUREEN FIEDLER: Let's begin with a theme in your autobiography, one that runs through the lives of a lot of people these days: the evolution from religion to spirituality. What's the difference, and how did that evolution take place in your life?

JOAN CHITTISTER: It *is* evolution, and I'm glad to hear someone phrase the question like that. It's not revolution, it's not opposite under any circumstances. Why? Because religion is about what we believe and why we believe it. Religions tell us our tradition, our founding, our origins, our ideals. Religion is an institution; it's a system. The function of religion is to make us spiritual people. The temptation is that we get stuck at the level of religion and miss the personal, the human, the cosmic relationship with God that is one of the dimensions of life. Spirituality, in other words, is what takes us beyond the rules to the reality of both faith and the spirit. When we stay only with the level of the rules, that's a type of spirituality. But it's not what, at least in Catholicism, we would call adult faith. Someplace along the line, you're responsible for taking your religion into your own hands.

FIEDLER: And would it be fair to say that in your life, as in anyone's who's going through this evolution, it's an ongoing process that stops only with the end of one's life?

CHITTISTER: Oh absolutely! Religion is a package. Spirituality is a process. The great mystics, the great saints of all the great traditions—the Sufi, Hindu, Christian, Jewish—had people who saw beyond the rules, who saw into the rules, who saw into what religion was about.

FIEDLER: You specifically embrace a feminist spirituality. What does feminist spirituality mean to you?

CHITTISTER: In the first place, it does *not* mean female spirituality. Feminists come in two genders, male and female. I have a good many feminist brothers on whom I can count for a good portion of my own hope in the development of humanity on earth.

Feminists are persons who believe in the equality, and the dignity, and the human rights of all. They do not believe that rights and dignity and equality are gender-specific.

It isn't maleness that is the opposite of feminism, it's patriarchy. It is the father system, as it was in Rome. Remember that the patriarch of the Roman family could snap his fingers and have his wife, his children, all of his servants murdered on the spot, and nobody was going to question it. Patriarchy gives total power to single figures, always male. Feminism says: No! That leaves out the gifts of half the population, and that's wrong.

FIEDLER: Some people would say, in that scheme, then, isn't God the ultimate patriarch? Is it possible to think of God as a feminist? Is there, in a sense, a divine feminine?

CHITTISTER: Oh, of course there is. If my second grade teacher was right, then all of the rest of this nonsense is wrong. She taught us that God is pure spirit. I haven't heard anybody teach it better, and as I understand it, she was teaching the very core and center of the tradition. God is pure spirit. God has no gender. Godliness is both male and female. As long as we keep separating and excluding, we are a long way from the mind of God.

FIEDLER: And so it's possible to say, "Our Father, Our Mother, who art in heaven?"

CHITTISTER: Let's put it this way, Maureen. At least in the Roman Catholic tradition, where we come from centuries of litanies, we have called God a good many things. We've called God Spirit, Rock, Door, Light. Apparently, we are allowed to call God absolutely everything but Mother. There has got be some very blatant sexism in that, whether people are willing to admit it or not.

FIEDLER: You're in the midst, of course, of another patriarchy, the structure of the Roman Catholic Church, where women are certainly treated as second-class, because they are denied access to any kind of formal ministry. Why this inferior status of women and what do you think needs to happen to change it?

CHITTISTER: I always maintain that we are the inheritors of a bad understanding of biology that has been theologized. Through the centuries, theologians thought the same thing: that the seed of life was in the male. The sperm was the seed. That's what they assumed was of the essence of creation. That's really why they named God Father. If God was the creator of all life, then in God was all the creative sperm, then God had to be male.

Not until the nineteenth century did theologians become aware of what some had assumed for a couple of hundred years before that—the sperm was not the only carrier of life. In the woman's body was a life-giving power, the ovum. When the microscope was invented, we saw the ovum for the first time. Believe it or not, Maureen, that's not all that long ago. It's a little over 150 years ago that we have had to deal with the notion that the woman too is a life-giving figure, and that life is created only when the two of them operate together on an equal basis.

That explains, I think, why we came so slowly to the notion of the woman as a full and rational adult preacher. For five thousand years before that, women knew intuitively that there was something wrong. Nevertheless they accepted the definition given to them by male theologians, male philosophers, and male scientists, that they were simply some kind of mobile birthing machine.

FIEDLER: Do you think that that mentality is still there in the hierarchy today? Why is it that they continue to deny women access to the priesthood, for example?

CHITTISTER: I wouldn't think that the concept of women as birthing machines is out there in almost anybody's mind anyplace in the civilized world anymore, at least not explicitly, not consciously, not in so many words.

FIEDLER: But there's a leftover from that?

CHITTISTER: What is left over is the tradition, and that's the answer they keep giving you—it's always been this way; it's always been that way.

FIEDLER: And what needs to happen to change that, Joan?

CHITTISTER: I really believe that if many of the men who are arguing this looked at their own theology, let alone at the gospels, they would have to rip the veil from their own eyes. So what are the implications of this ovum/sperm relationship?

This union of two people, both made in the image of God, is going to have consequences and implications everywhere. The churches are not safe havens from that awareness. And it isn't just the Roman Catholic Church.

I'll be conducting a retreat in Taiwan in a couple of weeks with Buddhist nuns, who are asking, "What is the role of the Buddhist nun in society now?" We're all dealing with it. It was a universal understanding that is now cracking like a window struck by a baseball bat. And that understanding is cracking everywhere. It's over. That past is over.

FIEDLER: You mentioned Buddhist nuns. What about Roman Catholic nuns, since you are one of them? What's their role in bringing change in the church, Joan?

CHITTISTER: I'm biased here, because I've seen it from the inside out. But I think our Roman Catholic orders of sisters have given the church a phenomenal gift. They've put three things together. They're merging the life of the poor, their identification with the gospel, and their education. Uplifting women has been the history of Roman Catholic nuns. Mother McCauley, for instance, as the foundress of the Sisters of Mercy in Ireland, was out there literally picking up girls and women from the gutters in Dublin, in order to teach them to read and write. That has been the history of Roman Catholic sisters everywhere. So it's not strange that we should find them now in peace and justice centers, working with women and their children in halfway houses, completely committed to the development of a feminist perspective on life, and calling for changes in the church as well.

FIEDLER: Anybody who knows the Catholic Church knows nuns have been in the forefront of calling for changes for women in the church. And you yourself have been an example of that. A few years ago, you were invited to speak at Women's Ordination Worldwide, a conference in Dublin, Ireland. The Vatican forbade you to speak, but you went anyway with the full support of your prioress and your community, and that became a kind of watershed moment in the contemporary church. Would you agree?

CHITTISTER: I'm not sure it was a watershed moment, but I certainly do know that it brought us all to ask the question, "What is really good for the church?" When we have an issue, we must face it, and we must face it with great honesty. We don't have to worry about being improper, or scandalous, or unfaithful, or disobedient, when we are simply raising questions that require new thinking, or at least a rethinking, so that they can be owned totally.

FIEDLER: And so you would favor open discussion and open theological inquiry in the church, and an end to the practice of trying to silence people on issues?

CHITTISTER: I would say absolutely, without any kind of equivocation. The gospel says: let the weeds and the fruits grow up together. You're not going to solve anything by stamping it out, by silencing it.

FIEDLER: One piece of unfinished human business has to do with gay and lesbian people in the church. Where do you stand on that issue, and how do you talk to gay and lesbian Catholics who have one foot out the door of the church because they feel persecuted?

CHITTISTER: In the first place, I'm completely committed to the achievement of full civil rights for gay and lesbian people. This is another point at which we have to deal with new information. Once, it was universally assumed that gays and lesbians consciously chose their sexual orientation. There's almost nobody in the scientific community that believes that anymore. They know that somehow or other this is an orientation with which a person is born. And so to deny those people their rights in the name of morality is an immoral thing to do.

FIEDLER: And that includes rights in the church?

CHITTISTER: Why wouldn't it? It doesn't make any difference whether someone is heterosexual or homosexual. However, there is still a long-standing and virulent debate going on. And gay and lesbian people that I have met everywhere, the faithful ones, the caring ones, the ones who really define themselves as any kind of churchgoer, Catholic or Protestant, are in great distress. They feel un-churched by the church, excluded, and marginalized.

To those people I say: the church is a human institution too. I spent years struggling with this question. Where did I come down? What did I think? I had to live into the information. I had to live into the experience of saying to these people, as I've said before, "The church is a human institution. It grows, but it grows slowly. And it grows only if it is confronted over and over again by the bold, the brave, and the beautiful faithful among us."

FIEDLER: Joan, your speeches often deal with public issues of justice, peace, and human rights. I wonder, as you survey the situation in the United States today, what you see as the most pressing issues of justice that we face?

CHITTISTER: We're facing so many at the present time; I almost hesitate to sound as if I prioritize them. But I'll tell you this much, there are things that may not look now as immediate as others, but which stand to erode this country dangerously. One is the so-called doctrine of preemptive war. It's one of the most dangerous things that has ever inserted itself into American history, and I'm a slightly used history teacher. I think the whole notion that, on a guess and a golly, we can invade anybody we want to because they might hurt us, has so clearly been disproven in the last four years, that it ought to be immediately outlawed. We are the people who stand to destroy this globe. We are more than capable of it. Would we do it? We love to tell ourselves we wouldn't, but we wouldn't have destroyed Iraq if we had known better either. There are lots of things we wouldn't do if we were doing them over. The notion that we can simply take this Godlike position upon ourselves and risk an entire people is absolutely unconscionable and unacceptable.

The second great issue is education. A little country like Ireland can educate every single member of its population and never charge them a penny. I have a friend whose daughter just finished med school. She has not paid one penny for that education. She is now a certified pediatric consultant. I have a cousin who went to med school who is still paying off thousands and thousands of dollars of debt. This is the richest country in the world. We seem to have plenty of money for our bombs; we have no money for our babies. We call ourselves pro-life, when we are actually pro-birth. We want to get babies born, but we have no commitment whatsoever to getting them housed, fed, and educated. We now give tax breaks to one percent of the richest in this country. I call it welfare for the rich, and we don't even have the grace to blush.

The third issue is our callous response, at the highest political levels, to questions of ecology and global warming. We are more responsible for the tentative state of the globe right now than any other nation on earth. We would not sign the Kyoto Treaty; we will not restrict ourselves in any way whatsoever. We are morally responsible for the planet now, technologically and militarily, as well as ecologically and sustainably.

FIEDLER: You're the co-chair of the Global Peace Initiative of Women, which is a partner organization at the UN. And I know you've been heavily involved in peace work for decades, and you've recently written a book called *The Tent of Abraham*, with Muslim and Jewish co-authors. What should the West do to make peace with the Muslim world, do you think?

CHITTISTER: In the first place we have to start understanding that we are not at war with the Muslim world. The Muslim world is no more monolithic than the Christian world is. We need to begin to study and understand Islam, the Qur'an, the people, their history. And we've got to realize that we share this globe, and it's time to quit acting as if it's ours to dominate.

FIEDLER: And finally, how important is prayer in sustaining a life like yours, and what type of prayer do you find most meaningful for the work you do?

CHITTISTER: Prayer is vitally important. I have told social workers, religious women all over the United States and the world, that without the prayer life out of which you grow, you will soon tire. You'll weary and you'll quit, and even if you don't, you're only going to be one more do-gooder. Prayer is that lifeline to the will of God, to the universe, for all people. That's the foundation on which you must stand.

I'm a Benedictine. That means I've been raised in the context of the daily choral prayer of the psalms, the cries of the prophets for justice, for equality, for dignity. Those words ring in my ears; I never cease hearing them. I'm convinced that they are the organic chemistry of my own soul.

When those go, when the mind of God for the world is not the cry you hear, then you can be sold a lot of other cries. Profit can become most important. You can be seduced by domination everywhere; you can certainly want to be totally militarily secure. You can forget the babies, and the birthing, and the life, because there's no reason not to. Without prayer, there'll always be something better for you than what is the mind of God.

Barbara Brown Taylor
on *Leaving Church: A Memoir of Faith*

Barbara Brown Taylor is an ordained Episcopal priest and former pastor. In 1996, Baylor University named her one of the most effective preachers in the English-speaking world. She currently teaches religion at Piedmont College in Georgia, serves as an at-large editor for *The Christian Century*, and sometimes provides commentaries for Georgia Public Radio. In her book, *Leaving*

Church: A Memoir of Faith, she tells—not about leaving church literally—but about moving from being clergy to being laity, and what difference that made in her life. This interview was conducted in October 2007.

MAUREEN FIEDLER: First, Barbara, I wonder about the title of your book. It seems to me that you really didn't leave the Episcopal Church *per se*. What do you mean leaving church?

BARBARA BROWN TAYLOR: You're right; I really did not leave *the* church, and the omission of that article was on purpose. I did leave Grace Calvary Episcopal Church in Parksville, Georgia, and the book is the story of my leaving that particular place.

FIEDLER: Let's go to the beginning of your life then, and what led you to your spirituality. You talk about your love of nature, of animals, of nursing injured birds, and ultimately falling in love with God. What do you mean?

TAYLOR: I think I mean I'm smitten—silly and giggly and hot in the face, and light headed, and happy.

FIEDLER: Literally?

TAYLOR: Literally. I think you could photograph me and capture my red face. But I also mean being so charmed that I want to know more. I want to learn as much as I can, experience as much as I can, spend as much time close to God as I can, so all of that's wrapped up in falling in love.

FIEDLER: And this revolves around the life of prayer.

TAYLOR: It does, and I want to stretch prayer to mean more than "on my knees, by my bed at night, with my hands folded," which I also do. But for me, hanging out the laundry, I sometimes see my husband's T-shirts as prayer flags. Thanking God for every star in the sky is a kind of prayer. I'm interested in embodied prayer as well as the verbal kind.

FIEDLER: Later, you were ordained to the priesthood in the Episcopal Church, and you served two congregations, one in urban Atlanta, and the other in Clarksville, Georgia. But in both places, you spent almost every waking hour in ministry, to the point of what you call "compassion fatigue." In the book you say, "My quest to serve God in the church had exhausted my spiritual savings. My desire to do all things well had kept me from doing the one thing within my power to do, which was to discover what it meant to be truly human." Why did that happen?

TAYLOR: There are probably a lot of ways to talk about it, but I'm very aware that with Jesus as one's model, it's hard to say no, or "Thank you, I've done enough. I'm going to bed now." It seemed like the only way was to give 150 percent, that it made no sense to turn in an 85 percent performance.

FIEDLER: But you're a highly educated woman; surely you have read all those psychologists who tell you to take time for yourself, to take care of your own needs so you can take care of the needs of others. Didn't any of that sink in?

TAYLOR: My father was psychologist and a psychotherapist, so I even got that advice at home. I did know the advice, and I gave it more readily than I took it.

FIEDLER: The upside is you left the country church that you loved, and you became, to all public appearances at least, a layperson again. And of course, that meant you took off the clerical collar. You mentioned a number of differences in the way people treated you after you had taken off the collar. What were some of those differences?

TAYLOR: I think the most noticeable and immediate difference was that people talked the way they really talk around me. Nobody saw the collar and then changed the subject.

FIEDLER: Does that mean they felt free to use a swear word . . . free to talk about sexuality?

TAYLOR: Or even stock markets, or stock car racing, or bellyaches, or all kinds of things that didn't come under the heading of spirituality or religion. Because with a collar on, even people who don't know you, can come to you and start talking about Sunday school. The collar evokes religious subjects, and it was a great relief to hear about ordinary things.

FIEDLER: But you noticed a difference in power.

TAYLOR: I did, because that's the flip side of the coin. The clerical collar will get you a seat on a bus, even better than gray hair will. It confers a kind of deference; all of that also vanished. I could find myself ignored in any crowd of middle-aged women just as well as the woman next to me. So that was humbling and necessary to find out how most people live most of the time.

FIEDLER: At one point in the book, after you left, you reflect on the role of clergy. And you say, maybe there's something wrong with giving one person so much power, so that the starring role in the drama every Sunday goes to the same person. Should the role of clergy be different, do you think, than in the past?

TAYLOR: I can't answer for all churches; they are so different. But for myself, I am very eager to find and participate in church "in the round." I'm really tired of sitting in pews looking at the backs of people's heads. And when I am the person that's up front, I have the best seat in the house. And it's not fair to everybody else.

FIEDLER: Would you change from having a single preacher to having the participants share their reflections on the scriptures?

TAYLOR: Yes, and that's being done already. At the very least I would get the homily down to four or five minutes, with perhaps fifteen minutes of responses from those present. I've been in congregations that do that, and it's wonderful.

FIEDLER: You're now an adjunct professor of Christian spirituality at Columbia Theological Seminary. But you're not a priest in that pastoral role anymore. Do you ever regret that?

TAYLOR: I do not regret it. There are things I miss, but I wouldn't go back. I haven't found a year in my life yet that I'd go back. But what I have found is a wider ministry, more service to the world, with a wider swath of humanity than I was able to serve in the two churches I worked for. So I feel no sense of regret, only a sense of great gratitude that I've been able to do both.

FIEDLER: Did you find that humanity that you felt you lost and overworked when you were in the pastor role?

TAYLOR: I guess we have to define humanity. I don't know that I'm any better a person, or any more generous, but I wear much longer earrings and more red. And have found myself much more comfortable among people than I was when I thought I was there to play a certain role.

FIEDLER: Is your struggle with faith? Do you find that a lot of other people share that struggle?

TAYLOR: I do believe I wrote this book for my friends. And for people who are struggling with the same things I am. I hear from many, many people—via email, mail, telephone—who are on the edges of faith, on the edges of the church, and who feel as if they failed somehow. So my mission in this book, if anything, is to give them good company and encouragement, and to say that I learned from the Bible that one of the best places to meet God is to go camping in the wilderness.

FIEDLER: It's okay to question?

TAYLOR: It's not only okay to question; it's essential to question.

FIEDLER: And finally Barbara, who is God for you today? Are you still in love with God?

TAYLOR: I am still in love with God. Who God is for me today is the God beyond all nouns and adjectives, the God beyond all names. I am aware that God for me today is the God between me and other people, and particularly between me and strangers. God for me today is the God within, the God whom I find is as close, as the Muslims say, as the beat of my heart and my neck. So a God beyond, a God between, a God within, is the God that I'm most aware of today.

Ann Lamott

on *Plan B: Further Thoughts on Faith*

"Laughter is carbonated holiness." Those are the words of Ann Lamott, a humorist and a progressive spiritual activist in the Evangelical Christian world. The *San Francisco Chronicle* said of Ann Lamott: "She is living proof that a person can be both reverent and irreverent in the same lifetime," sometimes even in the same breath. She is the author of several books, including *Traveling Mercies, Bird by Bird, Blue Shoe,* and *Crooked Little Heart.* She has an online column with salon.com. In June of 2006, I interviewed her about her book, *Plan B: Further Thoughts on Faith.*

MAUREEN FIEDLER: First, Ann, how did you come to own a religious faith?

ANN LAMOTT: I always believed in God when I was a child, even though I was raised by atheists. And I always found girlfriends to go to church with and temple with. I had Catholic friends, Jewish friends, Protestant friends. I always prayed and I always knew that something heard me.

FIEDLER: You had been a secret believer as a young person?

LAMOTT: Yes. All through my twenties I pursued a lot of different spiritual paths, and read everything Buddhist and Hindu and Christian, and a lot of mystics. And then, when I started to lose the battle with alcoholism in my early thirties, I was very hung-over at a flea market on a Sunday morning, and I heard this beautiful music. And I went over to it. It was African-American spirituals, the music of the Civil Rights Movement, which my parents had been very involved in. I'd grown up singing this stuff. And so I went into this church. There were more black people than white. The church was very small, and kind of crummy looking, but it felt very nourishing and sweet. And I felt the presence of something gentle and spiritual in that place.

I sat down on a chair, but I left when the Jesus part started, because I really was not interested in Jesus. I stayed for the singing and a little bit of prayer. But I came back a week later, and little by little, I made it a point to be there on Sundays. And little by little, I wanted to hear the sermons too, and then one day, really without meaning to, I experienced the presence of Jesus. In *Traveling Mercies* I described it as feeling like this little lost cat was running after me. And I finally got too tired to keep running from it, and I finally said okay, you can come in.

FIEDLER: And, little by little, did you move away from your alcoholism too?

LAMOTT: I actually converted drunk at thirty-one, and then at thirty-two, I got sober. So it's been twenty years that I've been sober, and twenty-one years since I've been going to this little church.

FIEDLER: How would you describe your own faith today?

LAMOTT: I'm very dedicated to my church; I'm an elder at St. Andrew Presbyterian Church in Marin City, California. I started the Sunday school program. And I'm a regular old garden-variety Christian. I'm extremely liberal politically, so I think maybe that is one thing that startles people. I'm such an old democratic precinct leader type, and a California birch and stock tree-hugger. But I'm also very devoted to Jesus.

FIEDLER: In your book you very clearly tie your faith to peace and justice. You talk about being in anti-war demonstrations and how angry you've been with Bush. And you say that there are rules like "you don't hit first." Is this why you are against preemptive war? Do you personally fit the faith and peace and justice together?

LAMOTT: Oh absolutely! As I said, this little church was very grounded in the Civil Rights Movement. Black people and white people had all been very, very committed to equality and social justice. I grew up worshiping the God of Dr. Martin Luther King, and I always could tell that what Jesus was talking about was equality, and kindness, and really, really tending to the weakest, to the poor, and to the hungry and thirsty. So I don't really have an interesting theology; I keep it very simple, and I try to take care of people who are suffering and hungry, people who really need a kind person to listen to them for a few minutes.

FIEDLER: In another part of your life, you're a single mother, and you have a son named Sam. In some religious circles, that would raise a lot of eyebrows. How does being a single mother relate to your faith life?

LAMOTT: My faith gave me the courage to go ahead and have a child instead of an abortion. I happen to be someone who's a very, very strong proponent of women's rights, so that would not have been immoral in my understanding if I thought that I could not care for a child. I was very, very poor at the time and the father didn't want anything to do with it. I turned it over to God completely. I said to Jesus, "I'm not going to make any kind of decision until I hear back from you." And I said, "Just let me know what to do. If you think I'd be a good enough mother then I'd like to have this child."

FIEDLER: How did God answer you?

LAMOTT: I had this amazing dream where I had dropped this baby boy into the waters of the San Francisco Bay, and I dove in after him, but he was getting farther and farther away into the darkness and chill of the bay. I finally got him and brought him up to the surface. Some friends were waiting for me, and I held him over my head and they reached for him, and I knew he was fine. I sat up in bed that morning and I said, "For goodness sake, I'm going to have a baby." And I never thought twice about it after that, until he got his driver's license.

FIEDLER: Another part of the book intrigued me, because I am an animal lover. I notice your faith is intertwined with animals, dogs especially. You had a dog named Sadie, whom you dearly loved, and in the end you had to put her to sleep. And I believe you now have one named Lily. How can pets be a part of someone's faith life?

LAMOTT: I also want to say, on my cat's behalf, that I'm totally devoted to her also.

FIEDLER: I'm a cat lover, too. I have two wonderful cats. My vet, a very religious man, says one of the reasons he loves to work with animals is that they remind him of the unconditional love of God.

LAMOTT: I love them. I grew up with animals. Their love is really purely unconditional. And I know that that's what God's love is like. And I know that that's how we are urged to love one another.

FIEDLER: You talk in another part of your book about trying to forgive Bush. Have you been successful?

LAMOTT: I am passionately against almost all of his policies. But I know that God loves Bush just like he loves my little three-year-old niece, Clara. And I know that I'm supposed to love him, and that we're here to learn to love and forgive everyone. And so I wrote a long piece in *Plan B* about going to church one Sunday and hearing the Holy Spirit talk about loving him, and forgiving him. And I got it, and I felt a softening in my heart, which I do feel sometimes for him. I don't judge him. I understand that he's another human being, and he's like all of us. So I felt this wonderful warmth and love.

But then of course, I eventually had to leave church and go home, and that was where my problems began. And when I went home, there was something infuriating to me on the news about him and Dick Cheney. Immediately my mind kicked in, judging it. I was furious and heartbroken, and I got all discombobulated again. And so peace is really about waking up and doing the best I can, and praying for that desire to change my heart.

Immaculée Ilibagiza

on *Left to Tell: Discovering God*
Amidst the Rwandan Holocaust

One of the most moving and heroic stories of deep spirituality I have heard in my entire time as a radio host was the experience of Immaculée Ilibagiza, a woman who survived the Rwandan genocide. Remarkably, she forgave those who slaughtered her family and friends. Today, when forgiveness is a major focus for authors and filmmakers, her experience and her writings make her a leader in this field. In 2007, she received the Mahatma Gandhi International Award for Reconciliation and Peace. She is the author of a book on her experience: *Left to Tell: Discovering God Amidst the Rwandan Holocaust*.

She currently resides in the United States. This interview took place in April 2006.

MAUREEN FIEDLER: On the Jewish calendar, April 25 is *Yom Hashoah*, or Holocaust Remembrance Day. It recalls the memory of the six million Jews who died as victims of the Nazi Holocaust in the 1940s. But in spite of pledges by people of many faiths that there would "never again" be a Holocaust, holocausts continue. One of the worst took place in Rwanda in 1994.

Immaculée, you're a part of the Tutsi tribe of Rwanda. And the genocide was committed in your country by Hutus against Tutsis. Almost a million Tutsis were slaughtered. What led the Hutus to commit such horrific violence?

IMMACULÉE ILIBAGIZA: I think it was a matter of reducing the number of Tutsis so that they would never win power again.

FIEDLER: Let's go into your own story. You grew up, by your own definition, in a very loving home. You received a good education, indeed a university education. But as you grew, you began to notice signs of tribal differences, which was something you had not been aware of as you were growing up. How did you become aware of those tribal animosities? What signs did you see?

ILIBAGIZA: When I was in primary school, in the fourth grade, the teacher used to make Tutsis and the Hutus stand separate groups. When I was a child, I used to take turns standing up with Hutus and Tutsis.

FIEDLER: Because you didn't even want to recognize the difference?

ILIBAGIZA: Yes! Then I started to realize that something has to be behind that separation.

FIEDLER: During the early days of the killing, you heard certain things on the radio.

ILIBAGIZA: When the president's plane crashed and he died, my friends asked me to go into hiding. And we heard many things on the radio saying how they should kill Tutsis. Now all of a sudden ministers, what we called ministers, started to say on national radio now that the Tutsis are enemies of the country, that they should be eliminated. I remember one minister saying that when they kill, they should start with babies.*

---

* The plane carrying Rwandan president Juvénal Habyarimana was shot down on the evening of April 6, 1994, as it prepared to land. Responsibility for the attack is disputed, but it was the proximate cause of the genocide.

FIEDLER: Start with babies?

ILIBAGIZA: Yes, with babies.

FIEDLER: And they called you snakes; they called you cockroaches.

ILIBAGIZA: They were killing Tutsi families in the capital. And then my brother and my dad told me that they were killing our people and said that if they come to our home, they might run after me, they might rape me, and they were very worried, because I was one girl among three boys. So they all insisted that I go to hide in the home of a Hutu pastor.

FIEDLER: And that's where you went, to this local Hutu pastor's house. According to your book—and this is incredible—you lived in a small, hidden bathroom for three months, with seven other Tutsi women? And at times the killers were outside screaming for you. What was that time like for you?

ILIBAGIZA: It's hard to describe, but I remember that there were eight of us in a very small bathroom. The pastor told us not to make any noise, not to speak. During the first week I was very angry and bored. I was tired of sitting down. Then in the second week, I started to change in my mind when they started to search for Tutsis. First, they were killing Tutsis who ran to stadiums, who ran to churches, and then groups of three to four hundred people in every small village. They came to our home. And I can never forget this, when they reached the house where we were hiding, they were standing five inches away from me.

And you know if they touch you, they will kill you; there is no pity. I was so scared. I started to pray like I never prayed in my life. We really felt that only the power of God stood between us and the killers. If they had discovered us, they would have killed us and maybe they would have killed the pastor too—for hiding so-called enemies of the country.

FIEDLER: And during this time, you could hear reports on his radio about the killings in the country?

ILIBAGIZA: I listened to that radio really, really carefully. And I made a decision I will never regret, maybe the best decision ever in my life. I told myself—I'm going to pray every single second.

FIEDLER: So prayer sustained you through this horrific time?

ILIBAGIZA: Transformed me completely.

FIEDLER: What happened to your parents and your family?

ILIBAGIZA: When I came out, everyone was dead.

FIEDLER: Then, after all this horrific experience, you came to forgive the people who did that. How did you come to that?

ILIBAGIZA: This was best grace I have had. I forgave the people who killed my family, who wanted to kill me when I [was] in that bathroom. When I started to pray our Lord's Prayer, I said, "Forgive us our trespasses, as we forgive those who trespass against us." But I felt, "This is not right," because I don't forgive them.

It was so hard to trust God, and it was like a fight in me—how do I continue to ask God to protect me, when I am holding so much hatred within me? And I had a good reason to hate them. And then I said, "You know what, God, I give you everything. I wish I could mean every prayer, by loving everyone and forgiving. But how can I do that?" And I said, "You know what, I don't know how to do it; I give it to you." That was a moment when I felt happy. And that was the first step of what became forgiveness.

FIEDLER: Surrendering yourself to God?

ILIBAGIZA: Yes, you surrender to God. I don't know how to forgive these people who are killing me. I give it to you. Help me out; show me how to do it. When I was able to do that, I was able to pray with conviction that my prayers now reached God.

Then the next step came. I was praying on the passion of Christ. And all of a sudden, I saw him on the cross, and he said, "Forgive them, Father, they don't know what they do." And that's exactly what I needed to hear. They don't know what they do. In that minute, I knew how to forgive. There was no way they, the Hutus, can understand fully what they are doing to me or what they were doing to people, to children, to everyone in the country. In that minute, I started to pray. I saw that it was evil *in* them, but I did not see the people themselves as evil. Then I was able to love them as creatures of God, but hate the evil that was in them.

FIEDLER: And you've been able to sit down and talk and eat with Hutus since?

ILIBAGIZA: Oh my, there are so many good Hutus. I can talk to them without putting everyone in the same box.

Next I wanted to find out, "Do I really forgive them?" Is it real? Because everyone is telling me, "You are crazy." So I went to the prison, and I met the man who killed my mom and my brother. And I'll never forget that. When I saw him, tears fell on my face. You know, this man was so respected, and all of a sudden because of the sin he had done, he was sitting in a prison. And when I looked at him I thought to myself, "If he can't love himself, how can he love me better?" And I knew that this is a case I have to pity. I had to work to love him.

FIEDLER: You were able to love even him?

ILIBAGIZA: I was able to know that I love him. I know justice has to go on, but once you forgive your enemies, you can send them love. That's how I understood my forgiveness. It wasn't like letting him out of the prison, but I was able to wish him well.

FIEDLER: Did he reciprocate?

ILIBAGIZA: He couldn't look in my eyes; he was looking down all the time. I could see he was so ashamed.

~~~~~~

Sharon Salzberg

on Buddhism in America

In the world of American Buddhism, the name Sharon Salzberg is everywhere. She is a well-known teacher of Buddhist meditation practices, working out of her Insight Meditation Center in Barry, Massachusetts. She is a prolific author in the field of Buddhist spirituality. One of her best-known works is *Lovingkindness: The Revolutionary Art of Happiness*. My interview with her, excerpted here, took place in May 2006 when she and Robert Thurman were conducting a joint workshop on Buddhism in Washington, DC.

MAUREEN FIEDLER: You are in Washington to speak at the Washington National Cathedral, to a diverse interfaith audience. And your workshop is sold out. Why is Buddhism so attractive to those of other faith traditions, Sharon?

SHARON SALZBERG: I think to some extent it's the attraction of meditation, and of an ethical view of life. Buddhism offers a vision of life that's inclusive and interconnected, where what we do matters, where our actions ripple out into the bigger world. It takes people away from helplessness and apathy. You don't have to subscribe to dogma, you don't have to reject anything. It's almost completely nonsectarian; it's a better way of life.

FIEDLER: How did you come to Buddhism yourself?

SALZBERG: I went to college at the age of sixteen, and when I was a sophomore, I took a class in Asian philosophy, which was really a course in Buddhism. I was attracted by the Buddha's breathtaking vision of human possibility. It was very inclusive. People of all kinds, not just special people, could change their lives with the tools of Buddhism.

FIEDLER: Buddhism provides a way for people to deal with negative emotions, and to move towards greater peacefulness and compassion. We think of "loving kindness," and many people know that meditation is a path to that. But some of our listeners might wonder, how do I get started with meditation?

SALZBERG: There are so many, many different ways of doing it. The simplest way to begin is to set aside ten minutes and sit in a comfortable position. You can sit in an armchair; it doesn't have to be full lotus on the ground. Close your eyes and have a meditation object through which you can focus your attention. Very commonly that's the breath—just normal, natural breath. I often choose the breath as what we call a primary object in this kind of meditation exercise for a number of reasons. One is you don't have to believe anything. You don't have to adopt a dogma or set of beliefs; you don't have to reject anything. If you're breathing, you can be meditating. And the breath is very portable. You can practice if you're standing impatiently in the grocery store, or waiting in traffic and getting infuriated. If you're breathing, you can be meditating. So we just sit, close our eyes, feel the normal natural breath at the nostrils, at the chest, or at the abdomen, center our attention there, settle, relax, feel the actual sensations of the breath.

A very crucial understanding is that it's not going to last long. It will be one breath, or two or three, and your mind will fly away somewhere else. The moment when we realize we have been distracted is a very important moment. Because that's the moment where we have the chance to stop judging ourselves, to have some compassion for ourselves and simply begin again.

FIEDLER: We often hear about something called Engaged Buddhism, which usually refers to Buddhists involved in social action or work for peace. How prevalent is Engaged Buddhism in North America today?

SALZBERG: On a personal level, I actually believe all Buddhism is Engaged Buddhism. Monks or nuns who spend great amounts of time in retreat have always done it with the intention or motivation to serve others. I just think the manifestation of that is very personal.

Sallie Tisdale

on *Women of the Way:*
Discovering 2,500 Years of Buddhist Wisdom

"I think there's not just a general trend; I think it's an inevitable tidal wave of change." Those were the words of Sallie Tisdale, describing the rise of Buddhist women over 2,500 years of history. She is an ordained Zen Buddhist, and a frequent contributor to *Harper's*, *Antioch Review*, and *Tricycle*, among other periodicals. The stories she tells in *Women of the Way: Discovering 2,500 Years of Buddhist Wisdom* will sound familiar to women in other faith traditions struggling for equality. This interview took place March 2006.

MAUREEN FIEDLER: You are an ordained Buddhist. Can you explain to our listeners what that means?

SALLIE TISDALE: I'm afraid that it doesn't mean all that much. It's more like being baptized. There are two levels of ordination in Buddhism. One is simply the act of becoming a Buddhist. I've been a lay ordained Buddhist for twenty-four years. Currently I have entered the novitiate stage of what you would think of as priest training. And sometime this year, I expect to be ordained as a priest. That's a different type of ordination.

FIEDLER: Is it unusual for a woman to be ordained a Buddhist priest?

TISDALE: Not in the United States. Women have always been a minority of the ordained in Buddhism. But throughout the entire history of Buddhism, there have been women who took that role.

FIEDLER: In your book, you describe a history of inspiration and of sexism that has characterized Buddhism. What has been the traditional, historical role of women in Buddhism?

TISDALE: In certain places and times, women have taken on very powerful roles, but they have largely been the exception. The more traditional roles that women have taken have been, as we've seen in all major world religions, second class to men, even though the lip service is very different.

There is a rhetoric of equality that is built very deeply into Buddhism, in that gender doesn't matter, that form is what we call "empty"; it has no essential nature, and yet humans tend to act as though there is some essential difference between the genders.

My entry into Buddhism twenty-four years ago was very unusual, in that I was ordained as a lay Buddhist by a woman. My teacher was her assistant, and I spent ten years as the assistant to a woman, and never had an issue with women taking the equal role. From the beginning, I saw women and men sharing roles equally. But over the years, it's become quite clear to me that America is an exception in some ways. American women have demanded and asserted themselves as equal holders. It's not true for most Buddhist women. Most Buddhist women in the world are still held back.

FIEDLER: So this desire to overcome a history and legacy of sexism is more an American phenomenon than in other cultures of the world, particularly in Asia where Buddhism predominates?

TISDALE: I have to give some credit to my sisters over there. There is a very strong and vocal movement beginning in Southeast Asia and Japan. We're seeing that some of the women in this lineage that I write about are women who at various times and places have put everything on the line to say, "It's ours too; we want a role."

FIEDLER: In Buddhism, when you look at the question of sexism, is it that Buddhist men claim a theological reason for treating women as second class? Or is it simply garden variety male dominance as we've seen elsewhere?

TISDALE: We've certainly seen both. But it begins with the sexism, not with the theology. It begins with this feeling a man has that it's not right for a woman to take the same role. And then they look for the theological reason to rationalize it. So over many centuries, there did develop a body of teaching.

FIEDLER: Let's get to the essence of your book, which is the history of Buddhist women, spanning 2,500 years. And of course, it's necessarily fragmented and incomplete, because like other faith traditions, women weren't written about for many centuries. But you do manage to relate the stories of several dozen women. Let me ask you to tell the stories of three or four of your favorites.

TISDALE: I want to say that I chose these women for their relationship to Zen Buddhism and the history of Zen Buddhism. So there are many, many more women that could be chosen if you were looking at other sects of Buddhism.

One of the women that I really love is a woman named Zenchin, because she was the first ordained Buddhist in Japan, and she was a teenage girl. She was probably around sixteen or seventeen years old. And this is when Buddhism first came to Japan. At the time there were no ordained Buddhists of any kind in Japan. The priests came from Korea. So this young girl and two of her friends were first ordained, then they were sent to Korea, to this very far away foreign land where they didn't speak the language, and trained as nuns. And then they came back to Japan and started a temple, essentially the first Japanese temple. And what struck me when I was in Japan doing research is that most Japanese Buddhists do not know who she is. But I wonder at the amount of persistence and bravery she must have had to survive and thrive.

FIEDLER: And another favorite?

TISDALE: Another one of my favorites is a Chinese woman. I call her the bathhouse attendant, because for a long time in her life that was her job. She ran a bathhouse. Her name was Kongshi Daoren. And she represents the frustration and obstacles women faced who were denied the right to be ordained. She was first denied by her father. Then, she became her brother's charge, and he denied her, so she was self-taught. She became quite famous, even though nobody knew her face. She wrote treatises that were very famous and learned. But she decided to run a bathhouse, and in the bathhouse she wrote poems and tested her customers' knowledge of Buddhism. Only at the very end of her life was she ordained, and it was almost as an afterthought. One of the important lessons of Buddhism is that these forms we think are so important, like ordination as a priest, are actually not that important. It's that personal experience that counts. And she really lived that.

And there are also Indian women from the time of the historical Buddha. The first one, of course, was Maha Pajapati, his aunt and his step-mother. The Buddha's mother died right after he was born, and he was raised by his aunt. And then, when he left home and founded Buddhism, a lot of men went with him, abandoning their families. It was said that wherever the Buddha went, women were widowed. And these women came to Pajapati and said, "Help us!" And they went eventually to the Buddha and begged for the chance to join the community. And at first the Buddha said no. In the myth, he turns her down at first, but eventually accepts her, and she becomes a very important teacher and brings hundreds and hundreds of women into the community. She lived to a ripe old age and performed miracles.

FIEDLER: So this is very early Buddhist India?

TISDALE: This is in Buddhist India 2,500 years ago. I'm very moved by the image of her standing in a dusty robe with sore feet, asking for the right to have the same opportunities as men. Women weeping is an image we all know, but she stood her ground while she cried. And there have been times in my own practice when I've wanted to cry, and I thought, "Well, you stand your ground while you do that."

FIEDLER: Do you believe that there is a general trend toward greater gender equality that's likely to shape the future of Buddhism?

TISDALE: I think there's not a general trend; I think it's an inevitable tidal wave of change.

LaDonna Harris

on Native American Spirituality

Native American spirituality, with its deep reverence for the earth, has emerged with a new importance in the twenty-first century as we confront the serious challenges of environmental destruction and climate change. LaDonna Harris is a woman of the Comanche Nation with a great deal of wisdom about Native American spiritual practices. She is the founder and president of Americans for Indian Opportunity. I interviewed her in March 2007.

MAUREEN FIEDLER: LaDonna, tell me a little bit about the Comanche Nation.

LADONNA HARRIS: Historically, it's said that we came out of the Montana Mountains in the 1600s. When the Spanish came, we became great horse thieves and, with the Spanish horse, we became quite powerful. We were called the Lords of the Southern Plains because, if you can imagine, it was like having a jet plane at that time.

FIEDLER: The horse was the latest technology of warfare, if you will. So the Comanche were, for awhile at least, a kind of Native American superpower.

HARRIS: Yes, I think you could say that.

FIEDLER: Tell us about your own upbringing, as a Comanche woman, particularly looking at the spirituality of the Comanche Nation.

HARRIS: It was a wonderful experience growing up with my grandparents on their farm during the depression. But it was very hard to find jobs, and so my father went out to California to find work. And Mother then went to work at the Indian hospital.

FIEDLER: Your mother is Comanche and your father is Irish. So you're actually half Comanche?

HARRIS: I am. But culturally I'm totally Comanche, because Comanche was spoken at home, and we still wore traditional clothes, and, although my mother became a Christian, her father, my grandfather, never accepted Christianity. He had eagle medicine from his father and then peyote. He would take us to church, but he would sit outside church and wait for us. Then we'd come home and he would then sing his peyote songs on the porch. And he never seemed to have a conflict, except sometimes when a missionary preacher would come through and speak against our language and dancing.

FIEDLER: In the Comanche spiritual world, who is God?

HARRIS: There is a great Creator. We are very related to the earth; everything is circular. We believe we are connected to all living things. We know that we are part of the stars and, before the scientists came along, we said that we have stardust in our DNA. We know all of these things; we know that we are connected to the universe. And we know that there is a greater being who created all of this.

FIEDLER: Were there ceremonies and rituals that worshiped God, or that celebrated the earth?

HARRIS: We are very individualistic, and people say that seems to conflict with belonging a tribe. But it doesn't, because you should become as strong as you possibly can, and have as much of what we call "medicine" so that you can contribute to the whole. It is all linked.

We don't have a religious hierarchy. If people have the values of the community, like generosity and wisdom, and reflect them in their daily lives, people follow them. We don't have chiefs; in fact the United States government gave us chiefs.

FIEDLER: Do have anything akin to a clergy?

HARRIS: Yes we do. They are usually the medicine men. We believe that everybody has "medicine," but some people cultivate it. And when it's cultivated, and used in a way that is beneficial to the group, we recognize it in that individual, and we go to them for guidance and direction.

FIEDLER: Are they all men?

HARRIS: No, there are women as well. In fact, outstanding women can also do healing. There isn't that kind of distinction, though there are certain roles that people play. Women are the ones who keep the culture, the balance in the community. If someone acts out, they take the initiative to correct them. Then, if there is damage done to you by some other family, your family goes and talks to them, and they figure out how to make things right. We don't believe in incarceration. If the crime is so enormous, and so unforgivable, they must leave us. And, if you're a tribal person and a communal person, to have to leave the group that defines you is worse than death.

FIEDLER: I'm hearing you talk about values like cherishing the community, reverencing the earth, compassion, generosity. Are these the elements of the code of conduct that the elders and the medicine men and women preach to the community?

HARRIS: We don't preach it so much as we live it. If someone has those values, people will follow him or her. And, if they know someone to be wise and smart and concerned about safety for the group, and to be generous in distributing whatever is caught or killed, that person would have a following. No one would follow someone who didn't have those characteristics.

FIEDLER: How do you ritualize these beliefs? Is there dancing? Are there fires? Are there storytelling sessions? Does your nation do the sweat lodge?

HARRIS: Yes, we do the sweat lodge. But mostly Comanche men go off and fast and have a vision. They pray to the great Creator, saying "I'm looking for direction, give me some sign." And so, with no food or water, a man might have a vision, and when his time is over, the first animal he sees, the first bird or some other creature, he takes that as his symbol. That will be his protection. He usually puts it on his clothing, and people come to know him by the symbol.

FIEDLER: Do men do this only when they are young?

HARRIS: Men of all ages do this. They do it when they are young, when they are going through puberty, because they are making their mark, so to speak, coming into the community. We have great ceremonies of dancing, and music, and storytelling. And grandfather told me that they have people who can talk to animals. They become so close to certain animals that they can communicate with them and they can tell you which way to go to avoid danger. He tells the story of the man who could communicate with coyotes. His father actually saw this, experienced it. And sure enough, they went all the way to Mexico and back, and never encountered any real, major danger, because they followed what the coyote had told them.

FIEDLER: I understand that there have been studies done of Native American spirituality across the continent. There were great divergences discovered, because these various nations didn't have close communication in earlier centuries. But there have been commonalties as well. Can you talk first about divergence?

HARRIS: Yes. You have to think about how large the United States is. In the not-too-distant past, the distances between tribes were so great that they might as well have been as far as England is from China. We are diverse culturally. Many of us used sweat lodges and had other kinds of religious ceremonies, mostly to pray and purge toxins.

FIEDLER: So there were very diverse cultures and very diverse ways of sustaining existence, whether by farming or hunting. And so differences developed in spirituality. But what did you find they had in common?

HARRIS: We were very democratic and participatory. It was inappropriate to impose our values. When the Spanish came, imposing their religious beliefs, it was such a foreign thing. And so was ownership of land. We had territories that we used for hunting and for other purposes that we tried to protect from other tribes, but we never felt that we *owned* the land.

FIEDLER: You didn't have a concept of private property?

HARRIS: In Comanche culture, you should never own anything that you can't give away, because material things can own you, and then you become selfish and greedy. And so, the more things that you have, the more you should give back.

So what were the common threads in our spirituality? We came up with what we called the four Rs.

The most important one is *relationships*. Because we're communal people, we have to think of the good of the whole. Be an individual, but think relational. We're connected to everything.

Then the next one is *responsibility* to those relationships. For instance, if we call earth our mother, then how do we take care of her? We have to make sure that she replenishes our food. We give back to Mother Earth in many of the ceremonies. I remember hearing about when the Comanche saw the first boot they loved it because it would protect legs from being scratched. But the heel was too harsh, because it would hurt Mother Earth to walk on it, so they cut the heels off.

The third one is *reciprocity*. You do good because it's the right thing to do, but it'll come back to you in some form. It may not come back immediately, but if you do the right thing, good things will happen to you.

The fourth one is *redistribution*. We had very sophisticated ways of redistributing the wealth, and we tried to keep the people on the same economic level.

FIEDLER: You didn't pay your chiefs 300 percent of what the poorest person earns?

HARRIS: You paid attention to the poorest person in the tribe. If a mother lost her sons and had nobody to hunt for her, you would make sure that she was provided for. But in formal ways, our tribe had "Giveaways." We still have them. When our daughter graduated from Stanford, we asked, "What do you want for graduation?" She said, "I'd like to have a Giveaway." And that's what we did. We gave gifts to people who helped her become who she is.

FIEDLER: How do the casinos fit into this?

HARRIS: Well, it may be our horse.

FIEDLER: Like the Spanish horse?

HARRIS: Yes, like the Spanish horse. We have tried ever since we've been organized to do economic development, to follow the Western style of economic development. But the casinos have brought economic balance to us. And unlike other casinos, like the ones Donald Trump owns, the money comes back into the community. The first thing they support is education from cradle to the grave. Anybody can go to any school they want to. They feed the elderly; they take them on trips; they see that they're healthy. They make sure that they get right diets. They do infrastructure for the tribe, because they own it in common.

FIEDLER: So the elements of your spirituality feed into what you do with the proceeds from the casinos? You redistribute, you take responsibility, there's reciprocity. And somebody doesn't make a whole lot of money, while other people have almost nothing?

HARRIS: If they do, they're not living by our ethic.

FIEDLER: Reverence for the earth is, of course, central to the spirituality you've described. What does it do to your heart when you hear the reports about global warming?

HARRIS: I just saw a film on the polar bear. They can't find enough ice in their hunting ground. It's gone. And that's just one species.

FIEDLER: But in your spirituality, this is not just a faraway polar bear; this is a relative.

HARRIS: That's exactly right. And we use kinship terms to refer to animals. We call them our brothers and sisters. When animals die, we are losing relatives.

FIEDLER: What would you counsel the United States, the nations of the globe, to do about this problem?

HARRIS: To immediately sign the Kyoto Treaty agreement. If we see the earth as Mother Earth and think of our kinship with her, if we see those animals and think of them as our relatives, then by wounding them or losing them, we lose a piece of ourselves. Because they have something in their DNA that is the same as ours, we should respect them and honor that.

The Reverend Dr. Renita Weems
on Womanist Spirituality

When "feminist" theology and spirituality developed, many African-American women saw it as inadequate for their needs because it did not address the full reality of the lives of African-American women. Thus they developed "womanist" theology and spirituality.

One of leaders in this field is the Reverend Dr. Renita Weems. She is a well-known preacher, scholar, and author in the African-Methodist Episcopal Church, and the William and Camille Cosby Visiting Professor of Humanities at Spellman College in Atlanta, Georgia, as well as a contributing writer to *Essence Magazine*. She is the author of many books on womanist spirituality, including *Listening to God*, which won the Religious Communications Council's 1999 Award for Excellence in Communicating Spiritual Values to the Secular Media. And her newest book is *What Matters Most: Ten Lessons in Living Passionately from the Song of Solomon*. This interview took place in December 2004.

MAUREEN FIEDLER: First of all, how are women's spiritual needs these days different from those of men?

RENITA WEEMS: I believe that to be created human is to be created with the capacity for spiritual consciousness. But I don't think that men's and women's spiritual needs are any different from each other. But it does seem to me that men and women think and talk about spiritual matters differently. It's my experience that women are more comfortable talking about such things as faith, prayer, love, hope, forgiveness, and surrendering to God, and those are intangible components of what it means to be alive and human.

FIEDLER: That raises the question of why there aren't more women preachers, doesn't it?

WEEMS: You raise an interesting question. Inasmuch as women are more comfortable in this area, and so many churches do, in fact, have women as the majority of members, why haven't we been seen in the pulpit? Obviously, it's because the church is pretty much patriarchal, and men have pretty much run the church in many ways.

FIEDLER: What does all of this suggest about women's spirituality?

WEEMS: One of the challenges for today's woman is learning the importance of prioritizing her spirituality, prioritizing her values, and taking the time to nurture her faith and her belief in God, her belief in mystery, learning to trust her inner ear, her spiritual consciousness, and the spirit of the creator that is within each of us. I think women and men, but certainly women, have been trained for a lifetime not to trust that voice.

FIEDLER: Is that what you mean when you say you understand your work as that of a "midwife of the inner wisdom"?

WEEMS: Very much so. It's very easy as a minister and a professor, perhaps even as a writer, for people to invest a lot of authority and special knowledge in me. "Tell me what I should do! Do you think that this is what I should do? Or what do you think God tried to tell me?" And part of my work as a minister and as a teacher is to use my writing, preaching, and teaching to help people tap into their own inner wisdom, and to draw on their own experiences and insights, and walk with God to help them find the answers they need to life's dilemmas.

FIEDLER: You consider yourself a womanist theologian and writer. What do you mean by that?

WEEMS: I borrow from a term that writer Alice Walker used to characterize the unique experiences of black women in America. It is a term coined from within the African-American culture. When you're a young girl and you're very precocious, you are acting very womanlike. Your mother, or the older women in your family, are apt to call you "womanish," meaning precocious beyond your age.

A lot of black women scholars have started using it as a way to unapologetically admit that much of our scholarship and our writing, and perhaps even the preaching that I do, I do it through the lens of a black woman's experience.

FIEDLER: You wrote one book called *Listening for God*, and it's subtitled *A Minister's Journey Through Silence and Doubt*. Have you doubted your faith? Has it waxed and waned for you?

WEEMS: Absolutely. Ministers rarely talk about the lonely, dry periods on their spiritual journey and I, like so many other ministers and people of faith, have lost my faith a thousand times, only to find it 999 times. And I wrote *Listening for God* as a way of helping people admit, and not be ashamed of admitting, that belief in God and mystery wax and wane throughout one's spiritual development.

FIEDLER: Another one of your books focuses on Mary, the Mother of Jesus. But your image of Mary is different from that of many popular models. How is she different for you?

WEEMS: In my book called *Showing Mary*, I was interested in Mary as a woman, the woman who found herself pulled into the role she didn't seek, and a place in history she never imagined for herself. So much of the scholarship that's done, or even research and preaching that's done on Mary, is about Mary only as a mother. And she is frozen in her life as the Mother of Jesus. But I'm also interested in Mary as a woman. What happens when your purpose and destiny lead you down paths you never imagined, paths for which you have little preparation? And so I was interested in the Mary who grows up from being a little-known, unwed mother, from the wrong side of the tracks, to Mary the icon, a leader, a thinking and praying woman.

FIEDLER: One of the things that was very interesting to me is that most spiritual writing about Mary has been done by Catholics. But you're a Methodist. Do you believe that Protestants need to reclaim Mary in some way?

WEEMS: I do, and I'm happy to say that I belong to a generation of Protestant women ministers and scholars doing lots of work to reclaim Mary. I think that's certainly one of the benefits of having women enter into ministry. We're beginning to hear about many women in the Bible that have not been heard about before. We reclaim a kind of balance within our faith, a balance between a male and female, a balance even within the sacred, the masculine and the feminine side of the sacred.

FIEDLER: The title of your new book is *What Matters Most: Ten Lessons in Living Passionately from the Song of Solomon*. What's important about living passionately, and what do you mean by that?

WEEMS: It is based on a book in the Bible that we hear very little about. The Book of Solomon is highly erotic and seductive poetry. And so I was very interested in reclaiming the woman in that story, who is a very erotic, seductive, sensual personality, probably *the* most sensual in all of scripture. And I talk about her in *What Matters Most* as a way of helping us think about what it means to be truly alive—not just through sex, sexuality, and romance, but alive in terms of ambitions, energy, and love. I'm talking about passion, not so much about sex. I talk about passion that is found in things you enjoy doing, things that give meaning to your life.

FIEDLER: What led you to ministry?

WEEMS: In my tradition, I'm supposed to give you one answer to that, and that is, "God called me, of course." And that was certainly my sense. A musical group called Sweet Honey in the Rock has a song that says, "I feel something pulling me, drawing me, urging me on." And I would say that, within my own tradition, I went into the ministry because I felt something urging me, pulling me, drawing me, into this line of work. It also happened that this line of work tapped into my best gifts, and my best talents.

~~~~~~

Jean Houston
on *Mystical Dogs: Animals as Guides to Our Inner Life*

People of many faith traditions recognize that animals often play a special role in human spiritual development. Jean Houston knows a great deal about this, with her "mystical dogs." She is a prolific author, and founder of the Human Potential Movement. In her book *Mystical Dogs: Animals as Guides to Our Inner Life*, Jean Houston shows how animals, and dogs in particular, can help restore us to our natural condition of oneness with nature.

This interview was conducted by Josephine Reed, a former producer for *Interfaith Voices*, in April 2004.

JOSEPHINE REED: Jean, those of us with pets know the solace and the love we receive from them, but is that the same thing as pets guiding us to a greater spiritual awareness?

JEAN HOUSTON: I think it can be. Animals are the great companions of our lives. They teach us, they love us, they care for us. Even when we're uncaring, they feed our souls. They always give us the benefit of the doubt, with natural grace, spiritual grace. You might say they give us insight into the nature of what is truly good, what is truly beautiful. And they often provide us with the mirror of our better nature. We talk about better angels, but maybe some of our better angels are our dogs and cats. We're really ignorant if we regard them as an inferior species— our poor, much-loved relations because they're different tribes, if you will, different nations. They look at the world differently than we do. And often they look at us in such a way that they evoke our higher selves. You know it's not for nothing that through the millennia ancient peoples deify animals, hoping to capture, in their deep presence, our now once-removed spirituality.

REED: Why do you think in Western culture there is this resistance to recognize animals as having a spirit or a soul?

HOUSTON: If you're talking about classical theological traditions, that's one thing. But then you have St. Francis of Assisi who always traveled with a crow on his back, buying the lambs and giving them to poor Clare to raise so they wouldn't go to the slaughter house, that's also a very deep tradition of loving animals.

REED: Dogs, you write, can be holy guides to unseen worlds. What do you mean by that?

HOUSTON: If I take a walk with my dog, he sniffs out things in the larger reality. He sniffs things in the grass, in the flowers. He's alert to a world that is larger than mine. And he enters into my world and, because of his extended sensorium, I enter into his. I become a citizen in a world larger than my aspiration, more complex than all my dreams. When we come back into the house, and I sit down at my computer, he's there sleeping on my feet, and his soft snuffling reminds me of another state of being. It's like a meditative trance; it's another order of reality.

REED: I'm struck by one of your statements—that animals need no priest or interpreter. What power are we talking about here?

HOUSTON: Animals have an essential power, a power that is in tune with the very rhythms of the universe. They have natural rhythms; they have a sense of their own authenticity, unless they've been terribly beaten or repressed. They come into the world, in a sense, complete. They have profound instincts and that's what makes them, I think, so very lovable, and so utterly enchanting.

REED: I've had animals literally my entire life. I was two and a half when I got my first dog, and I remember it vividly. My world changed that day, from black and white to color. And I think what other people find through meditation, I really find through my dogs, because I need time with them every day—where I'm simply focused on them. And there is a way in which they can bring one to sort of a transcendental state.

HOUSTON: Yes, because they are there both in loveliness and simplicity. And with them you relax deeply, and you become a part of their flow of life.

REED: I want to go back to that statement about animals needing no priest or interpreter. Because I think our need for a priest is very much informed by the fact that we know we're mortal, which is something animals don't know. They don't understand an end time for them. And I wonder if, in some ways, dogs are inviting us to forget about our mortality.

HOUSTON: Certainly we can forget about our clocks. Animals need no interpreters; they are not twice removed from life, as we often are. And because we're so adapted, we cannot grow beyond that adaptation. But I think with animals there is always that yearning. And what we learn from the dogs is both their authentic happiness in being dogs, and at the same time, a willingness to go beyond themselves. To me, that's a tremendous teaching to each one of us, that we are who we are, but we are also so much more than who and what we think we are.

REED: You wrote about Titan, your dog whom you said was a Buddha in training.

HOUSTON: Titan was born with terrible hips, so he was always in pain. But his love of people was so huge that it exceeded his pain. I'd have an intellectual soiree on Sundays, where there may be fifty, sixty, seventy people. Titan was a huge dog, 240 pounds. And, because his hips weren't working, he would drag himself from person to person. And literally, he gave *darshan*, deep-seeing. He would kiss everybody gently. You could not be around him and be less than all that you were, because you felt yourself so nourished in the field of knowing, the field of love. It was as if he carried this larger reality that evoked the deeper reality in you.

A very famous philosopher sat on the rug and held hands with Titan while talking into a tape recorder. He spoke some of his deepest reflections because being with Titan illumined him.

When I asked, "Why is it that you get so intellectually stimulated in the presence of Titan?" He said, "It's as if there are two realities here. The existential one of this marvelous dog in front of me, and essential one that is on a continuum with the source-mind of the universe." And Titan would thump his huge tail, and he would glow. That's the way he was.

Margaret Mead used to say to me (and she wasn't a dog person at all; she was a cat person), "I love being around Titan. I'm such a public person. Everybody projects on me, but when I'm with Titan, he sees me for who and what I really am. He has the most fragrant, pleasant breath I ever experienced." To which we replied, "The odor of sanctity is no mere metaphor, Margaret."

~~~~~~

Dr. Jeanette Rodriguez

on *Our Lady of Guadalupe: Faith and Empowerment among Mexican-American Women*

Many cultural icons symbolize the spirituality of an entire people. In Catholicism, these are often images of Mary, the Mother of Jesus. In Poland, it is the "black Madonna," or Our Lady of Czestochowa. In France, it is Our Lady of Lourdes. In Bosnia, it is Our Lady of Medjugorje. And in Mexico, it is clearly Our Lady of Guadalupe.

Dr. Jeanette Rodriguez is a professor of theology and religious studies at Seattle University in Washington. She is the author of *Our Lady of Guadalupe: Faith and Empowerment among Mexican-American Women*. I interviewed her in April 2004.

MAUREEN FIEDLER: Catholics have reported many appearances of Mary, the Mother of God. But in Mexico, no appearance is more central than that of Our Lady of Guadalupe in 1541. Dr. Rodriguez, you say that the context of this appearance is central, because it comes only ten years after the Spanish conquest of Mexico, the *Conquista*.

JEANETTE RODRIGUEZ: The context is one of a people grieving the loss of their lands, the death of their families, of their way of life, their way of worshiping. No conquest is a good conquest, but this conquest in particular was brutal, because the people came to believe that even the gods had abandoned them.

FIEDLER: The Virgin of Guadalupe reportedly appeared to an indigenous man, Juan Diego. And the belief that Mary honored such a humble man, considered inferior by the conquering Spanish, is central to the Mexican love for Guadalupe. Juan Diego may have been indigenous, an Indian, but the common description of him as a peasant is not quite accurate.

RODRIGUEZ: Juan Diego was a fifty-two-year-old man, an elder in his community, and a catechist. He was a baptized Christian; he had already come to the faith. You have to understand, a lot of the religious practices of the people at that time were very similar to those of Christianity. For example, they had a form of baptism, a form of anointing of the sick. They believed in the ancestors, which we translate as the Communion of Saints. And they believed in an ultimate God.

FIEDLER: What was the story of Juan Diego?

RODRIGUEZ: He was on his way to catechism class, or Sunday school, when he heard beautiful music. He followed the music, and he met up with Guadalupe. And he must have recognized her, because he fell to his knees. And she said to him: "Juanito, Juan Diego, the smallest of my children, where are you going?"

He told her, "I'm going to your house to hear the divine things that your priest has to tell us." And then she said the famous message, which is, "Juan Diego, the smallest of my children, I am the Holy Mother of God, the mother of the true God for whom one lives, and I have a great desire that there be built here a *casita*. Not a church, not a temple, but a home, where I can show forth my love and compassion, my help and my defense to you, to all of you, to all the inhabitants of this land. To all who call upon me, trust me, and love me, I will hear your pains and sorrows and lamentations, and I will respond."

When he returned to his parish and reported the apparition, his priest asked for proof that Mary had appeared to him. So he returned to the spot of his apparition, and Mary reappeared. He asked her for a sign to bring back. What she gave him, so the story goes, was her image, on the inside of his cloak. This is a highly significant picture that we know today as the image of the Virgin of Guadalupe. This image of the Virgin is that of a *mestiza*, someone who claims both indigenous and Spanish heritage, as do the majority of Mexicans. In other words, this Mary looked like a Mexican. And so she is recognized as a symbol of the Mexican culture and nation rising from the ashes of the conquest.

She came to offer a reframing of that birth as a new creation. She was not one of their ancient Gods; she was something new. And I think that this newness, and this ability to recreate oneself, is a significant gift that the Mexican people offer other communities.

FIEDLER: So she symbolizes a kind of a restoration of the human dignity that the Spaniards had denied them.

RODRIGUEZ: Denied and trampled on.

FIEDLER: This image enhances the Mexican sense of dignity and self-worth to such an extent that devotion to Our Lady of Guadalupe is not limited to Christians.

RODRIGUEZ: It is said in Mexico that not everyone is Catholic, but everyone is a *Guadalupana*. And I believe that's true. I think, as her story gets told, more and more people are tapping into that creative life force or divine force. I know a woman of the Jewish tradition who claims to be a Guadalupana. And I asked, "How is that possible; you're Jewish?" And she said, "Because I tap into that creative earth energy of Guadalupe." It's amazing to me that Guadalupe in many ways is like a prism people come to differently: either as the Mother of Jesus, the maternal face of God, or Spirit as creative force.

FIEDLER: Before the conquest, the indigenous peoples of Mexico worshiped goddesses as well as gods. Consequently some have suggested that the image of Mary at Guadalupe is that of a Goddess, or the feminine face of God. Is that the case?

RODRIGUEZ: By applying to Mary the attributes of the feminine face of God, we almost withdraw those attributes from God, and I think that's potentially dangerous. Or we promote stereotypes of what is feminine and masculine, and I don't want to do that. But what I do believe about Guadalupe is that there is something about her spirit that she really is the Spirit of God.

FIEDLER: There is no doubt that the image of Our Lady of Guadalupe is used in multiple settings, from homes and living rooms, to the massive Basilica in Mexico City, to the struggles for equality of Mexicans demonstrating in the streets.

RODRIGUEZ: This symbol has moved people, not only internally, but also politically, as with the farm workers who hold the banner of Guadalupe.

She's everywhere. Look at the streets of L.A., and you will see kids who are considered delinquents. And yet, they have her image tattooed on their skin; they have her hanging from the rear-view mirrors of their cars. People have her in their bakeries. She's everywhere.

FIEDLER: It is clear Our Lady of Guadalupe holds a unique place in the religious culture of Mexico, a place that speaks to intimacy, accompaniment, and identity.

RODRIGUEZ: One is intimately connected to Guadalupe in such a way that whether it's a quiet moment of intimacy, or accompaniment in a struggle, she's there, and she's never left.

Chapter 6
Women Leaders in Social Justice, Peace, and Ecology

Almost all religious denominations or traditions are engaged in transforming social reality. Most are actively concerned with improving the lot of the poor, peace-making, and most recently, saving planet Earth in the face of encroaching climate change.

Women have long been leaders in this arena. In the Quaker world, there was Jane Addams who founded Hull House in Chicago in 1889, the first "settlement house" in the United States for recently-arrived immigrants. There were the great Quaker women abolitionists like Lucretia Mott and Sarah and Angelina Grimke. Many of these same women also put energies into the struggle for women's suffrage.

Catherine Mumford Booth was one of the founders of the Salvation Army, with its extensive outreach to the poor. Olympia Brown, the first woman ordained a Unitarian minister, spent much of her life working for women's suffrage. Coretta Scott King, wife of Dr. Martin Luther King, became a leader in her own right in movements for racial and economic justice, as well as women's rights. Melissa Harris-Lacewell is an emerging leader in this arena. She is an authority on the black church, a political scientist at Princeton, and a student of theology who has merged these interests to become a "public intellectual" in her advocacy for racial and gender justice.

In Catholicism, Dorothy Day co-founded the Catholic Worker movement with its advocacy for peace and free hospitality to the poor. Many orders of Catholic nuns were founded to provide education and health care to poor children and families, often immigrants. In 2000, Maryknoll Sisters Maura Clarke and Ita Ford, Ursuline Sister Dorothy Kazel, and laywoman Jean Donovan were murdered by a death squad in El Salvador because they championed the cause of the poor. Sister of Notre Dame Dorothy Stang defended both the rights of the poor and the preservation of the rain forest in Brazil until she was martyred in 2005. Still others, like Dominican sisters

Ardeth Platte, Carol Gilbert, and Jackie Hudson, committed nonviolent civil disobedience in opposition to modern warfare.

In the Jewish tradition, nineteenth-century Emma Lazarus worked against anti-Semitism and championed immigrants' rights. Her values led her to write the words now on the Statue of Liberty: "Give me your tired, your poor, your huddled masses yearning to breathe free." Eve Fertig pioneered work for animal habitat and wildlife preservation. Betty Friedan was one of the founding mothers of the twentieth-century quest for gender equality.

In the Muslim tradition, Shirin Ebadi stands out as a champion of human rights. She won the 2003 Nobel Peace Prize for her work as a lawyer, defending the rights of religious minorities, women, and children in her native Iran. And Irene Zubaida Khan of Bangladesh served as secretary general of Amnesty International from 2001 to 2009. In the Hindu and Sikh traditions, women like Sarojini Naidu, Lakshmi Menon, Sushila Nayyar, and Rajkumari Amrit Kaur became leaders for justice and peace as collaborators with Mahatma Gandhi.

Among Buddhists, Aung San Suu Kyi, the Burmese champion of democracy and winner of the 1991 Nobel Peace Prize, is an example of women's leadership for human rights. She founded the National League for Democracy in Burma, which won an election in 1990, after which she should have become prime minister. But the military refused to relinquish power, and placed her under house arrest. Through all of her ordeals, she credits Buddhism with a prominent role in the development of her political philosophy.

Layli Miller-Muro

on Caring About Women's Rights in the Baha'i Tradition

Layli Miller-Muro is a woman of the Baha'i tradition. As an activist attorney seeking social justice for women, she founded—at age twenty-five—the Tahirih Justice Center on the outskirts of Washington, DC. The center defends the human rights of women immigrants in the United States. Its cases involve issues such as domestic violence, sex abuse, or helping women avoid deportation to countries where they face genital mutilation. When I interviewed her in February 2003, she testified that her Baha'i faith, which strongly advocates gender equality, had led her into this work.

MAUREEN FIEDLER: How did the Tahirih Center come into being?
LAYLI MILLER-MURO: The creation of the center was inspired largely by my beliefs as a Baha'i, particularly the Baha'i principles of the equality of

women and men, and the emphasis on justice in the Baha'i community. That led me to law school, down a certain career path, and ultimately led to the creation of Tahirih Justice Center.

FIEDLER: I understand that the center you founded is named after a woman martyr of the Baha'i tradition. Can you tell us about her?

MILLER-MURO: Tahirih is the name of a woman who lived in the mid-1800s. She lived in what was then Persia, now called Iran. She was very famous during her time, a very strong and audacious woman. She was considered very beautiful, and the Shah tried to marry her. She was known as a poet, a theologian, a community organizer. She had memorized the Qur'an by the time she was thirteen. And she would argue theology with the chief imams. Of course, she did that from behind a black curtain, because women couldn't be seen.

She was also one of the first believers in the Baha'i faith, one of the first nineteen believers, similar to the disciples in Christ's time. Tahirih was very audacious; she traveled around the countryside proclaiming that a new day had dawned for the status of women, and for humanity. Her most famous act of defiance was to remove her veil before an assemblage of men. And at the time she did this, the act was so shocking that a man who was in the audience stood up and slit his throat, because it was considered so dishonorable just to look at her face.

She was eventually killed for her beliefs at the age of thirty-six. Her last recorded words were, "You can kill me as soon as you like, but you will never stop the emancipation of women."

And here's something that's very interesting—in 1848, during the two-week period of time that Tahirih publicly removed her veil, there was a conference taking place, in a place called Seneca Falls, New York. And of course, that is considered the birth of the Women's Rights Movement in the West. So you had it virtually at the same time in human history, both in the East and in the West: symbolic pronouncements that a new day had dawned for women.

FIEDLER: The central focus of Tahirih Center is justice for women suffering human rights abuses. Cases often involve women brought to the United States to be domestic servants in household situations that prove abusive. How does the center help these women?

MILLER-MURO: Legal services are the core of what we do; most of us are attorneys, and we provide free legal services to women and girls who are fleeing from human rights abuses. So they are immigrant women. We have clients particularly in the Washington, DC, area, some of whom are trafficked by World Bank and IMF officials to work for them in their homes without pay, without any time off, and under abusive conditions. Those conditions are often physically, sometimes sexually, abusive.

FIEDLER: Between six hundred and seven hundred women come to the center for assistance each year. This results in approximately 100 to 150 legal cases. How do you handle so many calls for your assistance?

MILLER-MURO: We take a holistic approach, and we help our clients access a range of social and medical services, so that they can get back on their feet and make a life for themselves. The center's work involves these direct services, but in an effort to create systemic change, so that women can be protected from violence long-term, we also engage in public policy initiatives to try to make sure that legislation is adequate to protect women.

FIEDLER: I understand that a major initiative of the center this year grows from the use of the Internet.

MILLER-MURO: One of the most exciting public policy projects that we have right now is called the Campaign to End Exploitation by Internet Marriage Brokers. And this is a project that was developed because of a pattern that we noticed among our clients—immigrant women being abused by American men, and they had met these men through Internet marriage brokers. Some people refer to them as mail-order-bride agencies. Many of the men were predatory violent abusers who had been married, and this was their third, or fourth bride through these agencies. And the agencies were often complicit in the abuse. They lied to the women about their legal rights. They did not warn them that an individual, for example, had been charged with attempted murder in a domestic violence situation. They knowingly paired these men with women from abroad. And so we've engaged in a project that litigates against the agencies to try to create liability for them, as well as the abuser, so that they'll be held accountable for this kind of abuse.

The other part of the project promotes legislation. This is a virtually unregulated industry. And we are advocating legislation that will provide protection for the women by providing them with information about the criminal backgrounds of these men. It will provide them information about their legal rights when they're being abused, so that they're able to access resources and protection, even if they find themselves in a desperate situation.

FIEDLER: Layli, you were born into the Baha'i faith. Did you remain Baha'i just because it was your family legacy?

MILLER-MURO: There is a law in the Baha'i faith about individual investigation of truth. It's up to every individual to decide whether or not to become a Baha'i. So there was a stage in my teenage years when I investigated other religions. I went to mosques, temples, churches, a Hare Krishna meeting. And I came to the conclusion that the Baha'i faith was for me, that it provided the best balance between faith and reason.

The social laws and principles are very progressive, and seemed to apply best to the time that we're living in.

FIEDLER: Is there another basic principle of the Baha'i faith that is especially significant for you?

MILLER-MURO: There is a principle of the Baha'i faith known as the oneness of humankind. And the idea is that we are all a part of the same body. And if one part of the body is ailing, or is ill, or is facing injustice, that affects the whole body. The world is interconnected, which is why I, as a white American lawyer, care passionately about what's happening to women in Thailand, in Brazil, in Ghana. This principle, rooted in my motivations, comes from the Baha'i faith. We're all connected, and our health, our justice, our happiness, our advancement, in fact, helps others. I hope we understand that at some point as a society.

~~~~~~

Sr. Helen Prejean, CSJ
on *The Death of Innocents*

If any person of faith is a recognized leader in efforts to abolish the death penalty in the United States, it's Sr. Helen Prejean, CSJ. Her efforts became famous in the Academy Award–winning movie *Dead Man Walking*, in which she was portrayed by Susan Sarandon. She is a Sister of St. Joseph of Medaille, and has accompanied death row inmates, even until their final hours. In the process, she has become the most prominent religious voice in the United States against the death penalty. Her second book, *The Death of Innocents*, is an eyewitness account of wrongful executions. This interview took place in January 2005.

MAUREEN FIEDLER: Helen, your book *The Death of Innocents* lays out the injustices you see in the death penalty by telling two stories. Can you tell us about Dobie Gillis Williams?

SR. HELEN PREJEAN: Yes. Dobie was an African-American man from Louisiana, with an IQ of sixty-five. I knew him for seven years. He had been accused of the stabbing death of a woman in her bathroom in the little town of Manny, Louisiana. The police said they heard Dobie confess, but somehow misplaced the audio tape. The video tape malfunctioned. The prosecutor presented the most unbelievable scenario of the crime. The only witness was the victim, a woman by the name of Sonia Nippers. Her husband said he heard her yelling from the bathroom, where she was stabbed, that a black man was killing her. So the search was only for black men, and Dobie was pulled up in the net. He was convicted by an all-white jury whose members seemed ready to believe whatever the prosecution presented.

FIEDLER: An all-white jury in this day and age?

PREJEAN: In this day and age, yes. And not only that, no court in the land, the appeals courts or the Supreme Court, found that his constitutional right to an impartial jury of his peers had been violated. And two years after he was executed, the Supreme Court decided that we shouldn't kill the mentally retarded. So that didn't help him.

He had inadequate defense. His attorney, later disbarred, did no forensic evidence testing of any kind. And so Dobie spent about thirteen years of his life on death row. And he was very scared at the end.

I was right in there with him in those last hours, saying "Dobie, come on, you're about to do the bravest thing you ever did." And he was very brave the way he went to his death. He even forgave people. His last words were, "I don't have any hard feelings about anybody, and God bless." And then he got on the gurney.

FIEDLER: Are you convinced that Dobie was innocent?

PREJEAN: He never wavered in saying that he had not killed that lady. And when I really dug into the case and saw what had happened to him, I became convinced he was telling the truth.

FIEDLER: I understand that your latest book fulfills a promise to Dobie's mother.

PREJEAN: After Dobie was executed, I was at the house of Dobie's momma, Betty Williams. After the wake and funeral, she said to me, "You know, Sister Helen, nobody ever heard Dobie's voice. The local newspaper, they put down only what the prosecution said." And she asked, "Would you do a story so we can hear his voice?"

It took me five and a half years, but when I finished, I looked up, saying, "Dobie, I kept my word; I told your story." And just recently, I got a note from Betty Williams. I'd sent her the book. "Sister Helen," she said, "Took you a long time, but now Dobie's story is out of there and at last the truth is told, and everybody gets to hear his voice."

FIEDLER: You've been in a years-long dialogue with the hierarchy of the Catholic Church on the death penalty because the position of the church, until recently, still permitted executions. What did you do to change that?

PREJEAN: I sent a letter to the pope making the case for a principled opposition to the death penalty from the Catholic Church. Pope John Paul II, in the *Gospel of Life*, pushed the death penalty to the edge when he said, "Modern societies have a right to defend themselves, so we should choose bloodless means, therefore not the death penalty." But he left a huge loophole. He said, "In cases of absolute necessity, the state can execute."

I said in my letter, "Your Holiness, any state that executes claims it's an absolute necessity." And I emphasized the dignity of every human person when I asked, "Does the church uphold only the dignity of the innocent? What about the guilty?"

A friend of mine in the Vatican assured me that the pope read every word of my letter.

FIEDLER: And what happened?

PREJEAN: They changed the *Catholic Catechism* which stated the criteria that churches used for 1700 years, namely, that the state could execute for grave or grievous crimes. But now, there are no instances in which the death penalty is justified in church teaching. There's a lot of confusion, however. You still have priests, and even some bishops, saying that there may be some instances when execution is permitted, but in fact there are none in official Catholic teaching.

FIEDLER: In your latest book, you also take on a prominent, practicing Catholic who supports the death penalty, Justice Antonin Scalia of the Supreme Court. What has that exchange been like?

PREJEAN: Romans 13 says, and Scalia states this very boldly, "All government comes from God, the civil authorities were appointed by God." It also talks about authorities punishing evil-doers with the sword. Justice Scalia sees this sword as the death penalty. But in fact, the sword is a symbol of Roman authority, and in the historical context, Paul was really telling the followers of Jesus, "You know, you have to listen to civil authority"—not that you could execute individuals.

But Scalia goes even further and says, "The more Christian a government is, the more it practices the death penalty." He actually says Europe doesn't have a death penalty because it is post-Christian. And then he makes this little slight-of-hand saying, "Individuals have to practice what Jesus says about forgiveness." But not the government, because they're divinely appointed by God.

FIEDLER: You also took on President George Bush, especially in the case of Carla Faye Tucker, a woman whose death warrant he signed when he was governor of Texas. Talk about her case, and your discussion of it on *Larry King Live.*

PREJEAN: Carla Faye Tucker had changed her life in prison, clearly she had. The warden knew it. She was asking to live so that she could minister to people in prison for the rest of her life. Governor Bush was getting ready to campaign for president as a compassionate conservative, but he signed her death warrant. Carla Faye Tucker was on *Larry King* in the living rooms of many Americans shortly before her execution date, and they could see her beautiful face and hear her soft voice and they asked, "Why do you have to kill Carla Faye Tucker?" And what Bush said was, "We can't make an exception now; if you do a crime, you've got to pay for it."

But the thing that got me the most was, after Carla was executed, I was on *Larry King* and he read a press statement from George W. Bush, saying, "God bless Carla Faye Tucker," after he had just had her killed. Larry King came right to me and said, "Sister, what do you think about what the governor just said? You know, he invoked God." And I said, "God puts us in each other's hands to bless. He had a chance as governor to save her life, and he refused to take it." I was incensed at the obscenity of the way he used religion.

FIEDLER: You also say that the death penalty is a form of torture. And you compare it to elements of torture in the Abu Ghraib scandal. What's the similarity here?

PREJEAN: Amnesty International has defined torture as the extreme mental or physical assault on someone who has been rendered defenseless, as everyone on death row has. They're shackled hand and foot, and then led into this room to be killed. What made stomachs turn at the tortures at Abu Ghraib was clearly that the prisoners had been rendered defenseless. That's the essence in torture.

FIEDLER: Sister Helen, do you believe that states will ever begin to outlaw the death penalty?

PREJEAN: We're moving that way. Look at the polls. When the questions asked in the abstract, "Do you favor the death penalty?" the percentage is lower than it's been in twenty years. When people are given a choice between the death penalty or life without parole, support drops much further, to 50 percent or less. Now, with 117 wrongly convicted people off of death row and telling their horror stories on the nightly news, I think the American people are moving to a new place.

FIEDLER: Your mission now is what?

PREJEAN: To carry on the dialogue. I travel a lot; I speak a lot. I wrote *The Death of Innocents* to keep the dialogue going and to deepen it. I say to people who continue to believe in the death penalty, "Look at all the mistakes being made. You have no guarantee that all the people who have been executed weren't innocent. We have alternatives in place to keep ourselves safe from people who have done violent crimes. Most states have life without parole. So, you tell me now, why do you continue to favor the death penalty?"

Kathleen Kennedy Townsend

on Reclaiming the Catholic Social Justice Tradition

Very often, laywomen are leaders in the quest for social justice, and occasionally they are public office-holders. Kathleen Kennedy Townsend was the lieutenant governor of Maryland from 1995 to

2003. She is the eldest daughter of Robert and Ethel Kennedy, and the niece of former President John F. Kennedy. She wrote about her social justice beliefs in a book called *Failing America's Faithful: How Today's Churches Are Mixing God with Politics and Losing Their Way*. I interviewed her in May 2007.

MAUREEN FIEDLER: You note at the beginning of your book that the churches in this country have, as you put it, turned inward, become privatized. And you include your own Catholic Church in that critique. What do you mean by that?

KATHLEEN KENNEDY TOWNSEND: The God that I grew up with was a big God who cared about big issues: war and peace, poverty, discrimination, how we treat one another, how we care for the sick and the least among us. My father, in fact, wrote an article for *Look* magazine saying, "Suppose God is black." This was a God who cared about the justice issues in the world, whereas the God that people talk about today is a private kind of God. And the issues that they focus on are much smaller. God has shrunk to a God concerned only with abortion, stem cell research, gay marriage—all important issues, but not the largest challenges that we face.

FIEDLER: And by the same token you wouldn't negate the importance of a personal relationship with God, either?

KENNEDY TOWNSEND: Not at all, but I don't think that's the only thing that we need. There are *two* great commandments: love God and love your neighbor. And that neighbor seems to have been forgotten.

FIEDLER: You, of course, come out of the Catholic tradition. And out of that tradition, you paint a picture, a stirring picture, of a different kind of church than the one we see today: the outward-looking church of your youth that nourished you and your father, Robert Kennedy. And of course, this was the Catholic Church of the '60s; it was the church basking in the first light of the Second Vatican Council. What was the significance of that period for you?

KENNEDY TOWNSEND: It was also the church that had been an immigrant church, that said we are supposed to care for those who come to this country, that we're supposed to care for labor rights. For example, in the '30s, '40s, and '50s, the Jesuits had three hundred labor-organizing schools. Just the other day I was talking to John Sweeney, the president of the AFL-CIO, and told him about the three hundred labor workers' organizing schools. And he said, "Kathleen I know that; I went to one."

So we had the sense that we were building a community where we were caring for one another, and then with Vatican II came this openness to the world. We really *are* here on earth to change the world, to use God's spirit to make life better. And there was the sense of community, a sense that you shared the same traditions with Catholics all around the world. And it was really those lovely connections that gave me such a sense of belonging, and a sense of strength to go forward and try to do tough things.

FIEDLER: You quote a wonderful memo that you received from your father after your uncle, President Kennedy, was assassinated. And it says, "Be kind to others and work for your country. Love, Daddy." What did that mean to you?

KENNEDY TOWNSEND: What's stunning about that letter is that he wrote it three days after my uncle, Jack Kennedy, had been killed. He was in the White House planning the funeral arrangements. And you can imagine all the other things he could've been thinking about. Everything he'd worked for had just gone. How was he going to get along with President Johnson? How was Jackie going to be treated? Just the logistics, the sheer logistics of the funeral, not to mention how his life was transformed. And yet he wrote a letter about responsibility to family, about kindness to others, and working for your country. And it really goes back to this: his wasn't a private God, but a large God who cared. That sense of the transcendent is always with us, and I think it has been narrowed today.

FIEDLER: As much as you find the church your home, you revel in the social justice traditions.

KENNEDY TOWNSEND: I love the prayers and the rituals too, the sense of the communion with other Catholics. There's something spiritual, if you go into these beautiful churches with stained glass windows. There's beauty and aesthetics to the churches. So it's not just the social gospel which I love; there's also an aesthetic pleasure to the soul.

FIEDLER: In the midst of all those pleasures, you also exhibited a certain ambivalence toward the church and some of its teachings. For example, you have chapter in the book on the Catholic Church and women, and why it has alienated so many on reproductive issues, on women's ordination, and women's leadership.

You point out that you were even being attacked when you were running for office because you were pro-choice, or what you now call pro-conscience. But you stick with the church in spite of this.

KENNEDY TOWNSEND: I do because I'm an American. And Americans stick with their country even if they disagree with their political leaders. I stick with my family even though I may disagree with them at times. And I stick with my church, because that's who I am; it's part of the sinew and blood of my being. I think the church is wrong about so much having to do with women. I think they've been outrageous in the treatment of women throughout history. I titled the chapter, "Misbegotten Males and the Devil's Gateway," because theologians used to teach that women were misbegotten males and the devil's gateway.

Saint Augustine and Thomas Aquinas, even Tertullian, really do see women only as sex objects. Either we're virgins, or we're mothers. We are not leaders, we are not thinkers; we don't have any other role. There are a lot of men who have been in charge for two thousand years, and they're afraid of women. They don't know what to make of us. They don't know how to understand us; they don't know how to comprehend us, and so they react in fear. Some open their hearts and some close themselves down. And this church, male dominated as it is, has closed itself down. But as you know, it took them 350 years to apologize to Galileo. And so a part of us has to realize that our job is to be voices to help enlighten them.

FIEDLER: And hopefully it will take less than 350 years on women's issues.

KENNEDY TOWNSEND: I think it will; I hope it will take less. I think of what we've seen with Pope Benedict. When he gave that speech in Germany about Islam, he was roundly criticized.

And he was stunned, I think. He did not understand what he was saying. He did not understand who he was as pope. And he basically changed his position. Of course, the church never acknowledges that it has changed positions. It's what they've done forever, but a month and a half later, the Pope was in Turkey praying with the imams. So he was able to change pretty quickly under public pressure.

My hope is that I will bring many progressive Catholics back into the church and we will exert the grassroots pressure on the church. Too many times, Catholics in the United States think, "We'll just leave." I want them to come back and have their voices heard. As you know, I've talked to a number of nuns, and I asked them, what is it like to be in such a church and what do you do with those bishops? And they looked at me as if to say, "What are you talking about, Kathleen? We don't pay attention to them," which is one political tactic. But I think a great political tactic is not to ignore them, but to pay attention and make them pay attention to us.

FIEDLER: And that's also going on, as you cite a number of the Catholic reform organizations in your book.

KENNEDY TOWNSEND: Yes, that's absolutely true, organizations like Voice of the Faithful and the Call to Action. There are a number of laypeople who love the church as I do, and they have said, "We're not going to wait for the hierarchy to change; we've grown up in a democratic country. We know that reform comes from the ground up, and we're going to be proponents of reform."

FIEDLER: You have what you call your pro-conscience position on abortion. This is not a lightly taken position in your case?

KENNEDY TOWNSEND: No, it isn't. I explain in the book about having grown up Catholic, having gone to Catholic schools for ten years. I was a serious church-going Catholic, and believed what my church told me. And then, when I was in college, a friend of mine had an abortion. She didn't want to tell me about it for a while, because she knew that, given my background, I would be disturbed. And when she told me, I was disturbed. I was really torn. On one hand, I had this great friend who loved social justice, who had given up a lot in her life to help others, and yet my church would be willing to condemn her.

I was trying to reconcile my brain and my heart. So I decided to write my senior thesis on abortion to understand the church's position. What I learned was very interesting. Number one, they had changed their position over the years. At one time the teaching was that the soul entered the fetus at the quickening in the third or fourth month, not at the beginning.

I thought that was interesting; that was change. And the second thing I saw over and over again is that when they did change their position, they would always change it to have the fetus live rather than the mother, which underscored my suspicion that the church did not really like women, and that women had to trust their own conscience. What strikes me is that the church's credibility on abortion would gain a lot if they allowed women to be priests and bishops. Then it wouldn't look like all the men have chosen the one sin only a woman can commit. They're telling women that they do not have the ability to make moral choices. It's amazing how difficult it is for this Catholic hierarchy to acknowledge that women have brains, and hearts, and minds, and can use them just as well as anyone.

FIEDLER: You talk a lot about the social tradition of the Catholic Church that championed the rights of workers, the rights of immigrants, that supported the minimum wage and the Civil Rights Movement.

KENNEDY TOWNSEND: What's actually interesting now is that many priests and bishops have allowed abortion to trump everything because the headlines are all about abortion. In the last presidential election, you saw the pope have his picture taken with George Bush, a person with whom he disagreed on the war.

But it turned out that abortion was more important to him. Again: condemning women rather than focusing on what is a male-dominated issue. We really have to look at the gender issues involved in the Catholic Church. The fact is that most of the people who are poor are women. Most of the people who are abused are women. And it's very hard for a church to stand up for women and yet be guilty themselves of such blatant discrimination.

FIEDLER: You also trace a similar Protestant history with the social gospel, although the Protestant history on women is somewhat different. But that great social gospel tradition existed there in the nineteenth century as well.

KENNEDY TOWNSEND: All the great social movements in our country had a religious component. Because if you believe in a great big God of justice, you believe that you have to do something to change the conditions in which we live. So in the early eighteenth century, you had the first Great Awakening. People felt that God was in them, and therefore they didn't have to pay attention to the ministers, or even to the Crown, and you had the American Revolution.

And in the Second Great Awakening, people felt that God was within them and within the black slaves, and therefore you could have an abolitionist movement. And then later, in the nineteenth century, you had the Social Gospel Movement, which asked, "What would Jesus do?" The idea being that Jesus would not tolerate the unfair working conditions, the unsafe factory conditions that people found themselves in. He would not tolerate child labor and he would have called for reform in the prisons. In other words, there is a strong tradition in the Protestant faith about how we act in the world.

FIEDLER: Martin Luther King was probably the greatest contemporary spokesperson for that movement. But you point out he's not an aberration. He's the descendant of social gospel preachers. And of course it should be said that this tradition supported women's suffrage and ordained women in many of the Protestant traditions.

How in the world do you get from this social gospel tradition to the right-wing evangelical privatized agenda of today?

KENNEDY TOWNSEND: There is still a social gospel in the mainline Protestant churches. But they have weakened because the mainline lost, in some sense, that personal relationship to Jesus. But what happened in the right-wing churches was the anti-segregation decision, *Brown vs. the Board of Education*.

Town fathers, rather than integrate the public schools, started so-called Christian academies. They decided that they would rebel against the government, because they did not want to integrate. You know, just down the road from here, in Prince Edward County, schools in Virginia were closed for seven years.

FIEDLER: And this is in the South, principally?

KENNEDY TOWNSEND: Yes, but a number of Republican operatives, Richard Viguerie and others, went to leaders like Jerry Falwell, and suggested that he belonged at the forefront of the effort to revive Republicanism in the South by getting involved in politics.

Jerry Falwell said, when he was criticizing Martin Luther King, "Ministers should be out of politics." But when the Republican Party figured out that they were going to capture the Christian Right, that's just where they went.

FIEDLER: And so it was a reaction against the Civil Rights Movement. And, to some extent, the Women's Movement as well?

KENNEDY TOWNSEND: Originally it was really the Civil Rights Movement. I think later it came out against the ERA [Equal Rights Amendment].

FIEDLER: You're also critical of the leaders of the Religious Left, because you say they've silenced themselves.

KENNEDY TOWNSEND: I tried not to criticize the Religious Left very much, because there are so few members, and we need to encourage all our friends there. But in 1980, when the Moral Majority became such a force, there were people going around saying, "We are the Immoral Minority," making fun of the idea of morality. So suddenly it wasn't cool to be religious and the Democratic Party really didn't open itself up to people of faith.

FIEDLER: Is that changing now do you think?

KENNEDY TOWNSEND: Yes, I think a number of things have changed. I think there are people like me, who are outraged at the idea that Christianity has become, in the public eye, what the Christian Right defined as Christianity. I think it's anti-Christian, because it's so anti-the-poor. I think people are really disturbed, as well they should be, about the war in Iraq. So there are voices being heard today in a way that they hadn't been before. And then there's the sheer politics of it. Candidates such as Hillary Clinton and Barack Obama are saying, "We're not going to concede anything to the Christian Right. There are religious people out there and we're going to go out and get them." So it's very exciting to see the shift that's occurring. And that's always the hope. You can't control God, but when God gets to you, she might help you look around and say things could be better.

FIEDLER: And you want to get your "big God" back.

KENNEDY TOWNSEND: And I want my big God back.

Julia Butterfly Hill

on Saving the Redwoods

Julia Butterfly Hill does not identify with any particular religious denomination, but she is one of the most "spiritual" people I have ever interviewed. She is deeply in love with the earth, determined to save the planet. She is best known for living in an ancient redwood tree named Luna from December 1997 to December 1999, near the community of Stafford, California. Her act saved the tree and its companion trees from being cut down by the Pacific Lumber Company. She is a founder of the Circle of Life, and the author of *The Legacy of Luna: The Story of a Tree, a Woman, and the Struggle to Save the Redwoods*. I interviewed her in May 2004.

MAUREEN FIEDLER: Julia, can you describe your spiritual background and upbringing? I understand that both of your parents were preachers, and I'm wondering if you yourself claim a particular spiritual or faith tradition.

JULIA BUTTERFLY HILL: Both of my parents were actually raised Catholic. In my teenage years I started to veer away from Catholicism, because of what I felt were some discrepancies in that tradition, including the fact that I saw a profound lack of respect for women, and it felt alienating and hurtful to me growing up.

At first, I thought I no longer believed in God. But then I realized, I was angry at God and you can't be angry at something you don't believe in. That realization sent me on a spiritual journey to find what I really believe in. And now, I don't adhere to a particular faith-based tradition. For me, spirituality is not only a way of life, it *is* my life. It is something that I hold myself accountable to with every thought, word, and action. It's the very thread of the fabric of my existence. I feel that without it, I am not walking with integrity and being with integrity in the world.

FIEDLER: How do you name that which is holy for you?

BUTTERFLY HILL: I call it the Universal Spirit. And I call it that because one of the things that I realized while in the tree is that when I pray, it's about deep questioning, and I believe very strongly in deep questioning. Jesus encouraged all of his followers to deep question everything, including him. And somehow we get conditioned over time to deep question only certain things, and to silently agree with other things, even if our hearts might be asking us to question. And so I started questioning in the tree through my prayers. And in those prayers, I started realizing that I was receiving answers from so many different places, from the trees, from exchanges with animals, from people. And that's when I started calling it the Universal Spirit. I realized this divine is within all life. And as such, if we pray to that essence, to that spirit, to that sacred source, then the answers can come from all parts of life.

FIEDLER: What's an example of a deep question?

BUTTERFLY HILL: There are many jokes in my family about me. And one of them is that when I was born, my first cry was—"Why?" And I've been questioning things every since. And I think many people know of children who would ask a question of a parent or an elder, and would be given an answer, and then ask why. And then be given an answer to that, and ask why again. Deep questioning is about asking a question and then just because the answer comes, not taking that answer as fact, as solid truth, without doing a little more questioning.

In doing this work, I am asked a lot of questions all the time. And I do my best to answer them, but if I don't feel I've done enough questioning myself to know that my answer comes from a solid place, I'll say, "That's a great question, but I still have learning to do before I can answer." And those topics include deforestation, global warming, the prison industrial complex, the war.

I do not want to ask questions only of the people who think like me, but I also ask questions of people who wouldn't seem likely allies. Getting answers from diverse perspectives can help find a solution that will include as many of us as possible, in a healthier and more just world for all.

FIEDLER: What's the place of human beings in the midst of creation?

BUTTERFLY HILL: I think our challenge has been that we forget that we are just another species on this planet. And so we set ourselves apart and separate from the rest of creation. And one of the things I feel is that all of the issues facing our world are symptoms of one disease; I call that disease "separation syndrome," because when you're separated from something, you can destroy it. When you are connected to people or the planet, it's more difficult to destroy it. I feel that that disease of separation has led us to a point where we think we can manage nature. We think we are here to do with the planet as we will. And the reality is that because of that separation syndrome, we have become part of a disease that is eating us alive from the inside out. It is destroying communities, it's destroying air and water quality, it's destroying souls, and spirits, and hearts, and minds of people. And so much of our Western culture perpetuates separation that our challenge is to find ways to reconnect. And that is a very big challenge because it means swimming upstream. And we have to find the courage to swim upstream in very challenging times, and find new and creative, heartfelt and spirit-felt ways of connecting once again with the earth and with each other.

FIEDLER: And so your time in Luna was your time for reconnecting with the earth?

BUTTERFLY HILL: I feel that very deeply. I didn't go into the tree expecting to have a deep spiritual epiphany. I climbed into the tree only because it was all I could think of to do. I grew up with two brothers and no sisters, so I've climbed trees my whole life. And when I found out that over 97 percent of these original redwoods were already gone and that we're continuing to cut them down to this day in horrifically devastating and polluting ways, my heart compelled me to action. So when I found out that people were sitting in trees in order to protect them, I thought, "That's something I could do; I know how to sit in trees."

FIEDLER: And so essentially the tree drew you into a deeper spirituality?

BUTTERFLY HILL: Living in a tree during the worst winter in the recorded history of California, subjected to a company trying to destroy me with helicopters, and suffering sleep and food depravation, there were moments when I was literally in the fetal position and crying, and begging for help. I asked the creator, "Okay what did I do to deserve this? I'm sorry for whatever I did; whatever karma I'm having to work off, I apologize."

And then I realized that I was asking for strength, and that the universe said, "Fine, the way to strength is through challenges." And so it taught me that the power of prayer is phenomenal, but we also have to be willing to receive the answers. The blessing of having this experience while living in an ancient, ancient elder connected me to a deeper spiritual path than I ever could've imagined.

~~~~~~

Kim Bobo

on Defending the Rights of Working People

Workers' rights are central to movements for social justice. Today, Kim Bobo is the executive director of the National Interfaith Committee for Worker Justice. Before that, she was the organizing director of Bread for the World. She was raised in the evangelical Christian tradition. I interviewed her in June 2003.

MAUREEN FIEDLER: Kim, some people would say, "Look, these are economic issues. Why should people of faith be involved with issues having to do with workers and unions?"

KIM BOBO: The scriptures from all traditions are very clear about the requirement to help people in need, to help the least of these. And the labor movement is a vehicle, a way to help low-wage workers in this country.

FIEDLER: When was the Interfaith Committee for Worker Justice founded?

BOBO: The National Committee was founded in 1996, although it grew out of work developing a local group in Chicago in 1991.

FIEDLER: And are you truly interfaith? In other words, do you go beyond Christian denominations?

BOBO: Absolutely! We have very strong involvement from the Jewish community, and increasingly strong involvement from the Muslim community. In addition, we've also had some Buddhist and some Hindu involvement.

FIEDLER: Who funds the Interfaith Committee?

BOBO: At this point, the bulk of our funding is from foundations. But we do get strong support from the religious community, from denominations, from religious orders. We get some money from labor unions, and money from individuals.

FIEDLER: About what percent comes from labor unions?

BOBO: It varies between 10 and 15 percent, and the religious communities' support is about the same.

FIEDLER: So no one could say that you're providing a religious veneer for the agenda of the labor movement in this country based on your funding.

BOBO: That's right; that's just silly. And while we want to foster strong partnerships with the labor movement—because if you want to work with working people, you need to be in partnership with the labor movement—it doesn't mean that we do everything labor tells us, nor do we think labor is perfect. In fact, we believe that the labor union movement is frankly a lot like the religious community. It's composed of people who have high values, and often don't live up to those values.

FIEDLER: In general, what kind of projects do you sponsor?

BOBO: We're involved in a whole range of things. In a number of communities we're building worker centers, which are really drop-in centers primarily for immigrant workers, but for other low-wage workers as well. We're organizing courses to teach workers their rights in the workplace, to explain to them what unions are and to hook them up with unions if they're interested. And for those people who have problems in the workplace, we work with them to find ways to address those problems.

Sometimes we file complaints with the Department of Labor, or OSHA, or EEOC, and we have some terrific partnerships with government agencies to help us on this. Sometimes we work with some pro-bono attorneys to file lawsuits. And sometimes we take groups of workers and clergy to meet with employers to ask them why they're not paying people according to the law. And we get direct action and people get paid. Another thing we're doing is educating workers about their right to join a union without being fired, and without being harassed.

Right now in this country, over 80 percent of employers hire a firm to help them fight unions in the workplace to intimidate workers, and we think that's wrong. These are union busters. It's a big business in this country.

FIEDLER: How do you engage the clergy in this work?

BOBO: We do it a lot through workers. We'll get workers who come to us and we'll ask, "What current issue are you involved in?" When they tell us, we ask how they would feel if we help set up a meeting with their clergy. So together we educate their clergy, and involve them in these struggles.

FIEDLER: Do you ever encourage them to preach on labor issues, the clergy?

BOBO: Absolutely; we have a very wide program around Labor Day, called Labor in the Pulpit, where about 130 cities participate, where workers and labor union leaders speak in congregations.

FIEDLER: I noticed on your website that you have a special interest in poultry workers.

BOBO: Poultry is an area where we've heard numerous complaints. In fact, I was on the phone this morning, talking with one of our contacts in the Delaware area. She told me that she had talked to a worker in a poultry plant who wasn't allowed to get off the poultry line to go to the bathroom. So she urinated on herself, and when she did that, they fired her. This happens all the time in poultry plants.

FIEDLER: What would you do for this woman?

BOBO: She organized a group of clergy in the community and they went down to the plant and met with the manager. And they held a little demonstration and then insisted that he rehire this worker.

FIEDLER: And did he?

BOBO: Not yet. Although when I was talking to her on the phone, I suggested that OSHA may be able to help because it is against OSHA regulations to prevent people from going to the bathroom.

FIEDLER: I know that you challenge religious institutions. What are some of those challenges?

BOBO: This is probably the hardest part of our work. And frankly I find it most discouraging to realize that some of our religious institutions who do terrific work in terms of providing charity and reaching out to low income people will hire union busters and intimidate workers when they try and organize unions. This applies to Catholic, Lutheran, and Methodist organizations. It's multi-denominational.

FIEDLER: And what do you do about it?

BOBO: I go the extra mile with a religious institution. We try to have some sort of conversation, send a letter, or question what's going on. But frankly that seldom does anything. And at that point, we try to involve other area religious groups to encourage them to make changes in their policy.

FIEDLER: Is it ever in order to report them to the authorities, or to even initiate a lawsuit?

BOBO: If they are violating the law, yes. That's well within what we would do.

FIEDLER: Sometimes you also challenge unions; how do you do that?

Bobo: Unions have a history of operating in isolation from allies in the community. The first instinct of labor is to wait until the last minute of a crisis to call and say, "We need you to pray on the picket line." So we're also challenging labor to think about what's going on, to say that we've got to plan together. We can't be called at the last minute to pray on a picket line.

A second area of challenge is to encourage labor to talk in language that reaches out to broad numbers of people. When you're talking with low-wage workers in very harsh working conditions, the epitome of oppression and the evil that they experience is the boss. So what develops is a kind of anti-boss language. But I think that is not effective language for reaching out to people in general. We have to talk about the broader vision of a just society and fair wages.

Fiedler: What struggles lie ahead? Where is your movement going?

Bobo: One of our struggles is with the fact that we don't have an immigration reform package in this country, and the worst exploitation across the nation is the exploitation of immigrant workers. And part of the reason they can be exploited is because there's no way for them to become citizens.

Fiedler: Do you work with a lot of undocumented workers?

Bobo: Lots, in every rural area and every urban area. You can't work on worker issues and not be quickly drawn into immigration issues.

Fiedler: And do you collaborate fairly openly with the AFL-CIO?

Bobo: We partner with them whenever it makes sense for us and for them. In fact, one of the programs we're running this summer is a joint program called Seminary Summer, where we recruit seminary and rabbinical students, do some training, and place them in positions where they work directly for unions as their summer internship.

Fiedler: What other issues are on the horizon? What's coming up as you look ahead?

Bobo: In the public policy area, there's a bill in Congress called the Employee Free Choice Act. The bill would make it easier for workers in this country to organize a union without being fired and harassed. That kind of harassment is wrong. There's a fundamental right to organize. It's a human right.

Bishop Margaret Payne

on Seeking Peace and Human Rights in the Middle East

Margaret Payne is the bishop of the New England Synod of the Evangelical Lutheran Church in America, the largest Lutheran denomination in North America. She is both a denominational leader and a leading advocate for justice and peace, with a particular focus on the Middle East and the plight of Palestinians. There are many Palestinian Lutherans, and this interview took place after she visited them as part of a theological study retreat with other Lutheran bishops. This interview took place in March 2009.

MAUREEN FIEDLER: You were, I believe, one of fifty-nine bishops from the Lutheran Church who visited Israel, Jordan, and Palestine this January. What was the purpose of the visit?

MARGARET PAYNE: We have a longstanding relationship with the Palestinian Lutheran Church. This trip represented a strong commitment to walk with the Christians of Palestine, to accompany them and learn about their lives there. We also wanted to become more aware of what we call the facts on the ground, the reality of life for Palestinians and for everyone in the Middle East. That reality is not often very well communicated here. And then we returned to advocate for peace and justice in ways that we feel are important.

FIEDLER: I know this was not your first trip to the Holy Land. In fact, you've been there on several occasions. Why are you especially interested in this part of the world?

PAYNE: My interest began when I was first was elected bishop in 2000 and immediately traveled to the Holy Land, because we have what we call a "companion synod relationship" with the Lutheran Church there. The first time I went, I was astonished at the depth of the experience from a religious point of view. I encountered a reality that I had never really understood before about the lives of the Palestinian people there.

FIEDLER: On this trip, what did you learn about day-to-day life in those regions? Did anything surprise you?

PAYNE: I was surprised by a troubling, growing awareness of how much worse the situation is getting in daily life for the Palestinian people. The building of the wall, the separation barrier, limits their movement and causes daily harassment and humiliation. In fact it cuts them off from work, family, and even medical care. And things are getting more and more restricted for them. Each time we go, and especially on this trip, we witnessed many examples of that kind of restriction and the pain that it's causing.

FIEDLER: Can you give an example of something you saw?

PAYNE: We visited the Augusta Victoria Hospital, which is a hospital of the Lutheran World Federation. It's on the Mount of Olives. It's the only hospital in the country that provides cancer care and dialysis for Palestinians. But there are checkpoints between the hospital and the patients, and the doctors. Doctors have been held up for as long as eight hours or more when they were trying to get to the hospital to treat a patient. In fact, a man, a member of one of our Lutheran congregations, died of a heart attack at a checkpoint. He had been trying to get to the hospital. These kinds of instances rarely get reported, but are a daily fact of life for the Palestinian people.

FIEDLER: When you're talking about the Palestinians, you're talking about the West Bank, not about Gaza, where the recent war was, is that right?

PAYNE: Yes. My experience has been in the West Bank; I haven't traveled to Gaza. But in the West Bank the separation wall has intruded far into Palestinian territory; it's not on the border. And so it has cut apart Palestinian communities, and demolished houses, and divided people from their work and family.

FIEDLER: What would you say to the Israelis who claim that the separation barrier has prevented suicide bombers and other terrorists from entering Israel?

PAYNE: It's true that the wall has provided some protection against suicide bombers, and it is the position of our church and all the people that I know who traveled there that we are all adamantly opposed to violence against the Israeli people. But in reality, the location of the wall does more than just provide security. It also ruins, disrupts, and cuts apart Palestinian territory, where there is not a border between Israel and Palestine. So there really is not a reason for the wall to be there. For example, there is a thirty-foot concrete wall that completely surrounds the city of Bethlehem. The only way you can get into Bethlehem is through a checkpoint. Some tour buses still come in, stop for a half an hour at the Church of the Nativity, the site of Jesus' birth, and then go right back out again. So the people who come as tourists don't have a chance to shop and support the economy, and they don't have a chance to experience the vibrant life of the real people who live there.

FIEDLER: You were there in January during the war in Gaza, when Hamas, which of course is the party that controls Gaza, sent rockets into villages in southern Israel. And Israel, in response, bombed and invaded Gaza. Why did that happen?

PAYNE: We felt fortunate that we were able to be there during that time. Although it seemed like a dangerous time to travel, it was important to be there in solidarity with the Palestinian people. We were in the West Bank and not in Gaza, so we were not near the violence, but we talked with many Palestinians who had friends and relatives there. And their biggest concern was that the attack on Gaza was so out of proportion to the Hamas rockets. Those rockets had been going on for quite a few years. A number of people had been killed, but it was a small number.

The Israeli response killed a couple of thousand people, and left many injured and suffering. No medical aid was allowed in. And so, although we agree that retaliation should be allowed when there is a situation of violence, it seemed as though the disproportionate response, and the occupation and shutting off all the borders for humanitarian care, was way beyond what would be appropriate in a situation where it truly was a security issue.

FIEDLER: You are nonetheless critical of Hamas for sending the rockets into Israel?

PAYNE: We do not support any of the violence that Hamas uses against the Israeli people, and we think it should stop; there's no doubt about that. But we believe that the ultimate peace and security of Israel will not come with the attacks that have begun to take place, but rather with diplomacy and work toward a truly viable two-state solution that will provide security in the whole Middle East, not just the small area of Gaza and Israel.

FIEDLER: I'm wondering what you heard from Israelis about the war? Was it different from what you heard from Palestinians?

PAYNE: We found a wide range of opinion from very defensive and determined, saying that all of the actions were critical for the security of Israel, to other people who deeply love Israel questioning what the right path is to find security and safety, to live at peace with their neighbors.

FIEDLER: I understand there's a much more robust debate within Israel itself over these questions than there is here in the United States.

PAYNE: There is a debate in Israel. I think one of the biggest problems for us in this country is that we really do not get full communication and the whole picture, communication that would lead us to a well informed opinion about the truth of the situation, and what could be done moving forward.

FIEDLER: Many observers of the region say that one of the major barriers to a viable peace is the increasing number of Israeli settlements in the West Bank. How do you view the settlements?

PAYNE: I would agree that that's a major problem; the settlements are all illegal under international law, and some of them are even illegal under Israeli law. I find it enormously frustrating that international law is not being supported or enforced by countries around the world. And so the settlements are continuing to grow.

The settlements sound kind of like the Wild West. And it really is, in some cases. They're in rural areas, but sometimes they're in Palestinian territory, becoming more and more integrated with the land. So it seems almost impossible to try to disassemble them—to come to a place where we say, "Yes, settlements are illegal and now they have to go away." And that's one of the fears that the Palestinian people have.

On one of my previous trips, I visited a village in Hebron, where Palestinian land had been taken to develop a settlement, diverting all the water from the villages. And then, the settlers also began to interfere with the life of the Palestinian people outside the settlement. People from the settlement were attacking children on the way to school, in an effort to continue to expel the Palestinians from the land that they wanted. The settlements are much more than the subject of an academic debate.

FIEDLER: I'm wondering if religion plays a partial role in these settlements, one that we don't often hear about. I've heard some people say that settlers, in many of those areas, might be described as Jewish fundamentalists. We hear a lot about Muslim fundamentalists, Christian fundamentalists. What is your experience of Jewish fundamentalists who want to reclaim the West Bank for Israel?

PAYNE: There are many different kinds of settlers, and I think it is true that some of them are completely committed to regaining all of that land for Israel. I believe other people are more secular. It's really important for us in our work to differentiate between people of the Jewish faith and the actions of the Israeli government. When the two get mixed up, we combine political views with a long history, which is why anti-Semitism has been, and still continues to be, present in the world. And as the Lutheran Church, we really do want to oppose that and support the rights of the Jewish people to exist, to worship, and to have their own land. But that's different from what's going on in the settlements, with a wide range of different kinds of people with different kinds of reasons for being there. And the end result is that the Palestinian people are suffering, but there's no one person or group that can be blamed.

FIEDLER: I understand that the Lutheran Church is rethinking its investments in the region as well. Do you know what's been proposed, and if that might include divestment, that is, withdrawing money from groups that support Israel?

PAYNE: Our church does not have a policy of divestment. We invest in the places that we think are most valuable and most helpful for the sake of justice and peace, so we have a policy of active investment in the Palestinian economy. But we do not have plans to participate in any kind of divestment from companies that do business in Israel.

FIEDLER: Looking forward, do you see any way to a viable two-state solution to bring peace to this troubled area?

PAYNE: I'm glad you used the adjective "viable." Because a two-state solution sounds like it will make everybody happy. But the reality of what's going on is that Palestinian land is increasingly depleted and isolated. If you look at a map of the West Bank, it looks like a piece of Swiss cheese, because the Palestinian land has been isolated into small areas. These areas are surrounded by roads the Palestinians aren't allowed to drive on. The diversion of water and other infringements on human rights make it impossible to have a viable state, unless there are some radical changes.

FIEDLER: Someone who has put forward a point of view that sounds a bit like yours is former president Jimmy Carter. How do you view his work and his viewpoints?

PAYNE: First of all, I admire the man enormously. I think he's dedicated his life, perhaps even after his presidency more so than during it, to be a person who reveals the truth all over the world and says exactly what he thinks. His latest book was very controversial, because he compared the situation to apartheid.

He got a lot of criticism for that. But I think it is wonderful when people invite controversy, and make people wonder what the truth really is, and encourage them to look into any given subject more deeply. And so I admire the fact that he is working hard to seek to make the truth be told. Whether or not his analogy is right is unclear to me, but I greatly appreciate the fact that he's created more opportunity for discussion.

FIEDLER: If you had the opportunity, what advice would you give to the Obama administration, to Secretary of State Hillary Clinton, to promote peace in the region?

PAYNE: The only way to move forward is to end the occupation of the Palestinian territory. But along with that does *not* come a greater danger for Israel. What will come instead is the peace and security that both countries want and need. And so the end of the occupation is the answer to everything. Humanitarian aid is helpful, but it's not the answer. Understanding the facts won't change them. I believe that ending the occupation is the one way both countries really can get what everyone wants, which are lives that have peace and meaning.

FIEDLER: But the United States can't end the occupation; the State of Israel will have to do that. What should the United States do to push Israel in that direction?

PAYNE: The United States government has more clout with the State of Israel than any other entity in the world. The United States can bring the facts to the table, and encourage the pursuit of all the options. There just has to be honest strategizing—and a willingness to talk about peace.

Leymah Gbowee and Abigail Disney

on Christian and Muslim Women in Liberia,
Pray the Devil Back to Hell

Women leaders often create new grassroots movements for justice and peace. They discover leadership talent they never knew they had. Such was the case of Leymah Gbowee, a leader of the Christian and Muslim women in Liberia who came together to pray publicly, to take nonviolent direct action, to end their country's bloody civil war and the rule of the infamous dictator, Charles Taylor. These women succeeded, and in the process, formed a grassroots movement that helped put in office Africa's first democratically elected woman president, Ellen Johnson Sirleaf.

But when peace finally came, no major news outlet was there to cover the story of the women and their movement. Enter Abigail Disney, who produced a film about these women called *Pray the Devil Back to Hell*.

Leymah Gbowee has won the Gruber Women's Rights Prize, the Living Legends Award, and the Profile in Courage Award from the John F. Kennedy Foundation.

I interviewed Leymah Gbowee and Abigail Disney in November 2009.

MAUREEN FIEDLER: Leymah, as you watched your country slip into a bloody civil war in the 1990s, you brought together the women in your church to pray for peace. But some people would say, "Prayer is fine, but it is a very weak response to war." How would you respond to that kind of skepticism?

LEYMAH GBOWEE: Prayer is definitely *not* a weak response to war. Prayer, for me, is the strongest thing you can use. I saw it work in my own life during the crisis. Prayer was the thing that kept us going. There is no way anyone can survive peace activism in the midst of war without belief in a higher power. That is a solid conclusion I take from my experience.

FIEDLER: What exactly were you praying about, or protesting, in your movement?

GBOWEE: We had three basic concerns. One, we needed an end to this war. Fourteen years was enough. Two, we had no confidence in the ability of the government or the rebels to provide security for us as a nation, specifically for us as women. So we were praying also for the intervention of an international peacekeeping force.

And three, conflict cannot be solved by the barrel of the gun. And so we wanted a dialogue among all of the warring factions to chart the course for Liberia's future.

FIEDLER: You grew a huge nonviolent movement of women. And later, it wasn't just Christian women, but you came together with your Muslim sisters in Liberia and asked them to join. Was it difficult to build that alliance?

GBOWEE: Initially, it was. We had to do a lot of re-socialization and dialogue, to come to an understanding. We had to deal with the misconceptions, the prejudices and stereotypes that each group had about the other. It took us about two years to solidify the relationship between these groups. But even at that, at some point, the most difficult groups were often Christian women who brought their quotations from the Bible. At one point, we had a whole contingent of women from charismatic churches who felt that we were diluting their faith; it was not biblical to be praying alongside Muslim women. So it was really, really difficult.

FIEDLER: But you overcame that?

GBOWEE: Oh, definitely, because at the end of the day, we used our womanhood to unite us, and not to divide us. We had issues of faith, but also we had issues affecting all of us that cut across faith or ethnic lines.

FIEDLER: During this war, there were child soldiers, there was rape, and there was horrific violence. And you all prayed together, not privately, but publicly, right?

GBOWEE: We prayed together publicly. As a matter of fact, we pray together to this day, and some of the Christian women can now recite the Muslim prayers and Muslim women can recite the Lord's Prayer.

FIEDLER: Abigail, you document all this in *Pray the Devil Back to Hell*. Can you briefly describe the conflict, the civil war, in Liberia?

ABIGAIL DISNEY: Liberia had suffered 150 years of grotesque injustice. Tensions had built between ethnic groups, and the haves and have-nots. And in 1979 that burst in a coup that was destabilizing enough to lead to a whole series of power grabs. And unfortunately by the early 2000s you had many different groups who had an equal amount of power, and there was a conflict that looked like it was never going to end.

FIEDLER: Charles Taylor led one of those groups. This was the country where you had child soldiers, amputations—I believe—of the limbs of even small children, and horrible rape.

DISNEY: Yes, and a lot of the horrible things that we associate with modern conflict actually started with the colonial powers. But nevertheless, in this conflict, rubber, timber, and diamonds were all being actively and directly traded for weapons. Charles Taylor recruited child soldiers, because they're ideal soldiers once you've separated them from their families. And the weapons have gotten lighter, so it's easier for children to use them. Terrorizing civilian populations was the object of the battle, not the side effect. It was a way of creating a smoke screen behind which you can pull all these resources out of the earth and amass fortunes.

FIEDLER: How, in the end, from your perspective, as a producer, did the women achieve their goal? Some of them even traveled to Accra, Ghana for the peace talks, didn't they?

DISNEY: Yes, I think that they were incredibly strategic and smart. Once they had achieved their goal of persuading people to go to the peace talks, they didn't sit back and say, "OK, we've done the job." They understood that they had to go there and hold people's feet to the fire. A group of women, including Leymah, went to a refugee camp in Accra, where they organized the women there and brought them to the peace talks. They prayed, they sang, and fasted together.

FIEDLER: And there was a point, was there not, when the peace talks broke down? What did the women do then?

DISNEY: It was really an incredible moment in the history of nonviolent resistance. The women surrounded the building, they locked arms, and they sent a note inside saying, "We're taking you all hostage on behalf of the women of Liberia." And security came to arrest them, saying, "We're arresting you, Leymah, for obstructing justice."

As then Leymah says in the film, "I heard those words, and I just lost it." The word "justice" is an important word in any faith, but particularly in the Abrahamic religions. When she heard that word misused in that way it really did set her off, and she started to strip naked! They refused to arrest her. And so the tables were turned. It's classic nonviolence. One person has all the power until something small shifts, and the power shifts to the other side

FIEDLER: You really tried to strip naked, Leymah?

GBOWEE: Oh, yes. At that moment, it was life or death, not just death of our physical bodies, but death for the souls of our children and so I had come to the point where I had to fight against the misuse of the word, "justice." What I was saying was that people were destroying each other for selfish gains.

FIEDLER: And so, as a result of your actions, they went back to the peace talks?

GBOWEE: The peace talks became more focused. All of the merrymaking ceased.

FIEDLER: Abigail, the interesting thing is that these women were successful. The peace talks ended, in fact, in an accord, and ultimately led to the ouster of Charles Taylor as the dictator of Liberia. But no major media outlet covered the pivotal role of these women in the peace agreement. Why was this ignored?

DISNEY: I think there's a complex cocktail of reasons that go into it. Historically, there have not been many women in leadership positions, so we tend not to acknowledge that they look like leaders or like serious people. They don't look like George Washington. They don't look like Napoleon Bonaparte. So how can they possibly matter?

FIEDLER: They don't even look like Nelson Mandela!

DISNEY: Right, exactly. War is a man's realm. It's a completely masculine thing. The women didn't speak in the language of politics; they always took a stance that was *above* politics. I think that if you are a stringer or a news photographer or a journalist, it's hard to recognize history.

And they were making history, speaking outside the accepted vocabulary, and clinging to a moral discourse. I think the tendency is to dismiss that as irrelevant or impertinent or immature. And ultimately, I think that's why news sources tended to ignore the women.

FIEDLER: And when they actually did their public prayer by the thousands in the streets of Liberia, how did the culture react to them?

DISNEY: Locally, there was an enormous sense of relief that the women were stepping up. Some of the economic support that they got for that was from people inside the Taylor government, who, under cover of night, would show up and hand them a paper bag full of money.

For a lot of people in the government, this was the only way out. A man could not simply choose not to participate any more. There were really no options left. And the women were offering everyone a way out.

As we shot this film, we told people why we were there and people wanted to help, "What can I do for you? We'll do anything for the Women in White." There was a huge sense of gratitude.

FIEDLER: Abigail, why did you decide to do the movie?

DISNEY: I inherited a little bit of a story gene from my family, who made a lot of films. When I heard this story I knew it was really cinematic and hopeful. It was such an unusual story, a good-news story, a story of people succeeding in their fight for a change. I thought, if I stick my neck out in this way, I hope someone does me the courtesy of remembering what I have done.

FIEDLER: Liberia now has a woman president, Ellen John Sirleaf. She's the first woman democratically elected president of any nation in Africa. Did the movement of these women help bolster her chances for election?

DISNEY: I think there's no question about it. Leymah has a great line in the film: "There's no way the history of President Sirleaf could have been written without the history of the women. We were the cake; and she was the icing!" I love that! The women really got out there and pounded the pavement. They encouraged women to come out and vote. And one of the women says—and this line really curls my toes—"We campaigned in the night. We campaigned until we forgot we could be raped." It's an incredible line; it really jolts you back to the memory of exactly what it is they were up against.*

---

* To order the DVD of this movie, visit the website: PraytheDeviltoHell.com.

Chapter 7
Women Leaders in Interfaith Relations

A robust movement to forge collaborative interfaith relations is relatively recent, and it gained new importance after the attacks of September 11, 2001.

Before and since 9-11, many leaders of this movement in the United States and the world at large have been women. Some are prominent academics, like Karen Armstrong, an internationally acclaimed author of numerous books, including *The Battle for God: Fundamentalism in Judaism, Christianity and Islam*. In 2009, she launched her new Charter for Compassion, a document that is the product of her international and interfaith leadership. It names and promotes compassion as the core moral value of the world's faith traditions. Diana Eck directs the Pluralism Project at Harvard University, a program that is considered "the" source of information on interfaith activities in the United States. Others, like Susanna Heschel, the daughter of Rabbi Abraham Joshua Heschel—the rabbi who marched with Martin Luther King—follow the legacy of their forebears but take it in new directions.

Some are drawn to interfaith work by life experiences. Such is the Muslim woman, Asra Nomani, who was a journalist, colleague, and friend of Danny Pearl, murdered in Pakistan in 2002 in part because he was Jewish. Asra—whose story is told in the chapter on religious activists—has been active in seeking justice for Pearl, and in promoting positive Muslim/Jewish relations.

Women like Mary Heléne Rosenbaum deal with specific issues such as interfaith marriage, and still others like Ranya Idliby, Suzanne Oliver, and Priscilla Warner are grassroots women who launched interfaith dialogues in their living rooms—and then wrote a book to turn their dialogue experience into a nationwide movement.

At the local and regional level, thousands of women are members of councils and conferences, promoting interfaith cooperation through organizations like the Interfaith Alliance, the United Religions Initiative, and the Council for a Parliament of World Religions, or Religions for Peace.

Diana Eck

on *A New Religious America*

Perhaps no American interfaith leader is better known than Diana Eck, who founded and directs the Pluralism Project at Harvard University. She is the author of the key book documenting the growth of religious diversity in the United States: *A New Religious America: How a "Christian Country" Has Become the World's Most Religiously Diverse Nation*. I've talked to Diana Eck several times, but her presidential speech to the American Academy of Religion brought the often esoteric world of interfaith relations down to earth with concrete stories. The following extracts of that speech, which we aired on *Interfaith Voices*, illustrate how diverse we have become as a nation.

DIANA ECK: A North American Christian or Jew has a Hindu surgeon, a Buddhist co-worker, a Sikh roommate, a Muslim congressman. These are facts on the ground that require rethinking our understanding of the religious other.

In 1993, a Methodist church and an Islamic society in Freemont, California bought adjoining property, named their frontage road "Peace Terrace" and broke ground together. Then what happened? How are these communities related to one another over the years beyond landscaping and allocating parking? What happened when Christmas Eve and a Ramadan evening coincided? What happened after 9-11? What insights do these collaborations give us into new patterns of American religious life? And does it matter?

This East Bay city gives us much to think about. Its India Day parade attracts tens of thousands of people to downtown Freemont.

When the Sikh gurdwara was built on Hillside Terrace a decade ago, the Sikhs petitioned the city council to rename that street Gurdwara Road. "But I can't even pronounce Gurdwara," said a fellow citizen at the town hall meeting. "Well, I cannot pronounce the Paseo Padre Parkway," said a member of the Sikh community.

A few years later, the Freemont police chief was invited to the gurdwara and made an honorary Sikh with the presentation of a sword. The mayor of Freemont made sure that Muslims had a place to pray in the city hall during a town meeting and a Hindu woman was recently re-elected to the city council.

Freemont is fifty years old this year, celebrating its multicultural civic life with a hands-around-the-lake enactment in September. But just two weeks ago, an Afghan Muslim woman wearing hijab was shot and killed in a residential area while walking to school to pick up her children, her three-year-old in tow. And just last Monday, Freemont citizens organized a day in response to the violence in which hundreds of citizens wore head gear, hijabs or turbans, in public response.

My point is that we in the American Academy of Religion should be paying sustained attention to the Freemonts of America. What must catch our eye are not simply the mega-churches, important as they are, but these very micro-histories of hundreds of smaller religious communities and civic communities where America's prospects for pluralism are being worked out on the ground every day.

This fall, the Harvard Hindu community consecrated its first ever architecturally designed prayer space. On Yom Kippur, the Jewish day of fasting, Jewish students who had been fasting gathered for *iftar*, the meal that breaks the Muslim fast on the days of Ramadan, with members of the Harvard Islamic society who had also been fasting. And the next week, during Sukkot, the Jewish students invited the Muslims to an iftar in the *sukkot*, or tent. For more than a year a student group called JAM (Jews and Muslims) has met for a weekly discussion group.

A Presbyterian woman, Betsy Wiggins, brooded about rumors that Muslim women in Syracuse, New York were feeling unsafe in their homes. She invited one of the women from a local Islamic center for coffee in her kitchen. Each invited nine friends to another meeting, and the group, Women Transcending Boundaries, was born. The group kept meeting and growing, taking hold of critical issues, including the alarming arrest of local Muslims in upstate New York. With the impending war in Iraq, and their own life-cycle issues, they looked beyond Syracuse as well, linking their local concerns internationally to women around the world, raising money for a school in Pakistan, for example.

In Dearborn, Michigan, the Ford Motor Company has become convinced that pluralism is a workplace issue. And for some 350,000 people employed by Ford at a hundred plants around the world, they have created an interfaith network as an employee resource network to steer into the issues of religious diversity in the workplace. Their mission is to assist Ford Motor Company in becoming a worldwide corporate leader in promoting religious tolerance, corporate integrity, and human dignity. As one official said, "It's the right thing to do, and it's good for business."

What is at stake in the many highly contentious symbolic public controversies? In the Ten Commandments case, for example, what is at stake is not primarily Christian respect for the Ten Commandments, but Christian claims to public space. When Chief Justice Roy Moore in Alabama was challenged for installing a two-and-a-half ton monument of the Ten Commandments in the federal courthouse, he said, "We need to reclaim our biblical heritage." Well, which "we" is he invoking here exactly? Surely not "we the people of the United States of America." Are we a Christian nation? A Judeo-Christian-Muslim nation? A secular nation? A nation in which freedom of conscience is guaranteed for everyone, including everyone who is not religious? These are the issues.

As minorities become more visible, they also become more vulnerable. For example, even in 2006 an almost completed Hindu temple in Minneapolis in Maple Grove was vandalized, its sacred images smashed, followed by the uprooting of the flagpole and the burning of the Sikh flag at a gurdwara in South Salem, Oregon in July. Bullets were shot through the front door of a mosque in Michigan City, Indiana in July.

The public response to those issues of vandalism or violence has been to assert that that's *not* who we are in Maple Grove. Six hundred concerned citizens attended a public forum a week after the vandalism of the Hindu temple. The temple community worked hard to clean up the mess, and go ahead with the project. The nineteen-year-old vandals were apprehended. They were invited for a meeting at the temple. The temple representative said, "They're suffering as much, if not more, than we are." And when the young men were brought to court for sentencing, the representatives of the Hindu temple interceded with the judge for lighter sentences. Indeed, in their sentence was a course on Hinduism and two-hundred hours of community service.

MAUREEN FIEDLER: Religious pluralism is not just an American concern but a global issue, Dr. Eck concluded. Not long before, she had visited Indonesia at a time when some Muslim clerics had issued a *fatwa* [decree] denouncing religious pluralism, but that fatwa spawned debate and dissent within Indonesian society. She quoted from an editorial in the Indonesian newspaper, the *Jakarta Post*.

ECK: "We all need to build the bridges that somehow connect us in spite of our differences. If we want to go one step beyond unity and diversity, pluralism is the way forward." I could not have said it clearer or better.

Mary Heléne Rosenbaum
on the Challenges of Interfaith Marriage

Nothing challenges the ideals of interfaith relations more intimately than the issues raised by interfaith marriages. A few years ago, I came across Mary Heléne Rosenbaum, a leader in this field through the Dovetail Institute, which she founded with her husband. She counsels interfaith couples, and writes and speaks on the subject with a remarkable clarity that comes from her own experience. She is Catholic; her husband is Jewish. She is the co-author, with her husband, of *Celebrating Our Differences: Living Two Faiths in One Marriage.*

She lives in Louisville, Kentucky. This interview was broadcast in April 2006.

MAUREEN FIEDLER: Mary, first of all, what would you consider the most common challenges faced by interfaith couples today?

MARY HELÉNE ROSENBAUM: They mostly involve having to think about things that other people don't think about. If you're married to a person of your same faith, you can just slide into whatever practices you're used to. An interfaith couple has to consider almost everything they do in the light of their religious difference.

FIEDLER: So therefore they have to come out of themselves and listen to each other, maybe more deeply than a couple with the same faith tradition has to do?

ROSENBAUM: That's right. And they also have to look into their own hearts and see what their faith means to them, to what extent it is an identity with the community, and to what extent is it a belief, a set of propositions. There's also the challenge of sorting a religious question from some things it may be masking, like control issues. Is this really about my religion or is it about me getting my own way?

FIEDLER: Do most couples these days have the foresight to talk about interfaith issues before they get married?

ROSENBAUM: Yes, we find that, especially as intermarriages become more common, people do talk about them. And there are two possible pitfalls. They'll say either, "Oh, it will all work out one way or another," because it's too hard to talk about, or they'll try to nail down every single aspect in advance without allowing for the fact that people change, and circumstances may change.

FIEDLER: One thing they must talk about in advance though is the wedding service itself.

ROSENBAUM: That can be their first real experience in negotiating with each other and learning to accommodate each other. It's also easier nowadays.

My husband and I were married forty-two years ago. Nowadays, it's much easier to find a priest and a rabbi to cooperate in a wedding ceremony together.

FIEDLER: Then, we move to one of the stickiest issues: raising children in a faith tradition. What are some of the ways that couples deal with that?

ROSENBAUM: The two most common choices are to choose one religion for the household and for the children, or to try to celebrate both. And there's no one right answer here. Choosing one religion, if one partner is stronger in the faith than the other one, can be a way to go. If what the couple is after for their children is "God wrestling" and if the parents are interested enough in religion to do all the work that's involved with maintaining both, then that could be the way to go. And that can be very rewarding. That's the way my husband and I went, and we've never regretted it, and neither have our three children.

FIEDLER: And what tradition do they claim?

ROSENBAUM: Our daughter formally converted to Judaism and she is now married to a Japanese man whose tradition is Shinto and they're raising their child Jewish. But my daughter is very firm that the upbringing that she got, with the grounding in more than one religion, added to her understandings of the Judaism that she's chosen and was a very positive thing. So she is definitely giving little Benjamin Yoshito the understanding of his father's Shinto tradition as well as his Jewish education.

FIEDLER: And how about your other two children?

ROSENBAUM: Our older son considers himself to be a religious independent.

FIEDLER: What does that mean?

ROSENBAUM: It's complicated. I think one of the problems with looking at the children of intermarriages is that they don't often fit into preconceived categories, but he does spiritual exercises and prayers with his children.

FIEDLER: And how about your third child?

ROSENBAUM: He is uncommitted. He's the one of our three children that's been the most interested in Christianity. He told me once that he would consider the priesthood if they would bring back Latin and abolish celibacy. I could see a world in which either one of those might happen, but not both.

FIEDLER: It sounds to me like your whole household is a grand experiment in interfaith relations.

ROSENBAUM: We hadn't set out to make it that way. My father was a Lutheran, and when he and my Catholic mother were married in 1939, theirs was a "mixed marriage." And they agreed to raise my sister and me as Catholic, but my father was religiously marginalized in our family, and it's one of the reasons that I didn't want to go that way. I think the people who do choose one faith, that's what they need to watch out for—that the partner whose religion is not being followed doesn't get shoved to the sidelines.

The other potential complication is this: if the religion that's being chosen is not the religion of the mother, that means that the father's got to step up and do some of it. We very often see the situation in which they've decided on the father's religion but then he expects the mother to do all the driving to Sunday school or Hebrew school or whatever. Even if you've chosen one religion, you both still have to take part in that.

FIEDLER: Another issue that comes up is the one of special seasons or feasts. Like: do we celebrate Christmas? Do we have a Passover seder at home? How do you handle Ramadan if one is a Muslim? How do people resolve those questions?

ROSENBAUM: We solve them in various ways. One of the things that we recommend that they do first is try and sort out the questions of religion from questions of nostalgia or tradition, the things you remember as a kid. Not that those things aren't important, but once you're clear on the fact that the Christmas tree or the Easter bunny are not religious obligations, it makes it a little easier to talk about and to negotiate.

We talked to a couple once, and the Jewish husband said to his Catholic wife, "I don't care if you have an eight-foot crèche in our living room. That's your faith and I can respect that. I just don't want to deal with the damn tree!" Now that's not the way I think that most couples resolve that particular question, but I think the lesson is that you need to think about what's important to you and why.

FIEDLER: I would think for a Christian, celebrating Passover would not be difficult since that is the celebration from which the Eucharist grew.

ROSENBAUM: Theologically, it's not difficult, but practically it is. It takes a lot of work to prepare the house for Passover and then to celebrate Easter without Easter traditions that involve things like nice yeasty coffee cakes and marshmallow chicks that are not kosher. Whole new things rise up. I think Christians also need to be sensitive to how that season has been co-opted by Christianity. It's not entirely a warm fuzzy thing for Jews to have Christians participating in their seders. That time of year was historically a time of gloom and depression for Jews, so it's not just all skipping down the garden path; you have to really be mindful of those things.

FIEDLER: Do you ever encounter couples where one partner is of a more fundamentalist persuasion and desperately wants to convert the other?

ROSENBAUM: Rarely. I hate to get involved in people's personal relationships and give advice. What we mostly try to do is help people make their own choices, but that's a case in which I would really recommend that they seriously rethink the relationship. There's a play we saw a couple of years ago called *I Love You, You're Perfect, Now Change*. It seems to me that it really strikes at the roots of a partnership. If you strongly want your partner to change something that basic and that important, you may be with the wrong person.

FIEDLER: Are in-laws ever a problem that way?

ROSENBAUM: Sure they are. Sometimes they can be completely intransigent and the partners have no choice but to say, "You know, if you want to see the kids, you're going to have to stop this." But on the other hand, they're often simply afraid. They're afraid of losing you. They're afraid that their identity is getting watered down. They're afraid they're being rejected. One thing that can be helpful is if you have a pastor or a rabbi who is sympathetic and knowledgeable about interfaith relationships sit down with the parents of that person.

FIEDLER: Other potential problems might arise, it seems to me, with conflicts over moral codes. One example would be if one spouse is Christian Scientist and gets sick but doesn't believe in conventional medical care, but the other loves him and wants him to get it. Or another example that strikes me would be an Evangelical or a Catholic who is opposed to abortion, but whose wife decides she really needs to have one. What happens in cases like that?

ROSENBAUM: It's a very interesting question and there really isn't any one answer. The only thing I can say is that it can happen in any relationship, not only one that's technically interfaith. Institutional Judaism, for instance, has attitudes toward abortion that run through a whole continuum. Two Jews can easily disagree on this subject, as can two Catholics. These are very thorny issues. Now something like the case of the Christian Scientist is an issue that should be talked about beforehand.

FIEDLER: Are most interfaith marriages in the United States today Jewish-Christian, or are you seeing them more frequently with Muslims or Hindus or Buddhists?

ROSENBAUM: The majority of interfaith marriages are Jewish-Christian. Muslim intermarriage is the fastest growing kind of intermarriage in the United States and I would say that the institutional Muslim community is about where the institutional Jewish community was twenty-five years ago. They're hoping if they close their eyes real tight it will go away, and I don't think it's going to go away.

FIEDLER: You and your husband are co-founders of the Dovetail Institute. What is its mission?

ROSENBAUM: The mission is to help interfaith couples decide the best choices for them, and once they've made those decisions, to provide them with resources to help implement them. So we have books, we have a journal, we have a national conference every other year. We have a referral list of officiants who will do weddings and naming ceremonies for interfaith couples.

We are the only national organization that does not have a denominational agenda.

~~~~~~

Susanna Heschel

on the Interfaith Friendship
of Her Father and Dr. Martin Luther King

Susanna Heschel, who is Jewish, is deeply involved in interfaith scholarship and dialogue with Muslims and Christians. In a sense, she comes by it naturally. Her father was Rabbi Abraham Joshua Heschel, the prophetic rabbi who befriended, and marched with, Dr. Martin Luther King. It was an interfaith collaboration, and that friendship was recounted by Susanna Heschel, who is currently a professor of Jewish studies at Dartmouth College. This interview took place in January 2008.

MAUREEN FIEDLER: Susanna, how did your father and Martin Luther King meet?

SUSANNA HESCHEL: They met at a conference in Chicago in 1963. The conference, sponsored by the National Conference of Christians and Jews, was about religion and race, two words my father said should never be uttered in the same breath. What's so remarkable is that they met as two people from very different backgrounds. My father was born in Warsaw to a very pietistic Jewish family and was expected to become a Hasidic rabbi, and of course we know the biography of Martin Luther King. And if you think about it in terms of Jewish histories, it's remarkable that a Jew and a Christian, a rabbi and a preacher, would meet and form such an immediate strong bond.

FIEDLER: It became much more than a political alliance that developed between them. It was also a deep and genuine friendship. What do you remember your father saying about King or about that friendship?

HESCHEL: It was not so much what he said, but the way he felt. My father seemed to have found a "soul mate," one might say, in Dr. King. That is, these were people for whom the Bible was vivid and with them at every moment. They were very much inspired by the prophets and by the Exodus. And keep in mind my father came to this country in 1940. He had been a student at the University of Berlin starting in 1927 and he lived in Nazi Germany where he heard Protestant theologians saying that the Hebrew Bible, the Old Testament, should be thrown out of the

Christian Bible because it was a Jewish book. And then he came to this country, and there's Dr. King making the Exodus the central motif of the Civil Rights Movement. That was amazing. That was miraculous for my father.

FIEDLER: And for those who may not know, we should say the Exodus motif is the story of Moses leading the Israelites from slavery in Egypt to the Promised Land.

HESCHEL: That's right. And so many people felt that Dr. King was their Moses. African-Americans felt that way, and many white Americans did too. My father actually said, "If there's any hope for the future of Judaism in America, it lies with the black church." That is, there was so much the Jews could gain spiritually from the prayer and the wisdom of the black church. He felt it was a real gift to Jews to recover their Judaism through African-American Christians. And it's interesting that Dr. King relied more heavily on the Exodus, for example, than on the gospels and the story of Jesus.

FIEDLER: Do you know why that was?

HESCHEL: I'm not sure why but I wonder sometimes if he might have been, in part, influenced by the presence of so many Jews as his allies in the movement, if Dr. King was trying to create an inclusive voice in the Civil Rights Movement.

FIEDLER: You mentioned your father had to flee the Nazis and I'm wondering if that had a particular impact on his life, his theology, his identity with King.

HESCHEL: Yes. My father felt an inner compulsion to speak out. He saw around him people in Nazi Germany, including theologians, who didn't speak out, who supported the Nazis, and when he came to this country he felt it was imperative that a religious person speak out. Look at the prophets, look at God! What is God's message? God's message is about widows and orphans, injustice, economic injustice, the prophets tell us.

FIEDLER: And that's the essence of the social justice message of the prophets which he shared very deeply with King?

HESCHEL: Yes.

FIEDLER: Was there any shared sense of oppression between your father and King?

HESCHEL: Definitely. I grew up on Riverside Drive and 115th Street in New York at the edge of Harlem, and my father would often walk with me and describe what he had experienced as a child in Warsaw in a very poor family, and talk about what African-Americans were experiencing today in Harlem. He drew the comparison for me, over and over again. He knew about economic injustice. He knew that walls of a ghetto can be invisible, but no less harsh than the walls of the Warsaw ghetto.

FIEDLER: Could you describe your father's collaboration with King in the Civil Rights Movement? We know they marched together at Selma, but there was certainly more than that. How did they collaborate?

HESCHEL: They were often together at speeches, at rallies, at demonstrations of different kinds. The one that my father did not participate in was the March on Washington in August of 1963, because it was held on the Sabbath. But the others strikingly were on Sunday, including the march that started at Selma. My father was there.

In addition, right around that time when they met, my father had formed an organization of clergy and laymen concerned about Vietnam. And it was that organization that talked to Dr. King about speaking out against the war. It was a very difficult decision for Dr. King because he was under great pressure not to speak out. If he spoke out against the war in Vietnam, everybody warned him that the president would turn against him, that he would endanger the Civil Rights Movement. It was a very serious moral dilemma. I think that's how I experienced politics growing up.

FIEDLER: But your father helped to convince King to speak out against that war. What was the winning argument? What finally compelled King to do it then? Do you know?

HESCHEL: The motto of the Southern Christian Leadership Conference was to save the soul of America. And my father and Dr. King both felt that the war was damaging America's soul. In addition, it was a war that was drafting African-Americans disproportionately into the military and it was a war that was inflicting terrible civilian casualties in Vietnam. And my father said to pray and not speak out on Vietnam is blasphemous. And Dr. King felt that way too. It was a great act of courage for him to speak out publicly in April of 1967 against the war at Riverside Church in New York. I was present that evening and remember what a momentous occasion that was.

FIEDLER: What do you remember about that night?

HESCHEL: I was filled with a sense of the seriousness of Dr. King's decision and the possible consequences. I knew he was going to be harshly attacked by friends as well as enemies, by the Congress and so forth. But I knew it was a great act of bravery for which he might pay with his life, and indeed he was assassinated exactly one year later. I was also very proud of my father. I was very proud that moral issues were at the center of his life and that he was so courageous. And then I sometimes wonder: where's the courage today? When I sometimes speak out on issues, my friends say to me, "You're so courageous." I don't think of myself as particularly courageous. I think Dr. King was courageous. My father was courageous.

What has happened to our courage? I was raised to believe that that's what it is to be a human being.

FIEDLER: You mentioned the prophetic tradition and how important it was to both Dr. King and your father, and how each of them regarded the other as a prophet. In fact Dr. King spoke at a rabbinical conference only ten days before he was assassinated and your father was there. What happened?

HESCHEL: That was an extraordinary evening. It was a convention of conservative rabbis in the Catskills in the Concord Hotel, and there were a thousand rabbis. After dinner, everybody gathered in the auditorium and when Dr. King entered the room, all the rabbis stood up, linked arms, and they sang "We Shall Overcome" in Hebrew.

And Dr. King was so pleased. He said he had heard "We Shall Overcome" in many languages, but never before in Hebrew, and he was so moved by that. And again, he was very courageous in what he said that night and when he took difficult questions from the audience. He was a remarkable human being.

FIEDLER: And I believe that your father described King as a prophet.

HESCHEL: My father said, "Where in America today do we find a voice like the voice of the prophets of Israel? Dr. Martin Luther King has such a voice." My father didn't feel that one should call a person a prophet, because prophecy was something that was given by God, but to have a voice like the prophets, to live like the prophets—that was what was important.

FIEDLER: The march on Selma had very special significance for your father. He wrote that wonderful line later that said "his legs were praying" that day. Do you remember Selma and how your father saw that event?

HESCHEL: I do remember Selma, and of course that event was marked by several weeks of terrible conflicts, riots created by the police against the demonstrators who were trying to go from Selma to Montgomery on behalf of the Voting Rights Act. I'm sure everybody remembers Bloody Sunday, just two weeks earlier. People were severely beaten and Dr. King received a federal court injunction to protect the marchers with federal troops, and to hold the march again.

My father received a telegram on the Friday afternoon before the march, asking him to come down. And I remember that quite vividly, because the Sabbath was about to start in a couple of hours, and we had to buy him a plane ticket and pack his suitcase, and it was a very nervous Sabbath. And then Saturday night when the Sabbath was over, my mother and I went downstairs with my father and he kissed us goodbye. I remember that kiss and I remember watching him turn around and walk to the taxi and get in to go to the airport, and thinking he might not come back, and I might never see him again. And at the same time, I knew from him that this was the most important thing a person could be doing at that moment and I was very proud of him.

FIEDLER: You say in your own writing that both King and your father understood God in a very similar way. God was not some distant Unmoved Mover but rather was involved and engaged in human affairs. That surely had a great impact on the struggle they shared.

HESCHEL: Very much so. I found it striking that in their speeches both my father and Dr. King used that phrase, "God is not the Unmoved Mover," the way Aristotle speaks of God. But God is the most engaged, the most deeply moved Mover of the Bible. That is to say, God is affected by human deeds. God gets angry when we misbehave, when we are cruel to each other. There is a Jewish tradition that my father had written a great deal about, divine pathos. It says that if I injure another human being, I also injure God. So God is most profoundly affected by us. My father and Dr. King shared that belief. There are people nowadays who commit acts of violence in the name of religion, but if you believe that God is hurt when you hurt other people, how can you commit an act of violence?

FIEDLER: As we moved into the 1970s, the great and historic alliance of African-Americans and Jews during the Civil Rights Movement experienced a major rift, largely over policies of affirmative action. Your father died, I know, in 1972, but he saw at least the beginning of that. How did he respond to that growing rift?

HESCHEL: My father did support affirmative action and I wish he had lived longer. I think if my father had been alive, the rift wouldn't have occurred. I heard from many people, from Andrew Young for example, and Jesse Jackson, how much they missed my father and his guidance.

My father was the kind of person who could forgive and who could repair a relationship. I think the Jewish community was led in the 1970s by lawyers and businessmen and people who formulated positions in opposition to affirmative action for the wrong reasons. They were not moved by religious or theological reasons. And I regret that. I regret that many Jewish organizations were opposed to affirmative action and submitted court briefs in opposition to affirmative action.

FIEDLER: Of course, Martin Luther King and your father had a great interfaith relationship, but I'm wondering if they went further in interfaith dialogue and relationship. Did they enter into any kind of dialogue with Muslims or Buddhists or those of other faith traditions?

HESCHEL: Yes they did. And I hear that in Iran today there are Muslim theologians reading my father's work, translated into Farsi.

FIEDLER: Overall what do you see as the significance in the world today of this beautiful and historic friendship between your father and Dr. King?

HESCHEL: That friendship is, for many people, an inspiring symbol. I have to say that when my father went to Selma in 1965, not a lot of Jews were happy about it. Even the U.S. Congress wasn't happy about it. I'm not sure how many people realize that the march was condemned in ugly ways. It took more than ten years for people to begin to have a sense of pride as Jews in my father's involvement in the Civil Rights Movement.

And now of course they do, but I would add that although the march culminated in Congress' passing the Voting Rights Act, those voting rights have also been eroded. They're eroded by legislation that says, for example, if you were ever a convicted felon, even if you're out of jail, you're never allowed to vote. I would say frankly, although I'm very pleased that my father was at Selma, and I want us all to be inspired by that, *we* should be inspired to act today.

~~~~~~

Ranya Idliby, Suzanne Oliver, and Priscilla Warner

on *The Faith Club*—An Interfaith Movement in Living Rooms

Sometimes, ordinary women unwittingly assume interfaith leadership roles, and launch a movement—literally—in their living rooms. Such is the case of Ranya Idliby, Suzanne Oliver, and Priscilla Warner, who founded a faith club when they tried to understand each other's faith traditions so they could write an interfaith children's book together. In the process, they spawned a grassroots movement of faith clubs across the country. Their book is called *The Faith Club: A Muslim, a Christian, a Jew—Three Women Search for Understanding*, and it quickly dispels any misconception that interfaith dialogue is basically sweetness and light. This interview took place in February 2008.

MAUREEN FIEDLER: What stereotypes of each other did you carry into these conversations? Suzanne Oliver, let me begin with you. You're the Christian.

SUZANNE OLIVER: Sure, I walked in thinking of Islam as a violent religion, a religion of mistreated women, and an eye-for-an-eye justice system. It was right after 9-11, and I had jihad on my mind. And I met Ranya at the school bus stop and she was very different from what I was reading in the papers. I thought of Judaism as an ancient and exclusive faith, one built on the trials and survivals of one particular people, one that didn't benefit from Jesus' message of love and life everlasting.

FIEDLER: And what happened to those stereotypes as you exchanged ideas and feelings over many, many months with Priscilla and Ranya?

OLIVER: It was a gradual process. As I learned more about Islam, it was exciting news to me that we all traced our religious ancestry back to Abraham, that Muslims revered Jesus as a prophet. So fitting those things together with my stereotypes of Islam made me rethink Christianity and rethink Islam.

With Judaism what came right to the fore is what we call the crucifixion crisis. I was talking about the crucifixion, and Priscilla worried that I was blaming Jews for Jesus' death.

FIEDLER: Priscilla, you're the Jewish woman of the three. What stereotypes of Christians and Muslims did you carry into these conversations?

PRISCILLA WARNER: I think the stereotype I had of Christians was what made me basically jump down Suzanne's throat when we were talking about Jesus and the crucifixion, which was that there were a lot of Christians walking around feeling that we were Christ killers, that loving Jesus and following the teachings of Jesus were incompatible with respecting the traditions of Judaism. I was, I guess, a little paranoid.

The whole theme of anti-Semitism ran through the first several discussions that we had. I stereotyped Suzanne as somebody who would be anti-Semitic, which led to a whole series of conversations about anti-Semitism. I also stereotyped Ranya. I didn't know too much about Islam, but she's Palestinian, so I was surprised that a Palestinian woman would sit down face to face with me so calmly.

FIEDLER: And Ranya, as a Muslim, what were your stereotypes of Christians and Jews?

RANYA IDLIBY: I have to turn this one a little on its head because the biggest stereotypes I had were concerning my very own religion. I had faith, but no religion, when I first came to the faith club and today I know that I have both. I'm more confident and firm as a Muslim because I know that within Islam, there's that diversity of worship that is parallel to Reform, Conservative, or Orthodox Judaism, or to many denominations within Christianity.

And I know that there's a lot of room in the rich history of Islam for a woman who does not wear a veil, who enjoys her occasional glass of wine. And I think I came to the faith club most ignorant about my own religion. The fact that we as Muslims are required to believe, for instance, in the gospels and the Torah are things that I discovered and reconnected with through my journey, and I therefore credit this dialogue for my becoming the Muslim I am today.

FIEDLER: What interfaith issue was the most difficult for you to discuss, Suzanne and Priscilla? Was it the crucifixion of Jesus?

OLIVER: Certainly. Because I was telling a story that felt so true to me and that contained no judgment of other people, it was really a surprise to me to see what Priscilla believed. I read in a children's book about the crucifixion, "The wicked hands among you have slain Jesus," and close to this phrase, "House of Israel." And to me it was talking about all people who were present at the time. I think of myself as part of that House of Israel, having grown out of the Jewish tradition.

But Priscilla brought to the table so much history of Jewish persecution, that it led her to hear it differently. Also, it was eye opening for me to see how the gospel has been used to feed anti-Semitism, to justify slavery and, to hold up the inequality of women.

FIEDLER: Priscilla, when you heard those phrases that described the crucifixion of Jesus, how did you feel?

WARNER: I had a very primal reaction. Some sort of radar went off in me. I had never had a conversation with anyone about Jesus before in my life. I'd gone to a Hebrew day school and a Quaker girls' school. And whenever his name came up, frankly, I got a little tense. I really did not know as a Jew what my relationship to Jesus was.

FIEDLER: But you knew that Jews had been stereotyped as Christ-killers, and that that had been a basis for the pogroms and the Holocaust, for persecution through the centuries.

WARNER: Yes, and I didn't really know enough about the history of anti-Semitism to understand exactly where it came from, so I think I was ready on any front—ready to be set off.

FIEDLER: How did it get resolved, Priscilla?

WARNER: Ranya was the mediator. Ranya, the Muslim woman, stepped in between the two of us. I went home after our conversation and I was talking to some Catholic friends who had heard the word "Christ-killer," so I was a little suspicious. When I came to the next meeting, Ranya was there. Suzanne hadn't arrived yet and I poured my heart out and said, "You know, I don't know if I can be part of this conversation. I don't feel that Suzanne's validating me." Ranya played the role of peacemaker and said, "Why don't you sit down and see what she has to say? I'm sure Suzanne made a couple of adjustments." And she had, and when she read her story to me again, no bells or alarms went off. And we learned from that that just a few words can make a very big difference.

FIEDLER: In the world of difficult issues, the Israeli-Palestinian crisis was another one that you dealt with. Ranya, how did you grapple with that crisis with Priscilla?

IDLIBY: We certainly had to gain some level of trust and friendship before I could really have that honest dialogue. And I felt that for the longest time I was being cold. Pricilla talked about certain qualities in Islam, how Islam had been radicalized and politicized for violent ends and I was called upon to explain how that could be possible and why it happened. I eventually felt the need to ask my Jewish partner to do the same because, unfortunately, Islam is not the only religion to have been manipulated toward violence. There are people who have committed violence in the name of Israel, the Jewish state, and so this is why it becomes a religious issue.

FIEDLER: So you confronted Priscilla with the questions of Israel's treatment of the Palestinians?

IDLIBY: I think it was not so much confrontation as an exploration of my need for Priscilla to affirm and to hear my voice as one Palestinian's story. So what I brought to the table was a very personal narrative.

FIEDLER: Your own family lost land in what is present-day Israel, correct?

IDLIBY: This is true.

FIEDLER: But then, Priscilla, you are not what one would call a hard line Israel-can-do-no-wrong Jewish woman, right? You listened to this with a somewhat sympathetic ear.

WARNER: I knew the policies were those of the government, not part of the Jewish religion. I thought that I was a lonely voice as a Jewish person looking at Israel with some objectivity, and it turns out that I met Jews all across the country and the world who share my view. We can even talk about the wall—fence—whatever you want call it.

FIEDLER: And that's the wall between the West Bank and Israel.

WARNER: Yes. I was really perturbed. I had gone to my rabbi, who had given a sermon at my synagogue where he said he was no longer on the fence about the fence in Israel. I walked home with my husband and I said, "You know I don't know which side to be on. I don't know. I don't want to be on the Israeli side; I don't want to be on the Palestinian side." I was very confused. And Ranya said, "When you can see the fence from all sides, you're on the side of humanity." And I'm very proud to be on the side of humanity.

FIEDLER: In this process, you've found you had some things in common. What were some of the things that most surprised you, Suzanne, as a Christian woman?

OLIVER: For me it was a recognition that these religions worked beautifully for the faith of Ranya and Priscilla. Certainly there are lines in scripture that people can point to and say, "Christianity is exclusive; you have to profess faith in Jesus." But certainly the example of the way Jesus treated other people really allowed me to feel confident that I can affirm the faith of Ranya and Priscilla and still be an authentic Christian.

FIEDLER: Priscilla, did anything you had in common surprise you?

WARNER: I was really surprised by how much I fell in love with Jesus. I don't know how to put it. I wasn't being disloyal if I listened to what Suzanne read to me from the Sermon on the Mount and the Beatitudes, and I found enormous beauty and inspiration in those words. I was not a Jew for Jesus; I was a Jewish woman who appreciates Jesus as a human being and a teacher.

In terms of Islam, I was continuously surprised by how close we are. We really *are* family, you know; we're called cousins. We talked about the manna that fell from the skies that saved the Israelites in the desert, and Ranya and I know what manna is. I grew up in the Middle East eating manna. It's a type of candy. And when her mother came from the Middle East, she gave me a box of manna. So it was startling to me how we continue to have these things in common.

FIEDLER: And Ranya, what surprised you?

IDLIBY: Two things surprised me. I think that most people, when they hear of interfaith dialogue, often think of diluted religion. The reality is that through working out the tough questions and the issues between these different faiths, we become firmer in our own traditions. The second thing that surprised me is that in our three holy books are certain fundamentals, the fundamentals of loving my neighbor and a faith that's built on action, as opposed to a faith that is based on the worship of creed and rituals and religion.

FIEDLER: How did these conversations change your faith, Ranya? You said you found your faith through this.

IDLIBY: This is true. I knew that in my heart of hearts I couldn't believe in a God who was a discriminator at heart and luckily for me there are many verses in the Qur'an that tell us that diversity is indeed by God's intended design. For example, the Qur'an says that we have been made into different colors, tribes, creeds, and religions in order that we may know each other and prove ourselves through our actions.

My other issue was, of course, "Could this diversity be found within Islam?" I myself was vulnerable to the stereotype that would have me believe that perhaps you had to wear a veil a certain way or eat or live a certain way, in order to qualify as a true Muslim and that's because there are literal voices out there who perhaps have a lot of oil money, who want you to believe that there is only one true path in Islam.

FIEDLER: And now Priscilla, it seems to me that, as a Jewish woman, you went back and forth in this journey in regard to your own faith, belief in God even.

WARNER: I prayed to God all my life and this God was perhaps a God of the Old Testament, and the Hebrew Bible, a judgmental and wrathful and very powerful God, a father figure, and a protector. And after September 11, that definition no longer applied because I didn't feel very protected on that day. And so we had these conversations about "Do you believe in God?" "Does God exist?" And I said I really didn't know after September 11 if God did exist. These two women had faith, and I really wanted their faith to rub off on me.

FIEDLER: And did it?

WARNER: It did. Suzanne taught me a lot about how joy and pain can exist side by side. When I looked at the World Trade Center and I saw just the black evil hole of death, she saw all the love rushing down to that site. And it seemed like a very different place to her than it did to me. Ranya taught me that Islam means to submit and a big lesson for me was humility. Today I feel fine not being in control of it all. I kind of like my humble little spot in the universe.

FIEDLER: Suzanne, on the other hand, with your faith journey, you originally—before this club—were a Catholic. You left the Catholic Church because you were dissatisfied with a lot of its policies. You became an Episcopalian, but you say in the book that in the course of this faith club, you started to call yourself an "Episcopalian Universalist." What happened there?

OLIVER: At the beginning of this conversation, I felt that I was in the best place of the three of us. I had already made the spiritual journey. I thought about my faith; I was happy in the community where I was worshiping. But through these conversations I had to re-examine it. Questions like Jesus' divinity, salvation—what does all of this mean? I reached a real crisis of faith in our conversations. It was frightening and I ended up turning to a professional. I had access to a great priest at my church in the dark days of my doubt, who reassured me that the opposite of faith is not doubt, it's certainty. And I found doubt very useful. Doubt allowed my faith to grow and blossom. My conversations with a Jew and a Muslim led me to a new understanding of my Christian faith so that I'm much more confident about it than I was at the beginning.

FIEDLER: I was struck with the fact that you are all fairly knowledgeable about your respective faith traditions. Now maybe you researched a lot as you were in your faith club. How would other people that are less knowledgeable do what you did?

OLIVER: I didn't walk in knowing at the beginning of the book what I knew at the end. It was a journey of learning. We read a lot, but these books are at Barnes and Noble. We weren't taking courses at Columbia or anything. It is something that anybody can do.

FIEDLER: And Priscilla.

WARNER: Yes, in fact, there are faith clubs springing up all around the country in all different shapes and sizes and with people of all different kinds of backgrounds. And some of them are taking place in churches and temples and mosques, community centers, universities, neighborhoods. These people are not rushing out and taking theology courses. They are sitting down with other human beings and talking about the beliefs that they grew up with, rubbing up against other people, and through that kind of exchange really defining their faith in a very exciting way.

FIEDLER: You made an important point because of course what you three have done has now become a grassroots movement. Ranya, how do you feel about knowledge of a faith tradition in this?

IDLIBY: I think that life is the biggest source of information. And we delved into questions that are real now for most Americans, questions such as, "What does it mean to grow up with a Christmas tree and be Muslim?" One of the gifts I take away from these conversations is the belief that I can participate spiritually, and not just culturally, in Christmas, because I as a Muslim celebrate the birth of Jesus. So I think those are conversations and dialogues that everyone can have because they are derived from our everyday life and experiences.

FIEDLER: The other issue that comes to my mind is that you seem to be at the progressive end of your various faith traditions. For example, Ranya, you don't wear the Muslim head scarf and you like your glass of wine now and then. And Priscilla, you are a Reform Jew and you are willing to be critical of the state of Israel. And Suzanne, you were once a Catholic but became an Episcopalian because you disagreed with the way the Catholic Church treats women and other issues. Do you think that people of a more conservative ilk could do what you did?

WARNER: Listening to your description of us, I thought we sound so theoretically liberal, but you know, we're not. We're not as simple as that. I am certainly a Reform Jew, but I went to an Orthodox Hebrew day school, and I was married by an Orthodox rabbi at the oldest synagogue in the United States. I have friends who are Reform, Conservative, and Orthodox. I understand that you're saying that we came to this in an open-minded way, but we've grown through this process to really respect people all across the spectrum. Now we know that they can have these kinds of dialogues with different people because they've come to some of our events and they've talked to us about handling them.

FIEDLER: And Ranya, how about you?

IDLIBY: I think one of the stereotypes I had, especially as we were ready to go on the road and to speak to different audiences on our book tour, was that I wasn't sure how it would be received by those who are more conservative within my Muslim faith, by those women perhaps who choose to wear a veil. And again, a stereotype was busted for me because I have had nothing but wonderful embraces. I have had women come, sometimes in tears, saying to me, "Thank you for representing Islam the way you do, for highlighting those qualities that we love about it." So again, just because a woman chooses to be more traditional or conservative in her style of life or worship does not mean that she is as judgmental as sometimes we assume she is.

FIEDLER: And finally Suzanne, how about you? Could someone of a more conservative Christian ilk do this?

OLIVER: Certainly they can. I think the only thing that it requires is a willingness to express oneself and to listen. And if you're able to listen without trying to convert the other, I think any kind of a person can learn from this conversation.

Kathy Giese, Olivia Berardi, and Nafees Ahmed
on Conducting Teenage Interfaith Dialogue

Finally, we hear from *future* women leaders in the world of religion. I discovered this group when Nafees Ahmed interned with *Interfaith Voices* in August 2006. She told me that she had decided to follow the example of her father, the noted Islamic scholar, Dr. Akbar Ahmed, and initiate interfaith dialogue at her high school. We decided to try a radio discussion, and I was amazed at the sophistication with which three young women—all high school juniors—approached interfaith dialogue. They are Kathy Giese, a Christian; Olivia Berardi, a Jew; and Nafees Ahmed, a Muslim. At the time of this interview, they were students at Walt Whitman High School in Bethesda, Maryland. This conversation took place in November 2006.

MAUREEN FIEDLER: With all the other things that teenagers generally want to do, why did you choose to engage in interfaith dialogue? Nafees, do you want to get us started?

NAFEES AHMED: Maureen, as you know, my father, Professor Akbar Ahmed, has been a great influence on me in my life growing up. He's always encouraged me and supported me to participate in interfaith dialogue, reaching out to others of a different religion, making friends with them.

But I personally found the need and the necessity to partake fully in interfaith dialogue on September 11 because I had just made a home for myself in the States. I was ten years old when I heard the news, and I really grieved for the Americans because this was my home now. But when I found out that the media was equating those nineteen hijackers with Islam, I really found it hard to succumb to that fact and I thought that they had hijacked my religion, and I remember promising myself that I had to do something. I had to make people aware that Islam is not a religion of terrorism.

FIEDLER: How long after 9-11 did you actually begin to engage in this kind of dialogue?

AHMED: When I was fourteen, I gave a talk in Palm Beach to over a hundred eighth graders on Islam and the meaning of Islam. And they raised a lot of interesting questions.

FIEDLER: Kathy Giese, how did you get into this, and why?

KATHY GIESE: Olivia and Nafees and I were all talking in Nafees' kitchen—just talking about our own religions and how we felt about other religions and misconceptions of them. And we realized how people really don't recognize the difference between fact and fiction. So we decided to take action and Nafees thought of making a club at Whitman, our high school. So we decided to go to our counselor and we started the Interfaith Club.

FIEDLER: Olivia, what got you into this?

OLIVIA BERARDI: The concept of "interfaith" has always been a part of my life because my mom is Jewish but my dad was born Catholic. And when he moved away from home, he went to college, and he decided religion wasn't for him and he became an atheist. So as a part of interfaith discussions with my synagogue and the churches across the street, I became very interested in what different religions are and how people of different religions interact. People I knew were curious to find out why a religion like Catholicism didn't work out for my dad. And I wanted to figure out if maybe he would be interested in taking Judaism as his new religion, or if religion didn't work at all for him.

FIEDLER: What happened?

BERARDI: He remains an atheist and he says he wishes that he could believe in God, because whatever religion you are, you have a lot of faith.

FIEDLER: So you brought interfaith dialogue from your family into the school eventually?

BERARDI: Right.

GIESE: That's the amazing-ness of interfaith dialogue, because we have so many different religions in our club. We have atheists; we have Christians; we have Jews; we have Muslims. We have everyone and we all can sit at one table and discuss everyone's faith and grow to understand one another.

FIEDLER: Any Buddhists, Hindus, Baha'is?

AHMED: We have Hindus and Buddhists.

FIEDLER: What are some of the misconceptions you brought to this dialogue and how did they get cleared up? Kathy, as a Christian?

GIESE: Just from the media, I think that Muslims have been perceived as terrorists, or that they promote violence of some sort, and I've actually learned through Nafees and many others that the Qur'an is actually preaching peace, and I realized that you can't confuse nineteen hijackers with 1.4 billion people who partake in being Muslim.

FIEDLER: Nafees, as a Muslim, did you have misconceptions of Christians or Jews?

AHMED: I grew up in a Christian school in Cambridge, England, surrounded by Christians, so I didn't have that many misconceptions of Christianity. But I didn't encounter many Jews, even though my father was having dialogue with people like the chief rabbi of Great Britain. So my sources were from the media, and where I saw Jews and Muslims fighting in the Middle East and I always thought that they must be very different from me with so much warfare going on. So much religious warfare is going on in the world. But coming into the Interfaith Club, I really cleared that up a lot. Now I know that Jews and Muslims have a lot of similarities, like the one God. They believe in the same prophets. We're all Abrahamic faiths.

GIESE: And we all believe in the Ten Commandments.

FIEDLER: What other commonalities have you discovered among your faiths, Nafees?

AHMED: I think that on a personal level, Kathy and Olivia and I have really become good friends and they talk the same way I do.

FIEDLER: Did you discover any commonalities, Olivia?

BERARDI: Yes, when we talked about the histories of each religion, we realized that in Spain, before the inquisition in Spain, the Jews and the Muslims lived together in peace.

FIEDLER: Finally, what does your club do? Do you sit around a table and have a conversation? Do you have public events?

AHMED: At each session, we usually have a student speaker. They talk about their faith, their religion, what their religion says, how that influences their lives, and it's followed by a lot of questions just to clear the ground, and clear up the misconceptions. And I know that's really helped. We also did some projects. The last project we did was for a girls' school in northern Pakistan. They're trying to promote interfaith dialogue.

I would also like to say that the Interfaith Club is essential not only in the United States. It would be great if we could spread it through the Muslim world and Muslim countries, so that the Muslim students can get a firmer grasp on Judaism and Christianity and see the similarities among the three faiths.

Chapter 8
Women Leaders in Religious Media

Women are currently in the forefront of religious journalism. Membership in the Religion Newswriters Association is more than 50 percent women. One of the early pioneers was Helen Parmley, who covered the religion beat for the *Dallas Morning News* for more than two decades and served as president of the Religion Newswriters Association. Cathy Grossman of *USA Today* created the religion beat for this, the nation's largest newspaper, which may have the widest reading audience in the country. Virginia Culver is a veteran religion reporter for the *Denver Post*.

The chief religion correspondent for the *New York Times* is Laurie Goodstein. The managing editor of PBS' *Religion and Ethics Newsweekly* is Kim Lawton. At Religion News Service, Adelle Banks is a leading correspondent. And Asra Nomani, covered earlier in this book for her work as a Muslim feminist activist, was a pioneer journalist for the *Wall Street Journal*. In the world of conservative "Christian radio," women like Janet Parshall and Janet Mefferd are well-known broadcasters.

In public radio, the only nationally syndicated shows that deal with religion are hosted by women. They are *Speaking of Faith* with Krista Tippett and *Interfaith Voices*, which I host. Moreover, the leading religion correspondent for National Public Radio is a woman, Barbara Bradley Hagerty.

Barbara Bradley Hagerty
NPR Religion Correspondent, on *Fingerprints of God: The Search for the Science of Spirituality*

Barbara Bradley Hagerty is the leading religion journalist with National Public Radio. She has also explored "scientific" approaches to spirituality with depth and clarity. She published her findings in a book called *Fingerprints of God: The Search for the Science of Spirituality*. I interviewed Barbara in April 2009.

MAUREEN FIEDLER: Barbara, you began your book with the story of a woman with cancer, whom you were interviewing outside of Saddleback Church in California.

BARBARA BRADLEY HAGERTY: That's right. Saddleback at that point was not as well known as it is now. It was about 1995.

FIEDLER: And for the record, this is Rick Warren's church.

BRADLEY HAGERTY: Back then he had only ten thousand people or so.

FIEDLER: A piddling number.

BRADLEY HAGERTY: That's right! I was interviewing a woman named Kathy Young about her faith, because I was doing a story for the *LA Times Sunday Magazine* about why some churches are growing and others aren't. And as she was talking to me, she mentioned that her melanoma had returned and that she felt that its return was not intended by God to kill her, but to give her a transcendent purpose.

And as I was listening to her journey of faith, it was as if something shifted in the atmosphere. We were sitting there; it was night and we were under a street lamp, so there was a circle of light, but it was as if someone stepped into that circle of light and was breathing on us. The air grew thick and moist. And this wasn't just me. Kathy stopped mid-sentence, and we looked at each other. It was fairly spooky. The air stayed that way for, I'd say, thirty seconds and then it kind of receded. I shut down the interview quickly, and said thank you so much, and drove back to Los Angeles, where I was staying. I could not forget that moment. And I wondered, is it possible that there is a God who can breathe on you? Is it possible that there is a God who connects with us in some way? And even though I waited about fourteen or fifteen years to do this book, it was a question that dogged me for many years.

FIEDLER: In earlier centuries, people might've called what you described a mystical experience. And in this book you study such experiences. Can you talk about the range of spiritual and mystical experiences that you discovered?

BRADLEY HAGERTY: One of the interesting things was the commonalties. I was shocked. It almost didn't matter if you were Hindu, Buddhist, Christian, Protestant, Catholic, Muslim, spiritual but not religious, atheist. I talked to atheists who've had these moments, these spontaneous moments.

The experience would come upon them, and this is especially true with the spontaneous mystical experiences. It would come upon them, often in a period of brokenness, when they were searching, when they were having a hard time in life. And the experience itself was of a different world. They experienced light, love, often an out-of-body experience, a sense of boundlessness in spacelessness, as if they were connected to all things—a sense that that moment was more real to them than all their other waking moments, and also a sense that all will be well. And they returned absolutely transformed in the sense that their ambitions, what they valued in life, radically changed. William Miller at the University of New Mexico calls it a quantum change.

FIEDLER: Did anyone have voices or visions?

BRADLEY HAGERTY: Yes, they did. The way they described it, it was not so much a person speaking, but almost as if love were speaking to them. It was a disembodied kind of voice. It was almost a knowing, rather than an auditory thing, and people had visions as well.

FIEDLER: You say in your book that having one of these spiritual experiences is not the same thing as being a part of a religious tradition, or believing in certain doctrines, or going through an external ritual. What's the difference?

BRADLEY HAGERTY: Psychologists have actually looked at religious people versus spiritual people, and they've found that they are different categories. People who are spiritual often tend not to be joiners. They often don't join a church. Theirs is very much an individual experience, as opposed to people who subscribe to church and doctrines. So these are very different categories. That isn't to say that people who are spiritual don't go to church. All I'm saying is that psychologically, they're different sets of people.

FIEDLER: You report that, unlike in the past, scientists are now studying these spiritual experiences. Why were they reluctant to study them before?

BRADLEY HAGERTY: I think the major reason is because scientists didn't feel they had the tools that could investigate these kinds of things. I mean, by definition, God is outside of time and space. So how is anyone going to study God? Also, I think materialism and reductionism have reigned triumphant ever since Freud declared God was an illusion. And I think they felt it was off the table. They didn't really want to get into the God issue. But in the last twenty or thirty years, I think scientists have begun to see a kind of circumstantial evidence of God. By that I mean they can't investigate God directly, but they *can* look at the brain, and see what the brain does, like when you're meditating, or praying—and realize that this is a very real experience. Spiritual experience unfolds in the brain; it's not a delusion. It actually happens.

FIEDLER: You describe actual physiological changes in the human brain, whether it's a Buddhist monk or a Franciscan nun. What happens?

BRADLEY HAGERTY: It's unbelievable. It's so interesting. And you can place chanting Sikhs into that category, as it turns out. I checked in with Andrew Newberg, the University of Pennsylvania scientist who did all of this. What they have found is that when people pray, or meditate deeply—and not just anyone, not me for example—but people whom I consider to be spiritual virtuosos, people who spend a lot of time in prayer and meditation, like Franciscan nuns, or Buddhist monks. When they pray deeply, two things happen in their brains. One is the front part of their brain, the frontal lobes, light up, because meditation and prayer are essentially a lot of concentration, a lot of focus. But the other fascinating thing that happens is that the parietal lobes, the part of the brain that orients you in time and space, that tells you where your body ends and the universe begins—that part of the brain goes dark.

And what that creates is a sense that you're connected with all things, or connected with God, or the Ground of Being. There's a timelessness and spacelessness about it. The brain physiology mirrors what the mystics tell you.

FIEDLER: I find it interesting that no matter what the faith tradition, the same thing happens. Does that suggest perhaps that any path to God, if this is indeed the presence of God, will do it?

BRADLEY HAGERTY: How many angry letters do you want? I think it's theological dynamite. It's as if the monks took Mapquest and the nuns took Google Maps, and they arrived at the same place through the same neural networks. From the point of view of a brain, spiritual experience is spiritual experience. Now some people who believe that there's only one way to God, or that they have a corner on doctrinal truth, will have a problem with that. And I'm not saying that they're wrong. All I'm saying is that this is what the brain scans seem to tell us.

FIEDLER: You note that there's a propensity for spiritual experience to run in families. Is this an inherited tendency? Is there a God gene?

BRADLEY HAGERTY: The God gene is an area of research that is probably the least developed. But studies of twins show that between 37 and 50 percent of one's tendency towards the transcendent, or tendency to be spiritual, is inherited, is genetic. So part is nature and the rest is nurture. I think it is safe to say that scientists will begin to identify a cluster of genes that may point toward someone who is spiritual, versus not—just like any personality trait.

FIEDLER: You were raised a Christian Scientist.

BRADLEY HAGERTY: I was.

FIEDLER: But then you had a friendly encounter with a bottle of Tylenol. Can you talk about that?

BRADLEY HAGERTY: Tylenol changed my life. I think it was the winter of '92 or '93, and I was up at New Haven at grad school, and I had the flu.

I was slipping in and out of consciousness. I was feverish. I was shaking, shivering, and in a moment of lucidity, I remembered that there was a bottle of Tylenol in my medicine cabinet that a friend had left there. And so I crawled out of bed, crawled to the cabinet, took one pill and crawled back to bed, and within about five minutes, I thought, "Gosh, I'm feeling pretty good. I'm not shaking anymore, I'm feeling, gee, I feel awfully well." And what I realized is that the Tylenol worked very, very well.

It took another year and a half or so to leave Christian Science. I eventually did incorporate medicine into my life. And to tell you the truth, I've never looked back. But I should also say that Christian Science has been very instrumental even in the research that I did for this book.

Mary Baker Eddy, the founder of Christian Science back in the 1800s, was a hundred years ahead of her time. She believed in the power of prayer: that one can pray and get better. We now would call that mind-body medicine, or psycho-neuro immunology, that my thoughts affect my brain chemistry, which affects my immune system. We now understand the mechanism. And what I gained through all of this was a profound respect for how far ahead Christian Science was.

FIEDLER: You also looked at near-death experiences, and we all know that hundreds of people have reported such experiences. You actually went to a convention of people who have had these. Did anything surprise you?

BRADLEY HAGERTY: Yes, it really surprised me. In the first place, I should say that I don't know how you ever confirm that someone's had a near-death experience. Because you can't kill Mrs. Smith and then follow her through the tunnel to the light, with a clipboard, watching what happens, checking if she sees dead relatives. You can't conduct that kind of experiment. However, let's step back for a second and look at something else that's really interesting. And that is: can my consciousness operate when my brain is not functioning well, or not functioning at all?

FIEDLER: You talk about Pam, who underwent brain surgery. What happened? I found this utterly fascinating.

BRADLEY HAGERTY: In 1991, Pam Reynolds had a brain aneurysm, and they had to do a very radical surgery on her, a "cardiac standstill" operation, in which they lowered her body temperature to sixty degrees, and drained all the blood out of her head, like oil from a car engine.

It was about an eight-hour operation. And she was anesthetized for all of it. Her eyes were taped shut, and her ears had ear speakers in them that made a sound as loud as a jet plane taking off. The reason they did that was so that they could see whether she had any brainstem activity, because they weren't going to drain the blood from her head if she did. So she had no vision, no hearing.

But she observed a large part of the operation. She heard conversations; she heard one surgeon saying that one left femoral vein is too small, and the other surgeon saying, "Well then, try the right one." She saw the Midas Rex bone saw, which she described as looking like an old electric toothbrush. She knew how many people were standing around the operating room. And then she had her near-death experience, and kind of lost it. She came back and saw them resuscitate her twice.

About a year later, she told the details of this experience to her neurosurgeon who confirmed them all. And then a cardiologist got interested in her story, confirmed all the details by looking at the records, talking to people. She was able to perceive when she was anesthetized, when her ears were being blasted away with these ear speakers.

Others might tell you that the ear speakers were loose; she could've heard; she could have been conscious; she could've had anesthesia awareness and everything she described as a visual, she reconstructed. She created a picture in her head. She heard sawing and it sounded like a drill, a dentist's drill. So she said it must've looked like an electric toothbrush.

But to me, that view strains credibility. I think her story is quite remarkable, and I think, at the very least, it raises the question of whether someone's mind can operate when their brain is not functioning well. Her doctors say she could not have formed or retained memories. So even if she had some kind of brain activity, she couldn't have come back with a coherent narrative of what's happened. I think this was a very, very interesting case.

FIEDLER: Would you say that reports like this prove the existence of an afterlife or a soul, or the existence of God, or something else?

BRADLEY HAGERTY: I'm not prepared to say that. I think whether you believe there's an afterlife, or a soul, is a matter not of science, but of faith. I think people can look at the evidence, and say, "You know what, this is brain chemistry; this is what a brain does when it's shutting down. There is no soul; there is no afterlife." And another person can look at it and say, "You know, to me there is an afterlife." But I don't think that science can say one way or the other.

FIEDLER: But yet, this is consistent with the belief that those things exist.

BRADLEY HAGERTY: Oh, absolutely! I have interviewed so many people about their near-death experiences. And one of the interesting things is that they describe, not only the tunnel, the light, the seeing of dead relatives, but they also describe a heaven and a hellish experience too, which we read about in scripture. They describe alienation from God, that's a hellish experience. The main hellish experience is pain about what you have done in your life to hurt others. But they also feel the enormous love, the inconceivably wonderful love of the light, of God. And so everything we read about in scripture is something that people will tell you about today if they've had a near-death experience.

FIEDLER: Can drugs induce spiritual experiences? I know you spent some time with Native Americans who used the drug peyote.

BRADLEY HAGERTY: All I can say about drugs is they can create a synthetic spiritual experience. We know that drugs like LSD, magic mushrooms, peyote, look a lot like serotonin to the brain, and they activate the same serotonin receptor. And when they do that, it creates a cascade of mystical experiences: sights, sounds, out-of-body experiences. So we know that you can create a synthetic mystical experience with drugs. Is that the real thing? To tell you the truth, I have my doubts.

I've interviewed people who had both spontaneous mystical experiences and drug experiences. And what they will tell you is that when you take a magic mushroom, you feel like there is a poison mushroom in your system. It doesn't feel like the presence of God. The other experience, the spontaneous mystical experience, feels like you've reached another world, that you have touched the Infinite, the Transcendent. And it feels somehow of a different sort than the drug experience.

FIEDLER: Do you think that scientists, as a whole, are getting closer to acknowledging that there might be a spiritual aspect to the universe?

BRADLEY HAGERTY: I think scientists do it at their peril still. It's not acceptable. But I also believe that we're seeing the young scientists getting restless. I've talked to enough scientists who have said that young scientists have come to them and said, "You know, I really admire the work you're doing, but I believe that we are more than just nerve cells, that we're more than chemical reactions, that there is another dimension." And I think, as more and more scientists begin to do some of this research, and do it well, which is what we're seeing, that's going to open the door to more and more scientific exploration. And so I may be wrong, but what I believe is that we're on the cusp of a paradigm shift.

~~~~~~

Krista Tippett

on *Speaking of Faith*

Krista Tippett and I have a great deal in common. Several years ago we both saw the crying need for a public radio show that dealt with religious and spiritual themes, but did not proselytize. We welcomed the views and experiences of believers from all major faith traditions. Her vision became the show *Speaking of Faith*, produced by American Public Media. Mine became *Interfaith*

Voices, which is independently produced. We take different approaches to our subject, and we're heard in different parts of the country. Krista Tippett has written about her life and experiences in a book called *Speaking of Faith*. I interviewed Krista Tippett in April 2007.

MAUREEN FIEDLER: In *Speaking of Faith*, Krista, you emphasize first-person experiences of faith. So let me ask you to speak in the first person about your own faith journey. What were your early experiences of faith, and who was influential in your formative years?

KRISTA TIPPETT: The idea behind speaking in the first person is that we have become used to religious people standing up and speaking the truth, not only for themselves, but for all of us. They're speaking for God, or the Bible, but it's important to me that we learn to speak *our* truth. So what I try to do in the book is trace that line for myself, as I ask my guests to do.

I was raised Southern Baptist in Oklahoma. The very formative person for me was my grandfather, who was a Southern Baptist preacher. I did eventually turn my back on his way of approaching faith. But I think, as I've grown older, I realize how he instilled in me some basic knowledge and some sense of God, and of love. It really stayed with me.

I spent a good decade as a non-religious person. I think that's a common trajectory in our time. I was very involved in politics, and I felt that all the interesting problems and all the interesting solutions in the world must be political. I spent some time in divided Berlin, as a journalist and diplomat in the '80s. And I found my way back to spiritual questions, coming out of that total immersion in high policy, and politics, and a secular take on life.

FIEDLER: You talk in your book about moving to England after that period in Berlin. And there was a quiet period in your life that helped transform you.

TIPPETT: In the latter years of my time in Berlin, I was working with very powerful people on what seemed to be the largest issues, the largest possible issues—the nuclear arms race, capitalism versus communism. I was working with people who were literally running the world, and yet, at that young age there were disconnects for me. There was a disconnect between the ideals of capitalism and democracy and the realities of human life. Then I started to ask spiritual questions: "What does this all mean? How do I want to spend my life?"

I would not have believed that I was religious or heading towards religion. But that is what happened when I got quiet, when I spent some time in Spain, and then England. Only later would I have called what started to happen "prayer." I was experiencing in silence and in beauty something that dwarfed nuclear weapons and did urge me to reexamine what I thought was ultimately important.

FIEDLER: You would not say, I presume, that issues like nuclear weapons or economic structures are of no consequence from a religious, moral, or social justice perspective?

TIPPETT: I would not say that. But I think for a time, I saw those things only from a political perspective. And I had to work on the part of me that would be morally discerning.

FIEDLER: Did you work for the state department in those days?

TIPPETT: I was the special assistant to our ambassador to West Germany. It was an amazing experience, I wouldn't trade it, but it did confuse me and exhaust me.

FIEDLER: All that led you to Yale Divinity School?

TIPPETT: Right!

FIEDLER: Why did you go to divinity school?

TIPPETT: When I was in England and I got quiet, I started reading Buddhist texts and English mystics. I started reading the Bible for the first time since I left Oklahoma. But I was coming back to it now by choice, with my mind open. And I did feel myself becoming a religious person. I felt that I had to believe that I could reconcile everything I knew about the world—all its hardness and complexity and excitement—with the practice of religion. So I didn't go to divinity school to become a clergyperson. I wanted to get a theological education; I wanted to think these things through.

FIEDLER: What did you hope to do with the theology degree?

TIPPETT: I didn't know. I felt like I was on this different path, and I needed to keep walking it. I did come out of it and started listening to the news. I was a late lover of public radio, wanting to hear some of the richness and relevance of theology, and of the religious conversation that I had experienced at divinity school, but it wasn't there. And this was the '90s, when we still had Pat Robertson and Jerry Falwell defining not only what Christianity was about, but what it meant to be religious, what religious people sound like, and advocate for. And in public radio, I felt there was this silence. There was this black hole where I felt an intelligent, broad, generous discussion of religion should be, with many, many voices.

FIEDLER: You pitched an idea for the show that ultimately became *Speaking of Faith* to Minnesota Public Radio. Did you have a hard time convincing people that the subject of religion belonged on public radio?

TIPPETT: I had a terrible time. That was in 1998. And the great fortune I had was that Bill Busenberg had just come to Minnesota Public Radio from running the news at National Public Radio. At National Public

Radio, he created the religion desk in the late '90s, because he saw this subject bubbling up in culture. When I pitched the idea of a radio show about religion to him, he was receptive to it. There was much skepticism, especially in the newsroom and throughout the public radio system. But basically I was saying, "Look, this is a part of life as diverse as our culture and humanity, but we don't know how to talk about it."

FIEDLER: How much of this resistance do you think was due to the image of "Christian Broadcasting," that was, and still is, on commercial radio?

TIPPETT: I think you know.

FIEDLER: Because religious broadcasting essentially means preaching?

TIPPETT: Yes, and I think that is the problem. When you start talking about doing a program about religion, about faith, the models that came up in people's minds were proselytizing, polarizing, excluding, and inflaming, or other kinds of un-public-radio-like behavior.

And what upsets me about those messages is that they are also alien to the spirit of the great traditions. But that wasn't upsetting to people at the public radio newsroom. They said, "You can't do this without making people mad, without offending and excluding."

But I answered, "This subject is too important for public radio not to innovate new ways to talk about it. If it's that hard, we have to try that much harder."

I think journalists in every medium are grappling with this now. And the answers are going to look different in print, they're going to look different on television, and they're going to sound different on radio, but this is important work.

FIEDLER: Needless to say, I agree. Now, looking at our common enterprise, as you survey the religious landscape in the United States, indeed perhaps the world, what do you think the most pressing needs are that shows like ours can or should address?

TIPPETT: I think that people are understandably curious about what makes religious people tick and about the different traditions. Understanding those things may just be part of being a good citizen in the twenty-first century. At the simplest level, of course, there's a lot that is frightening in some of the religious voices. There are people using religion toward violent ends, not that religion itself is violent. But people want to understand and think that through.

FIEDLER: And then of course we have this incredible religious diversity here in the United States. And when you talk about some of the voices that frighten people, there are some very tiny minorities within Islam, for example, that do that.

TIPPETT: People like us have to find ways to open that up. How valid is what these people are saying about Islam? Did the Qur'an really say that, and if it did, how does that fit into the whole context of what it means to be Muslim? People need to understand the diversity of Islamic practice, the different traditions within Islam.

FIEDLER: I always think when you ask, "Does the Qur'an really say that?" the next question should be, "What does the Bible say?" There are violent passages in the Bible. And when we talk about the use of religion in fomenting violence, Christians are not exempt. I think of the Crusades or the Inquisition.

TIPPETT: It is crucial to know when a verse of the Bible is thrown out of context, and we need to have places where these contentious issues can be looked at deeply and carefully.

FIEDLER: I think there is a delicious irony here in what we are about, because formal religion, as both of us know, tends to be male-dominated. And here we are, two women who have inaugurated shows about religion on public radio. I find the stories of women who challenge religious institutions very interesting, whether it's women in Catholicism seeking ordination or whether it's Muslim women who kneel down to pray in a mosque with the men.

TIPPETT: And there are people like Joan Chittister whose voices simply have to be out there. There may not be a woman Catholic bishop in our lifetime, but I feel that she's such an important presence.

FIEDLER: There are those who feel that if there is a woman Catholic bishop, Joan Chittister is as close as it comes.

Finally, Krista, do you believe that public radio, if you'll excuse the phrase, has finally seen the light? And shows about religion and spirituality—broadly conceived—will remain a part of the public radio landscape?

TIPPETT: I do. I think that what everyone is waking up to is the fact that this is not an isolated niche in society. Religious people are everywhere doing everything. And we have to find ways to delve into this subject, to explore it, to explain it, because this is the world we inhabit. And if you look at the big picture of history, there was a little blip of about fifty years in the twentieth century where only in the United States and in Western Europe did religion—which didn't ever go away—slip under the radar.

Peter Berger, a Boston sociologist, said religion was something that was discussed by consenting adults, in private. Those days are gone. People are trying to figure out how to integrate, not religious doctrine, but spiritual values, how to live those things. It's thrilling, and it's not the stuff of stereotypes.

FIEDLER: And so people will continue speaking of faith, and many interfaith voices will be heard?

TIPPETT: Yes!

Epilogue

This is only the beginning. Women are taking on many leadership roles in the world of religion. As we move into the middle and late decades of the twenty-first century, with rapid communications and cultural change, it seems likely that women will draw equal to men in the leadership of most faith traditions.

There will be holdouts, yes. Some faith traditions will move more rapidly than others to accept women in official roles. But in time, a secondary role for women will be seen to be just as archaic and as discriminatory as racial prejudice is seen in North America today.

Meanwhile, women will continue to make stellar contributions in the field of theology, the study of sacred texts, interfaith relations, religious media, and in religious movements for justice, peace, and equality.

And all generations will . . . ultimately . . . call them blessed.

Maureen Fiedler, SL

Bibliography

This bibliography is a guide to the books that were referenced in the course of the interviews. Many of these women have written multiple volumes.

Armstrong, Karen. *The Battle for God: Fundamentalism in Judaism, Christianity and Islam.* New York: Ballantine/Random House, 2001.

Brock, Rita Nakashima and Rebecca Ann Parker. *Saving Paradise: How Christianity Traded Love of This World for Crucifixion and Empire.* Boston: Beacon Press, 2008.

Chittister, Joan. *Called to Question: A Spiritual Memoir.* Oxford: Sheed and Ward, 2004.

Disney, Abigail, Producer and Gini Reticker, Director. *Pray the Devil Back to Hell.* New York: Fork Films LLC, 2008.

Eck, Diana. *A New Religious America: How a "Christian Country" Has Become the World's Most Religiously Diverse Nation.* San Francisco: HarperSanFrancisco, 1997.

Galambush, Julie. *The Reluctant Parting: How the New Testament's Jewish Writers Created a Christian Book.* San Franciso: HarperSanFrancisco, 2005.

Hagerty, Barbara Bradley. *Fingerprints of God: The Search for the Science of Spirituality.* New York: Penguin Group USA, 2009.

Hill, Julia Butterfly. *The Legacy of Luna: The Story of a Tree, a Woman, and the Struggle to Save the Redwoods.* San Francisco: HarperSanFrancisco, 2001.

Houston, Jean. *Mystical Dogs: Animals as Guides to Our Inner Life.* Novato, CA: New World Library, 2002.

Hunt, Mary. *A Guide for Women in Religion: Making Your Way from A to Z.* New York: Palgrave Macmillan, 2004.

Idliby, Ranya, Oliver, Suzanne, and Warner, Priscilla. *The Faith Club: A Muslim, A Christian, A Jew—Three Women Search for Understanding.* New York: Free Press, 2006.

Ilibagiza, Immaculée. *Left to Tell: Discovering God Amidst the Rwandan Holocaust.* Carlsbad, CA: Hay House, 2006.

Johnson, Elizabeth. *She Who Is: The Mystery of God in Feminist Theological Discourse.* New York: Crossroad, 1992.

Lamott, Ann. *Plan B: Further Thoughts on Faith*. New York: Riverhead/ Penguin, 2006.

Levine, Amy-Jill. *The Misunderstood Jew: The Church and the Scandal of the Jewish Jesus*. New York: HarperOne, 2007.

Nomani, Asra. *Standing Alone in Mecca: An American Woman's Struggle for the Soul of Islam*. New York: HarperCollins, 2005.

Pacelis, Karen. *The Graceful Guru: Hindu Female Gurus in India and the United States*. New York: Oxford University Press, 2004.

Pagels, Elaine. *The Gnostic Gospels*. New York: Random House, 1979.

Pagels, Elaine, with Karen King. *Reading Judas: The Gospel of Judas and the Shaping of Christianity*. New York: Penguin Group USA, 2007.

Beyond Belief: The Secret Gospel of Thomas. New York: Random House, 2003.

Pederson, Rena. *The Lost Apostle: Searching for the Truth about Junia*. San Francisco: Jossey-Bass, 2006.

Plaskow, Judith. *Standing Again at Sinai: Judaism from a Feminist Perspective*. New York: HarperCollins, 1991.

Prejean, Sr. Helen. *Dead Man Walking*. New York: Random House, 1994.

———*The Death of Innocents*. New York: Random House, 2005.

Rodriguez, Jeanette. *Our Lady of Guadalupe: Faith and Empowerment among Mexican-American Women*. Austin, TX: University of Texas Press, 1994.

———*Stories We Live = Cuentos Que Vivimos: Hispanic Women's Spirituality*. Mahwah, NJ: Paulist Press, 1996.

Rosenbaum, Mary Heléne and Stanley Ned Rosenbaum. *Celebrating Our Differences: Living Two Faiths in One Marriage*. Shippensburg, PA: White Mane, 1994.

Ruether, Rosemary Radford. *Goddesses and the Divine Feminine: A Western Religious History*. Berkeley: University of California Press, 2005.

Salzberg, Sharon. *Lovingkindness: The Revolutionary Art of Happiness*. Rev. Ed. Boston: Shambhala Press, 2002.

Salzberg, Sharon, and Joseph Goldstein. *Insight Meditation: A Step-by-Step Course on How to Meditate* (workbook and audio CDs). Louisville, CO: Sounds True, 2006.

Schori, Bishop Katharine Jefferts. *Wing and a Prayer*. Harrisburg, PA: Morehouse Publishing, 2007.

Starhawk. *The Spiral Dance: A Rebirth of the Ancient Religion of the Great Goddess*. New York: HarperOne, 1999.

———*The Earth Path: Grounding Your Spirit in the Rhythms of Nature*. New York: HarperOne, 2005.

Taylor, Barbara Brown. *Leaving Church: A Memoir of Faith*. New York: HarperOne, 2007.

Tippett, Krista. *Speaking of Faith: Why Religion Matters—and How to Talk about It.* New York: Penguin Group USA, 2008.

Tisdale, Sallie. *Women of the Way: Dicovering 2,500 Years of Buddhist Wisdom.* New York: HarperOne, 2006.

Townsend, Kathleen Kennedy. *Failing America's Faithful: How Today's Churches Are Mixing God with Politics and Losing Their Way.* Boston: Hachette Book Group/Grand Central Publishing, 2007.

Trible, Phyllis. *Hagar, Sarah, and Their Children: Jewish, Christian, and Muslim Perspectives.* Louisville, KY: Westminster John Knox Press, 2006.

Wadud, Amina. *Inside the Gender Jihad: Women's Reform in Islam.* Oxford: Oneworld Publications, 2006.

Weems, Renita. *Listening for God: A Ministers's Journey through Silence and Doubt.* New York: Simon and Schuster, 1999.

——*Showing Mary: How Women Can Share Prayers, Wisdom and the Blessings of God.* West Bloomfield, MI: Walk Worthy Press, 2002.

——*What Matters Most: Ten Lessons in Living Passionately from the Song of Solomon.* West Bloomfield, MI: Walk Worthy Press, 2004.

Williams, Delores. *Sisters in the Wilderness: The Challenge of Womanist God-Talk.* Maryknoll, NY: Orbis Books, 1995.

9-18-10